RUMI'S
SECRET

ALSO BY BRAD GOOCH

Smash Cut: A Memoir of Howard & Art & the '70s & the '80s

Flannery: A Life of Flannery O'Connor

City Poet: The Life and Times of Frank O'Hara

Scary Kisses

Zombie00

The Golden Age of Promiscuity

Godtalk: Travels in Spiritual America

Finding the Boyfriend Within

Dating the Greek Gods

Jailbait and Other Stories

The Daily News

RUMI'S SECRET

The LIFE *of the*
SUFI POET *of* LOVE

BRAD GOOCH

HARPER
An Imprint of HarperCollins*Publishers*

HarperCollins books may be purchased for educational, business, or sales pro-
motional use. For information, please email the Special Markets Department
at SPsales@harpercollins.com.

FIRST EDITION

Designed by Fritz Metsch

Library of Congress Cataloging-in-Publication Data has been applied for.

ISBN 978-0-06-199914-7

17 18 19 20 21   RRD   10 9 8 7 6 5 4 3 2 1

For Walter

CONTENTS

Love stole my prayer beads and gave me poetry and song

—RUMI

RUMI'S
SECRET

Prologue

ONE Friday morning, I wandered, nearly alone, through the
Grand Bazaar, in Aleppo, Syria. Most of the shops in the usually
frenetic indoor market—a warren of dank crosshatching pas-
sageways, lined by fluorescent-lit counters piled high with figs,
pistachios, djellabas, even toy trucks and cleaning products—
were closing for noonday services. I could already see clumps
of men depositing their scuffed shoes outside the Umayyad
Mosque, its stately courtyard with old square brick minaret,
tilted slightly to the right, visible through a pointed archway ad-
mitting a shaft of warm sunlight. It was nearly the beginning of
springtime, March 18, 2011, and by day's end, unanticipated by
me, as well as a surprise to most of the world, a Syrian civil upris-
ing would erupt that within a few years would destroy much of
this medieval bazaar and the historic mosque thriving nearby.

The only sounds in the bazaar that morning, though, were the
cooing of doves, fluttering in stone ceilings vaulted high above a
darkened second story, and the clanging shut of a few shop grates.
Taking advantage of this pause in all the jostling, I pulled out a
little notebook and began drawing a map, trying to figure out the
architecture extant from the thirteenth century, when the young
Rumi had been a student in this thrumming Arabic trading town.
I was penciling in an axial line for the straight street east to west,

when a black-haired twenty-something-year-old, pedaling by on his bike, came to a sharp stop.

"Where are you from?" he asked in impeccable British English. "America."

"Are you a spy?" he said, pointing toward my notebook.

No sooner did I shoot him an alarmed look than he broke into an infectious "just kidding" giggle. "Sebastian," as he told me his name was, quickly filled in that he had been schooled in England and was now home helping his family with their carpet shop. When he poked for more information about my note taking, I started filling in quickly, too.

"I'm writing a biography of Rumi . . . the Persian Sufi poet . . . he's famous now in . . ."

I didn't need to continue spelling out the ABCs of Rumi's life. Sebastian was jolted by my response and erupted into a swoon of rapid questions and comments.

"You're writing about Rumi? He's one of my favorite two or three poets in the entire world. He reminds me of your American poet Whitman because he's so universal!"

Now I, too, was surprised. Not only was Sebastian one of Rumi's passionate fans, but he also made an apt comparison, which had never occurred to me, with Whitman, likewise a poet of epic intimacy. As we walked a few more steps together, he startled me even more by breaking into a flawless recitation of the opening of Rumi's major poem, *Masnavi*, not in the original Persian, as I might have guessed, but in singsong stanzas translated in the last century by the eminent orientalist Cambridge don R. A. Nicholson:

> *Hearken to this reed forlorn,*
> *Breathing, ever since was torn*
> *From its rushy bed, a strain*
> *Of impassioned love and pain*

The lines were lovely, if dated, and created a heady effect. But their curious spell didn't last. Sebastian needed to get back to his pile of camel hair carpets and Ottoman blue tiles.

"Rumi is in a small group of the greatest poets of all time," he said, as his parting thought. "Why? Because, like Whitman, or like Shakespeare, he never tells his secret!"

After slipping me his business card, he was gone, a silhouette riding his bike through many receding arches, past the shuttered shops of the spice and jewelry markets.

❖

I instantly felt as if Sebastian, with his dashed, provocative comment, had also handed me—as we stood on that basalt slab walkway in the deserted souk—an important passkey to the poetry, life, and thought of Rumi. For just a few lines further along in the same poem that he had practically been singing to me, Rumi's reed flute itself sings:

> *The secret of my song, though near,*
> *None can see and none can hear*

And then, plangently:

> *Oh, for a friend to know the sign*
> *And mingle all his soul with mine!*

Yes, I thought. Rumi did have secrets—personal, poetic, and theological—that he was always both revealing and concealing. His was a life full of both mystery and meaning.

I was in town investigating one piece of the life of Rumi, who had likely been a theological student in Aleppo in the 1230s, perhaps at the former college, which I could just make out across the black-and-white marbled square. Yet I'd been in thrall to Rumi for much longer, beginning with the seductive lines of his verse. For years the poems of Rumi were my steady pleasure, ever since discovering a paperback of translations by A. J. Arberry—a student of Nicholson's at Cambridge—on a friend's bookshelf in Miami. I spent most of a week's visit reading one after another, drawn in by their ecstatic imagery, if not always understanding their mesh of flashes of wisdom on human and divine love:

> *I am the black cloud in the night of grief who*
> *Gladdened the day of festival.*
> *I am the amazing earth who out of the fire of love*
> *Filled with air the brain of the sky.*

A decade later I found myself among a group of young Muslim Americans in a Sufi group—the mystical branch of Islam—as I was researching a chapter about Islam in New York City for my book *Godtalk*. We met Friday evenings in a modest apartment on the Upper West Side of Manhattan. By then Rumi was something of a sensation in America, similar to the craze, in Victorian England, for Omar Khayyam ("A Jug of Wine, a Loaf of Bread—and Thou!"). Because of popular translations by Coleman Barks, *Time* magazine labeled Rumi the "best-selling poet in the U.S." Extraordinarily prolific, he had indeed composed a six-book spiritual epic, as well as over three thousand lyric *ghazals* and two thousand four-line *robais*.

But this circle was less interested in the compelling single lines of verse ("Out beyond ideas of wrongdoing and rightdoing / there is a field. I'll meet you there"—in Barks's famous version) than with meditations their leader read aloud from Rumi's talks, transcribed and collected in a book titled, simply, *Fihe ma fih,* or *In It Is What Is in It*:

If you accustom yourself to speak well of others, you are always in a paradise. When you do a good deed for someone else you become a friend to him, and whenever he thinks of you he will think of you as a friend—and thinking of a friend is as restful as a flower garden.

Together the group constituted a Noah's Ark of stripes and strains of Muslims in America, and from these young men and women of Central Asian, Pakistani, Middle Eastern, North African, Turkish, European, or Canadian background, I learned much more about Rumi's life story, and the importance of his religious background and beliefs.

❖

The map of Rumi's life stretches over 2,500 miles, and I soon began to travel, trying to put a face and a place to this name and ecstatic style glowing in my mind. I spent two summers—in Austin, Texas, and Madison, Wisconsin—in intensive Persian programs, getting closer to his native language, and beginning to translate his elusive poetry, as all the translations in this biography are mine in collaboration with the Iranian-American writer Maryam Mortaz. I visited Samarkand, in Uzbekistan, the site of a traumatic siege during his boyhood. I followed the old Silk Road into Iran, thinking of the adolescent Rumi, traveling west with his family, lulled to sleep by the tinkling saddle bells and Arabic love songs of the camel drivers on endless caravans. I stood at dusk on the bare, rocky rise of Mount Qasiyun, overlooking Damascus—for the mature Rumi, "paradise on earth." I was struck by similarities between his own violent and tumultuous times and our own. I also realized that all the dots of his life might never be connected, some secrets remaining intact. For this mystic of eight hundred years ago, poems were occasionally our only hard facts.

Interest in Rumi inevitably leads to Konya, in south-central Turkey, where he lived most of the nearly fifty years of his adult life. I visited Konya on the most auspicious and crowded week of the commemoration of Rumi's death, spun by him in advance as his "Wedding Night," on December 17, 1273. My guide was a raven-haired Turkish woman, in her early twenties, drawn to Sufism by reading a popular Turkish novel about Rumi. One afternoon she drove me to a thirteenth-century Seljuk inn, or caravanserai, the stone remains of its courtyard and stables outlined against the sky of a flat, grassy Anatolian steppe—like so many where Rumi had lodged. Having passed a peripatetic boyhood, he found in these way stations a metaphor for human experience:

> *The mind is a caravanserai*
> *Each morning, new guests arrive . . .*
> *All thoughts, happy or sad,*
> *Are guests. Welcome them.*

On our way back into Konya, rising on its outskirts like a punctuation mark of devotion to Rumi, not only as a poet but also as a saint, was the turquoise-tiled cylindrical tower, wrapped in a band of blue-and-gold calligraphy, of his shrine. The burial site is a rose garden, given as a gift for his father's tomb by their patron, the Seljuk Sultan Alaoddin Kayqobad I. Along with the nearly five thousand daily visitors, I filed through the chamber, crowded with women sobbing and praying, drawing scarves devoutly over their heads, while men and boys read aloud from books of his poetry, murmuring the words in Persian or Turkish. Rumi's elevated tomb, covered in gold-embroidered black

velvet, is placed near those of sixty-five members of his immedi-
ate family, including his second wife.

My guide finally dropped me at a private home, for a gath-
ering for whirling, the dance central to Rumi's own meditat-
ing. I was stopped at the door and said the password "*zekr*," a
word for Sufi prayer I'd learned at the Manhattan group. Inside,
one by one, men and women whirled on a low table, in a heat
of fast drumbeats. The next night I attended the more official
ceremony, or *sama*, at a stadium-size venue, where dozens of
"whirling dervishes" in tan felt tombstone hats, accompanied by
flutes and drums, shed their black woolen cloaks, looking, as
they spun, like white flowers opening, or orbiting planets. Like
his contemporary Francis of Assisi, whose Franciscan Order co-
hered mostly after his death, Rumi's circle only later became a
standard Sufi order—the Mevlevis—and his practice of meditat-
ing while spinning to music was codified into this elegant dance.

During the week in 1273 that we were commemorating,
Konya had been keyed up, too, with much of the population on
a deathwatch for the sixty-six-year-old Rumi—who was as much
a public figure as a mystic and poet. His chambers had been
hushed for months, except for the mewing of a favorite cat. In
those final days, Rumi's thoughts were often on Shams, the
transformative friend he felt had opened spiritual dimensions
of love and creativity for him—the supposed site of their meet-
ing now marked by a modest octagonal glass and turquoise-
painted metal shrine, resembling a bus stop, on Konya's main
boulevard. On his deathbed, Rumi had murmured that while
loved ones pulled at him to remain alive, Shams "calls me from
the other side." And he dictated a number of urgent poems
about his impending death, conveying fresh, upbeat messages,
including the joyfully brash lines that we visitors could now
study carved into the ornate calligraphy of his sarcophagus:

If you visit my grave
My tomb will make you dance
Be sure to bring a tambourine

Rumi's funeral on a gray December day was more like the heated frenzy of whirling I'd witnessed in the Sufi home rather than in the official *sama* ceremony. The turbulent procession originated in his home and school, a site now occupied—as pointed out to me by the director of the Mevlana Museum—by a flimsy, pale-blue, modern apartment house slated for demolition. Rumi's coffin was carried forth in the morning and did not arrive at the rose garden until sunset, its lid needing to be replaced after being torn off by mourners. Following behind, bareheaded, were not only Muslim imams, Quran reciters, bands of musicians playing tambourines and trumpets Sufi-style, as well as singers of Rumi's odes, but also Jewish rabbis, reciting psalms, and Christian priests, reading from the Gospels. They passed through the turreted walls of Konya, which endured into the early twentieth century but have since been reduced to a lonely gate here, some stonework there, such as the archway nearest to the rose garden, still intact, in the midst of a busy traffic circle.

Attending those services, which extended long into the night and still stand out in Konya's civic history, was Eraqi, a Sufi poet, not a close friend of Rumi's, more of an acquaintance. On his way out of the cemetery, and over the years whenever asked, his takeaway remark on Rumi voiced an essential insight that had been echoed, too, unintentionally, by Sebastian in the Aleppo bazaar and remains a through-line in history: "No one understood him properly. He came into this world as a stranger, and he left as a stranger."

PART I

CHAPTER I

"In a lightning flash from here to Vakhsh"

WHEN Rumi was five years old, he saw angels and would occasionally jump up and grow agitated at these visions. A few of the students gathered around his father, Baha Valad, then held the boy to their chests to try to calm him. "These are angels from the unseen world," his father reassured him. "They are showing themselves to you to offer you their favors and they have brought visible and invisible gifts for you." He emphasized that these unsettling episodes were nothing to fear but a sign of being blessed.

Baha Valad also recalled neighborhood children once visiting his son, when he was about five or six years old, on their rooftop on a Friday morning. "Let's jump from this roof to the other roof!" a friend shouted. They made a wager on the daring feat, just as his son, scoffing at their game, somehow vanished, causing a clamor. When he reappeared, a few minutes later, he announced, "While I was talking to you, I saw some people in green robes. They took me away and helped me to fly and showed me the sky and the planets. When I heard your shouts and screams, they brought me back." This report of a mystical adventure cinched his status among his amazed group of playmates.

In several such stories about Rumi's early childhood passed down from his father and his father's pupils, a coherent picture emerges that is consistent with the boy who saw angels yet managed often enough to stay a step ahead of his peers. The young Rumi was sensitive, nervous, and excitable, but he was also clever, warm, and engaging. The warmth emanated from a family life that he experienced as positive and loving. As he later wrote, "Love is your father and your family." He was eagerly absorbed in childhood fantasy and imagination, yet, given his family and community, this invisible world was mostly religiously tinged. Descended from a line of eminent preachers, his father assumed that his precocious son would follow in his footsteps to the mosque *minbar,* or pulpit.

While aspiring later in life to the ecstatic condition of having "no name," Rumi was truly a boy, and man, wrapped in layers of names and titles. His given name was Mohammad, like his father, and like so many of the boys in his neighborhood. Because the name was so common—if glorified—nicknames were useful, such as "Khodavandgar," a title usually reserved for adult spiritual leaders or seers, as the term was Persian for "Lord" or "Master," which his father conferred on him soon after he began seeing angels. Another of Rumi's honorifics, likewise given by his father, "Jalaloddin," means "Splendor of the Faith." In an account in one of his notebooks, Baha Valad tenderly referred to his son as "My Jalaloddin Mohammad." Later in life he tended to be addressed with the title "Mowlana," for "Our Master" or "Our Teacher." Indeed "Rumi," the single name by which he is now known—derived from "Rum," or "Rome," referring to Byzantium, the eastern half of the Roman Empire, including present-day Turkey, where he spent most of his adult life—was used for identifying him by few, if any, during his lifetime.

Like most young children, until puberty Rumi spent his earliest childhood years behind the protective walls of the harem, a more intimate and separate domain in a traditional Muslim household, where the women lived and walked about unveiled.

He stayed not only with his mother, Momene, about whom little is known, though she was later credited with the honor of descent from the house of the Prophet Mohammad, but also with his father's other wives, his difficult paternal grandmother, "Mami," whom Baha Valad complained about in his diaries, for her "mean temper . . . always screaming, yelling, and fighting," and a nanny, Nosob, with whom he was especially close. Given the intricate dynamics of multiple wives, Rumi had both siblings and half-siblings. His older brother, Alaoddin, was born to Rumi's mother two years before him. He also had an older married sister, Fateme, and at least one half-brother, Hosayn. Rumi was the youngest, as his father was already in his early fifties when he was born.

According to Baha Valad's diaries, he was living with his family in Vakhsh, on the banks of the Vakhsh River, in present-day Tajikistan, when Rumi was born on September 30, 1207. Both vital water source and geographical marker for this somewhat obscure town, the Vakhsh River flowed down from the Pamir Mountains—dubbed the "Roof of the World" by the Persians—replenished by glaciers, then cut its way nearly five hundred miles southward to disappear into the broader river whose name it vaguely echoed, the Oxus. The Oxus served as a vast natural divide in Central Asia, now the border between Tajikistan and northern Afghanistan, or, in Rumi's time, between Transoxania, "the lands beyond the Oxus," and Greater Khorasan, the eastern half of the old Persian Empire.

Vakhsh was a modest one-mosque town, memorable for its stone bridge spanning a deep gorge of the river. The entire valley remained true to its description by one Muslim geographer as "very fertile, and famous for its fine horses and sumpter beasts; having many great towns on the banks of its numerous streams, where corn lands and fruit orchards gave abundant crops." Its soft green fields were filled with willow and mulberry trees, and

irises and crocuses in spring. Beyond Vakhsh to the mountain-
ous north and east, in the direction of China, were trade routes,
where caravans descended bringing slaves to market, as well as
musk, the aroma of male deer, a coveted ingredient in perfume,
synonymous in Rumi's poetry with spiritual awakening—"your
sweet scent."

When asked in future travels about their origins, Rumi's
family tended to say they were "from Balkh," the capital of the
Balkh region—of which Vakhsh was an outpost—on the south-
ern shore of the Oxus River, in modern-day Afghanistan—and
so the phrase "al-Balkhi" became yet another tag attached to
Rumi. This better-known city helped fix them on the map, as
Balkh, known by the Arabs as "Mother of Cities," was one of four
capitals of Khorasan, its round central town with over two dozen
mosques fortified by triple-gated walls, its markets stocked with
oranges, lilies, and sugarcane. Living in Vakhsh between 1204
and 1210, Baha Valad still claimed ties to this metropolis, as
Rumi's great-grandfather led Friday prayers and gave the offi-
cial sermon in one of its largest mosques.

Rumi matured into the boldest of believers in the oneness of
the "religion of lovers," and few areas could have offered as nur-
turing (if regularly violent) an experience of religious diversity
as Central Asia in these early years of the thirteenth century.
Fittingly, he came of age on the edge of several cultures, several
languages, and many living faiths. As he insisted, "If he is Turk
or Tajik, I am close to him." In the vicinity of Balkh, for instance,
were the ruins of a Zoroastrian fire temple, its priests known as
Magi, which had itself been converted from a Buddhist monas-
tery. (Zoroastrianism was the imperial religion of the Persians
before the Arab Muslim invasions of the seventh century.) Rumi
noticed, a bit subversively, in a later poem, the quality of divinity
to transcend divisions, when he wrote, "Why is divine light glow-
ing in this Magi Temple?"

The adult Rumi liked to tell his students of a mystic Sufi of Balkh so used to bolting upright at the call to prayer that on his deathbed, when he heard the chant wailed from the minaret, he stood. Recurring in his poems, too, was Ebrahim ebn Adham, the so-called "Buddha of Balkh," an eighth-century Muslim prince who earned his epithet by giving up his kingdom for a life of poverty, and traveling off toward Mecca and Syria:

> *Joyful Prince ebn Adham rode his horse away*
> *Turning that day into a great king of justice*

The rising smoke of Zoroastrian holy fires, Buddhist renunciation, and the colorful mystics of Balkh all show up faintly in Rumi's later poetry, like a palimpsest of his childhood in Central Asia, registering the different influences he assimilated naturally.

❖

Rumi looked to his father with the admiring and idealizing eyes of a young boy, and strikingly continued to exhibit that attitude well into adulthood. Baha Valad was the single most important influence on his son during the first half of his life, not only emotionally, but spiritually and intellectually, as well. As a little boy, Rumi would watch as his father stood and repeated over and over, "Allah, Allah, Allah," as he himself would pray as a grown man, in a loud voice, during the long nights, his head resting against a wall. He so devotedly studied and recopied his father's personal meditations—written during their time in Vakhsh—that he was able to recite large prose swathes by heart.

Yet Baha Valad was more complex than the figure idolized by his son, and, as his diaries revealed, more transparently human.

Tall, big boned, and strong, he was a compelling, argumentative figure, full of great spiritual longing and honest outpourings, but also susceptible to tremendous pride and ambition. Rumi once told his students a story of Baha Valad, so rapt at the set time for prayer that he had forgotten to turn his prayer rug to Mecca. Two of his pupils paid him the ultimate respect of continuing to face his back rather than turning their own rugs in the proper direction. Adoringly, Rumi concluded that his pious father had been "the light of God." His father did inspire such feelings, but for some, especially during his years in Vakhsh, he could also arouse dismissive ire.

Baha Valad's main work was as an occasional preacher, as well as a Sunni jurist, grounded in the moderate Hanafi School of law that allowed for personal reasoning in decision making. Popular in Central Asia, the Hanafi approach was followed by his family, and eventually by Rumi. As Baha Valad was not the main preacher at the mosque, he did not deliver the Friday sermons, as his more celebrated grandfather had in Balkh. Instead he spoke on weekdays and taught a circle of young men to whom he was committed for spiritual direction. He was strict and insisted on fasting, proper washing before the daily ritual prayers, and tithing for the poor. When a group of local Sufis slept in the sanctuary to be closer to God, Baha Valad lectured them the next day on the commonsensical virtues of a good night's rest at home rather than pursuing such bliss. Sufism was the mystical branch of Islam, and while Baha Valad was close to the Sufis in many of his spiritual practices, teachings, and writings, he was not publicly identified simply as a Sufi and could be more insistent on keeping to religious rules and regulations.

Each morning Baha Valad sat in the mosque, flattered by the respectful *salam*s of the worshipers. He passed some of the rest of his day walking the streets, engaging with the townspeople.

He advised the town clown to become a vegetable peddler, so that he might live a more honest life and become pure and sincere. He spoke with a local astrologer about the limits of his predictions, and with a silk weaver about the power of the Islamic prophets. He spent enough time in the bazaar to be able to tell yellow Baghdad glass from crimson Samarkand and the round crystal flasks of Bukhara; or to consider the merits of violet-root with sugar over crushed birdlime for a stomachache. He watched as villagers picked mulberry leaves to feed their silkworms to make cocoons.

The current events and issues of Central Asia all filtered through Baha Valad's alert, theological intelligence as he sifted for morals and lessons. Temple statues of Hindu deities—dragons, snakes, scorpions—fascinated him as he wondered if a graphic illustration of a thief with his head stuck in the mouth of a fiery dragon, or a traitor eaten by a snake, frightened Hindus enough to prevent them from practicing vices. He was disturbed to learn of an ancient clitoridectomy initiation practiced on women in Muslim Turkic tribes in the Khotan region of China, though his horror over the ceremony mostly concerned the scandal of uncovered women, public lovemaking, and wine drinking.

Baha Valad possessed a healthy sexual appetite, both a delight and a challenge. Waking up one dawn to the sound of a barking dog, his eyes fell on his wife "Bibi Alavi," perhaps a pet name for Rumi's mother, and, aroused by her, he wondered, "This arousal was also caused by God. So why did I have a feeling of torment and distraction?" Another wife put him in mind of the virgins of paradise: "Maybe like the morning I had a sensation when I was embracing the daughter of Judge Sharaf, and kissing her lips, and joyfully holding her. I saw that her skirt was rolling up, like a little girl's. She kept saying, 'Oh, God!' The same God who at that moment made my spirit happy." He reconciled any conflict over being distracted from God by feminine sensuality, unusually, when he wrote, "Embrace God, and God will hug you to his bosom, and kiss you."

Yet Baha Valad was pained by the limits of small-town life, and beneath the pleasures of the daily round he chafed at his rank. He experienced Vakhsh as an exile. His conviction of his importance in the spiritual scheme of things did not match his post at a minor mosque. "I began to wonder, why Vakhsh?" he vented in his journal. "Others are in Samarkand, or Baghdad, or Balkh, or other glorious cities. I'm stuck in this bare, boring, and forgotten corner!" And he confessed misgivings that he knew revealed a lack of a deep faith: "Sometimes I feel as if I'm a king without a kingdom, a judge without authority, a man of position without a position, and a wealthy man without any money."

Baha Valad backed up his sense of destiny with a grand title that he attached to his signature—"Sultan al-Olama," or "King of the Clerics." Supposedly this title came to at least one of his friends and students in a dream. In this shared dream, a radiant old man stood on a hill and called out "King of the Clerics!" to Baha Valad, inviting him to make his true status known to the whole world. A eunuch servant from Merv told him of a similar dream of his exaltation, and of crowds shouting in acclamation. And a Turk dreamed of him leading hundreds in Friday prayer. Yet when Baha Valad used his lofty title to sign a *fatwa*, or legal ruling by a religious scholar on questions of Islamic jurisprudence, the judge of Vakhsh dismissively crossed it out.

Baha Valad had a number of exalted enemies, if only in his own mind. One was Khwarazmshah, the ruler of much of Khorasan after his conquests of 1204. Baha Valad labeled him a religious "deviant," an insult that might have explained his unimportant post in Vakhsh, if expressed publicly. Even more heated was his dislike of the king's favorite preacher, Fakhroddin Razi of Herat, whose preaching the king so loved that he stationed a representative in regal gold cap and belt, as a seal of approval, at the foot of any pulpit where Razi appeared. Baha Valad did not hide his envy when a friend described being present when Razi, known for bringing his congregation to tears, spoke with barely enough room for the many listeners who entered to hear him, all bearing candles.

Yet Baha Valad's aversion was not only a matter of petty jealousy. Known by the title "Chief of the Skeptics," Razi used his defense of reason and science, which made him a famous scholar, as well, in a vendetta directed against Sufis and other mystics. To convince Khwarazmshah, Razi once staged an elaborate hoax. He dressed the king's stablemen in Sufi robes, surrounded with extras posing as disciples. When the king solicited their spiritual advice, Razi exposed his prank, illustrating the potential for charlatanism in such claims. The lesson stuck, as Khwarazmshah ordered a leading Sufi drowned in the Oxus a decade later—an obvious threat to men such as Rumi's father.

When he later wished to personify reckless use of power, Rumi, in poems and talks, reached back to Khwarazmshah and, as the very symbol of intellect befuddled by logic rather than love, Razi—the two men his father classified as "useless" philosophers, comparing them to locusts. Some consolation to both father and son was Razi's change of heart as he neared death, in 1209. The skeptic had dramatically reproached himself for devoting his life to logical sciences that did not lead to truth. In a deathbed "Testament," Razi admitted that he had studied philosophical methods, "But I have not found in them either satisfaction or comfort to equal which I have found in reading the Quran." Rumi made a vignette of this deathbed scene from his childhood in Book IV of his *Masnavi*:

> *That philosopher on the day of his death*
> *Saw intellect as a tree with no fruit or leaves*

Baha Valad was hardly averse to conflict and spent hours, and piled up hundreds of manuscript pages, settling such scores. (If his son had not heard rants against Razi as a boy, he could have relived them by reading later.) Yet he also had a remarkably soft core, a delicacy of sentiment, as he expressed musings, prayers, and dreams, which revealed hints of an extraordinary spirit. He loved music and visualized his prayers as songs played singly by a small, stringed, violin-like rabab, tambourine, and flute, and then by all three. Awaking one morning, he imagined himself as a tree beginning to branch with eyesight, to flower with feelings, to bear fruit with prayer, and to touch the skies with language. Cutting a loaf of bread, he retraced in his mind its cycle from wheat to grist to oven. He recorded a dream of learning the secret language of a flock of large white flying birds.

This journal was Baha Valad's most durable gift to his son. After his father's death, when Rumi was in his mid-twenties, he was emboldened to listen for internal guidance by the divine messages included in the manuscript, such as Baha Valad's record of fears of failure, revealed by the voice of God to be in fact a test of his fortitude. As he had transcribed into his journal: "God inspired me with this thought: 'If you are with Me, I will be your companion. You won't be in any one place—not Vakhsh, nor Baghdad, nor Samarkand. You won't be with anyone, nor will you be outwardly adorned.'"

Rumi also borrowed material from his father. Baha Valad's commentary on a passage in the Quran on the four birds God uses to prove to Abraham that He can resurrect the dead is spun in the *Masnavi* into over a thousand lines on the duck of greed, rooster of lust, peacock of pride, and crow of avarice. Inherited, too, was his bold and confessional voice, an intimate yell. Baha Valad experienced a midlife crisis in Vakhsh, and his articulation of its dark nights remained vibrant: "I will be fifty-five years old on the first day of Ramadan. I've heard my life span will be another ten years, since the average life span is sixty to seventy years. When I added up ten years, I found that would amount to 3,600 days. I want to be sure to spend those 3,600 days in the best way . . . remembering the splendor and greatness of God."

❖

The dominant force in his son's emotional and even literary development, Baha Valad was not Rumi's sole influence, though, as the world of Khorasan was rife with stimulation for a boy with an active imagination and an early curiosity about matters spiritual and heroic. Trances and the supernatural were popular elements in the storytelling culture that filtered through Vakhsh and Balkh, both for entertainment, or when shared by wandering holy men, for moral wisdom. Fantastical tales were retold, embroidered, and exchanged among Rumi and his friends. Favorites were stories of good and evil genies, demons and angels, as well as the exploits of legendary kings and princes, judges and warriors. Within earshot, too, were teasing riddles, jokes, and obscene remarks or curses that were particularly colorful. Even as an adult, Rumi could startle by occasionally letting fly with the common Khorasani insult "You brother of a whore!"

The most persistent of these boyhood spells was cast on Rumi by the animal fables of friendship and betrayal collected in the famed tale collection *Kalile and Demne* named for its vivid pair of squabbling jackals. Dating back at least as far as the ancient Sanskrit *Panchatantra*, these enchanting tales were translated in the sixth century into Pahlavi Persian, and then into early Modern Persian in the eleventh century by Nasrullah, as "The Fables of Bidpai." The stories had such force that when the Abbasid Caliphate of Baghdad conceived an ambitious project to translate the Greek and Persian classics into Arabic, *Kalile and Demne* was among the first—an edition popular in Rumi's time.

The Arabic and Persian collections hung on the pretext of a Sassanian emperor hearing rumors of the existence of an ancient book of wisdom for rulers hidden at the court of an Indian king, and dispatching his learned physician to surreptitiously copy down its stories, with the help of a wise sage. The tales often cleverly open up into other tales-within-tales. Animating all the plot trickery is a bestiary of scampering, cognizant species: a hare outwits a lion, luring him to dive into his own reflection in a well; a crow shuttles a mouse, nearly trapped in the nets of a hunter, to the safety of a tortoise pond.

Rumi showed how avidly he absorbed these stories when he revisited them in the last two decades of his life while composing his *Masnavi*, described by one literary scholar as "a grand Storybook." Early in Book I, he unrolls its tale of the crafty hare outwitting a powerful and arrogant lion, in nearly five hundred lines of verse, baldly introduced:

> *Go ask Kalile about that story*
> *And seek out the moral there*

In Rumi's adaptation, the story transforms into a debate on faith and works. In Book II appears the fox from *Kalile,* tearing down a hollow drum hanging from a tree branch, believing its rattling in the wind is the sound of an edible pig. In Book IV, the three great fish of *Kalile*—one wise, one clever, one stupid—meet differing outcomes at the hook of the fisherman, with a caveat from Rumi that his storytelling is strategic:

> *You must have read the story in* Kalile
> *That was the husk, this is the kernel*

The cautionary tale of the three fish leads him to meditate on wisdom as a solitary path, as the surviving fish had figured out his escape on his own, through independent thinking.

The other monumental storyline for Persian-speaking adults and children, especially in Khorasan, was set in marble in the epic *Shahname,* or *The Book of Kings,* written in the eleventh century by Ferdowsi, in the rhyming-couplet *masnavi* form that Rumi would use for his own spiritual epic. A mythologized history of the Persians from Creation until the toppling of the Sassanid Dynasty, the poem is set in the land of Rumi's birth. Like Greece and Troy in the *Iliad,* the opposing sides in this heroic tale, which is described in the *Shahname*'s second third, are Turan, in Transoxania, and Iran, already another name for Persia, in Khorasan, with the river Oxus as the divide between the two fighting clans. At a climactic moment, the Iranian king Khosrow rides his black stallion across the Oxus to the amazement of a boatman, who exclaims: "No one has ever seen horsemen in full armor crossing the river in the height of spring!"

Rumi's imagination was filled with the kings and princes of *Shahname,* its fathers and sons. In his lyric poems, the mythic fourth king of the world, Jamshid, again "sets the world on fire," and he evokes the evil Zahhak, snakes coiled on each shoulder:

> *Anywhere you find anger, you will also see pride*
> *If you're happy with these snakes, turn into Zahhak*

Rumi was most smitten with Rostam, son of Zal, who excelled, Hercules-like, at completing seven labors while riding his mighty steed Rakhsh. (In the tragedy at the heart of the poem, a reversal of *Oedipus Rex,* Rostam unknowingly kills his son in battle.) Rostam was to become his epitome of the spiritual hero, comparable to Joseph, or Ali:

When the perfume of your grace arrives
All Zals become Rostams, ready for battle

These heroes from Rumi's boyhood became familiar pres-
ences scattered throughout his work. Yet he was never nostalgic.
He looked back on his childhood in Khorasan as a stage of de-
velopment in learning to see through surface to meaning. To be
a boy was to ask literal questions, about how two jackals could
speak, or how a moon could fill an elephant with fear. As a man,
his subject became "meanings inside," and mature heroism:

> *The hero gives a wooden sword to his son*
> *Until he learns to use a real battle sword*
> *Human love is a wooden sword*
> *Until he learns to battle hurt with mercy.*

❖

Between 1210 and 1212, Baha Valad finally resolved to leave
Vakhsh. His motives might have been political. The cities and
towns of Transoxania were forever being sequestered and re-
claimed in shifting territorial allegiances, mostly between the
Khwarazmshah and other dynasties, such as the Ghurids, from
a central province in Afghanistan. The king of Ghur ruled in
Vakhsh during at least part of the stay of his family; when this
king came to town in 1204 to settle a policy dispute with a minor
vizier, Baha Valad remained neutral, invoking uncertainty about
the ultimate will of God.

Yet Baha Valad did not need an excuse to abandon Vakhsh.
Near the end of his family's stay in the town, he worked through
his ambivalence about making a move westward. He worried
about leaving friends and securing a stable living situation for

his mother. Taking into account his age and chronic diabetes, he wrote: "It occurred to me: I am sick and am in no state to travel, for I have always stayed in a fixed place. What should I do?" Eventually he felt as if he received direction through prayer, and grew resolved: "God gave the inspiration: 'If you want to travel and to gain endurance, begin to go, little by little, in heat and in cold, every day, and then return home, until you get used to it!'"

Baha Valad did lead his family out of Khorasan in half steps. Their first destination was Samarkand, one of the enviable three cities on his wish list. After their departure from Vakhsh, or later from Samarkand, or perhaps both, they halted in Balkh. Yet clearly when they left humble Vakhsh, traveling "little by little," the family of Baha Valad, and certainly their youngest son, Rumi, did not know they were embarked on a perpetual journey with no fixed conclusion that would last nearly two decades and constitute a grand, if not always voluntary, tour of the vital Muslim civilizations of the Middle East.

CHAPTER 2

Samarkand

WHILE still a boy no more than six years old, Rumi, around the year 1212, traveled with his family to Samarkand. Located only 150 miles northwest of Vakhsh, in modern-day Uzbekistan, this most fabled capital of Central Asia would have been reached most directly by his father's caravan crossing the Zarafshan mountain range into a region ruled by the Karakhanids, one of the Turkic dynasties in the region vying for its control. In Rumi's later poems, such Turk warriors were often romantically frozen in time, nomadic on the steppes, and riding wild horses, as in one of his Ramadan poems:

> *Inside this month is a hidden moon*
> *Hidden like a Turk inside the tent of fasting*

Yet by the time Baha Valad and his family arrived in Samarkand, their new Turk rulers, like many such roving clans, had long ago abandoned their ancient, shamanic practices for more urbane and cosmopolitan lives while adopting, as well, the Sunni Islam of their subjects.

Samarkand was certainly the grandest, busiest, and most eclectic city the boy had yet witnessed, even more so than Balkh because of its crucial location at the crossing of several important trade routes, bringing traders and their curious goods from farther away. Samarkand was also at a poetic crossroads, one of the cities where innovative poems were first composed and sung a couple centuries earlier in the Persian his family spoke, rather than a more ancient, classical form. Samarkand tasted and sounded sweet to the young Rumi, though he would also experience within its walls some of the dark tumult released by the historical forces into which his family was now unwittingly traveling.

The first glimpse of Samarkand for any caravan crossing the Zarafshan River and making its way through surrounding peach orchards and tall cypress trees, irrigated by numerous canals, was the impressive Sharestan, the old district, commanding the highest ground above the city bulwarks—built in clay in pre-Muslim times. Circular in the Persian manner, and protected by a round wall, Sharestan could only be entered through one of the four royal gates: the China Gate to the east, with its many ter-raced steps, led down to the river. Visible everywhere were lead pipes on stone supports carrying water to most of the homes and the markets. Arcing overhead was the expansive pale blue sky described by one Syrian traveler, with a memory perhaps tinted by nostalgia, as "perpetually clear."

Rumi's family likely settled in a more modest but popu-lar neighborhood nestled below the promontory, along the riverbank—flooded sometimes in spring, when mountain snows thawed, just south of the Kish or "Great Gate." This newer, almost suburban area was protected by its own seven-mile, semi-circular wall, which was pierced by eight gates. Here were clus-tered most of the wood and clay brick houses of an estimated hundred thousand families, so many with gardens that a guard looking down from the fortress of the Citadel might not see any buildings at all, just brick minarets and a forest of trees. Cutting through the district were flagstone streets converging onto the great marketplace Ras al-Taq, in the square that connected the neighborhood to the old city of Sharestan.

Fifty years later Rumi would faintly evoke this largely merchant neighborhood in the opening story of the first book of the *Masnavi*—the tale of the goldsmith of Samarkand, told not simply as a spiritual parable, but also with a feel for the texture of its setting, the sense of place that comes from being a resident rather than a mere visitor. The story turns on a pretty slave girl adored by a much older king. As she remains so wan and unresponsive to his advances, the king dispatches his trusted physician to diagnose the problem. Cleverly, the royal physician, taking her pulse, asks leading questions until a quickening occurs at the mention of "sweet" Samarkand, and of her own abduction from her beloved there:

> *Her pulse was beating normally and evenly*
> *Until he asked about Samarkand, sweet as sugar,*
> *Her pulse quickened, her face turned red and white*
> *She had been carried off from a man of Samarkand, a goldsmith.*
> *As the physician uncovered the secret of her illness*
> *The source of all that pain and misery*
> *He asked, "Where is his street, and which way?"*
> *She answered, "By the bridge, at Ghatafar Street."*

Ghatafar quarter, with its small bridge, was located in the market district near Kish Gate, fitting for a goldsmith. And the couplet offers a rarity in Rumi's verse: an address.

The casting of his main character as an artisan was not apt for just the neighborhood of Ghatafar, but for all Samarkand, where commerce was king. Rumi would later include lots of imagery of bazaars piled high with products, drawn mostly from Konya—he was taken by the bazaar as a symbol of the seductions of material life, sensuous, though finally evanescent. Yet during the time his family visited Samarkand, the immense square of Ras al-Taq, just steps away, offered exposure to shopkeepers and artisans more lavish than anything he might ever again have known.

Throughout the city, but especially near its chief bazaar, two thousand stations were set up for obtaining iced water, kept chilled in tiled fountains, copper cisterns, or clay jugs. In spite of some of the stricter rules of Islam against representation, lifelike statues of animals had once been arranged about the square as a folly, as recorded by one tenth-century geographer: "Astonishing figures are cut out of cypresses of horses, oxen, camels, and wild beasts; they stand opposite the other, as though surveying each other and on the eve of engaging in a struggle or combat." Still milling in Ras al-Taq in the evenings, by oil lamplight, were storytellers, snake charmers, and backgammon players.

Samarkand products carried mystique. Looms spun red and silver cloth, as well as brocades and raw silk. Coppersmiths hammered gigantic brass pots. Craftsmen fashioned stirrups, harnesses, and goblets. Farmers grew walnuts and hazelnuts. Famous worldwide was Samarkand silk paper, originally a product of China. Handmade from the bark of mulberry trees, the smooth paper—dyed in many colors, using henna, rosewater, or saffron—had a sheen almost tactile in the sheets scattered throughout Rumi's poems, as he exclaimed: "Spread out the paper and break the pen. The wine-server has arrived!"

Still being sung in Ras al-Taq Square when Rumi was growing up were the odes of Rudaki, lovingly recorded on those sheets of fine Samarkand paper. This tenth-century innovator in "New Persian" poetry, the language and style in which Rumi would write all his works, was born in a small village near Samarkand. Rudaki became one of the first to write poetry in Modern Persian, its alphabet in phonetic Arabic script—very close to contemporary Farsi—rather than ancient Pahlavi Middle Persian ideograms. He had begun by versifying tales from *Kalile and Demne* and went on to compose in all genres used by Persian poets from then on. Rudaki was said to have invented the *robai* quatrain form based on a jingle he heard chanted by children as they were rolling walnuts down the streets of Bukhara— the nearby twin city of Samarkand, famous for its library, and twinned by Rumi in his poetry, too:

> *Sugar comes from Samarkand, but his lips*
> *Found sweetness in Bukhara, so he stayed*

Rudaki's lyrics remained humming in Rumi's mind throughout his life, like the songs of childhood. Sometimes he borrowed lines directly, taking a half line from Rudaki's elegy about a friend for his own elegy for the mystic poet Sanai: "The death of a great man is no small matter." The most famous of Rudaki's poems was a ballad composed to convince the king to return home to his court in Bukhara after summering in Herat, lured by a wide variety of grapes for fine wine. As the story went, by the last strum of Rudaki's lyre, the king had already mounted his horse for the return trip. "Now stirs the scent of the Muliyan brook," Rudaki sang, "the memory of dear friends." Rumi adapted the line, giving a more romantic and spiritual sense to its longing for home and companions:

> *Now stirs the scent of garden and gardener*
> *Now stirs the scent of the beloved friend*

Not all of Rumi's memories of Samarkand, though, were filled with melodic odes and lively marketplaces. Soon after his family's arrival, still around 1212, he had his first brush with a frightening siege, by none other than his father's nemesis, the Khwarazmshah, who felt ready and powerful enough to annex this most attractive of the capitals of Central Asia. Using as his excuse the supposed mistreatment of his daughter, one of the wives of the Karakhanid ruler, he massed soldiers at the city walls and conducted an aggressive three-day siege. This was Rumi's earliest recorded memory, and he relived the events years later, in a talk to students, dwelling on the plight of a lady he remembered watching, and interpreting the scene, in retrospect, with more than a boy's maturity:

> We were in Samarkand and Khwarazmshah had surrounded the city, with his soldiers in ranks. In that neighborhood, there was an extremely beautiful lady, without compare in the entire city. I kept hearing her say, "Oh God, how could you let me fall into the hands of tyrants? I know you would never permit such a thing, I trust you." They looted the city, and were taking everyone captive, including the lady's maids, but nothing happened to her. Even though she was very beautiful, no one even looked at her. So you should know that whoever trusts in God will be safe from all harm.

The onslaught was relentless enough for Khawarazmshah to emerge as the new ruler of Samarkand and fierce enough for him to live on in Rumi's poetry for his weaponry and violence: "The word is an arrow, and the tongue the bow of the Khwarazmians." Any victory for Khwarazmshah marked a setback for Baha Valad. Yet no record exists of the family fleeing Samarkand, or even leaving soon afterward. This change of power at the top was assimilated by a city well used to such shakeups. Life went on, and in some ways the city became even more lustrous, as Khwarazmshah memorialized his victory by building a cathedral mosque and a lofty edifice of a palace.

The impression left by Samarkand in the poetry of Rumi was

certainly warm, tender, and nostalgic—a wide-eyed apprecia-
tion shared by many other Persian poets:

> *Join together the fractured bits of your intellect with love*
> *So you may become as sweet as Samarkand and Damascus*

He often talked about his entire homeland as "Khwarazm,"
which included Samarkand, now subsumed within Khwarazm,
and more than once remarked on its beautiful people:

> Someone said, "No one falls in love in Khwarazm: there
> are so many beauties that as soon as you see one and
> become infatuated, you see another even more beautiful,
> and forget about the first." If you don't dare fall in love
> with the beauties of Khwarazm, better fall in love with
> Khwarazm itself, which has many inner beauties.

He associated both the city and his homeland with this inner
beauty, outlasting even the striking beauty of the people on its
streets, and holding a quality heartfelt and enduring.

❖

By the time of the siege of Samarkand, six-year-old Rumi was old
enough to attend one of the *maktabs,* or elementary schools, at-
tached to the local mosques. While no sure record exists of Rumi
enrolled in any of the *maktabs* of Samarkand, stories of him as a
pupil in learned settings come from Sharafoddin Samarqandi,
an eminent citizen of the city, as well as a follower of Baha Valad.
Sharaf liked to tell of Rumi as a nine-year-old—three years after
the siege of Khwarazmshah—asking tricky questions of the

local scholars, but being too polite to contradict his elders when they were mistaken. "He went to exaggerated lengths in respecting the religious scholars," Sharaf reported. Sharaf's wife was also devoted to Baha Valad, and first taught Rumi a juvenile version of *sama*—meditating while listening to poetry and music—though he only went as far as "waving his hands about."

Whether Rumi's knowledge of *maktab* schooling came from Samarkand, Balkh, or elsewhere, the experience of this early education was nearly standard throughout Khwarazm, as the curriculum was controlled through the network of mosques. Most subjects were related back to knowledge needed for better reading the Quran. Here Rumi would have learned the technique for properly intoning the holy book and studied the lives of the prophets, and sayings of caliphs, imams, and companions of the Prophet Mohammad. Many proverbs were set to verse for easy memorizing. Yet language, mathematics, and science were taught, as well. As with Quranic proverbs, Arabic lessons were versified into catchy lines matching Arabic terms with Persian definitions, including vocabulary from astronomy or geography. The popularity of such *maktab* schools helped explain the high literacy rates of the medieval Islamic world, said to have surpassed medieval Europe.

Like love and religion, school, for Rumi, was blurred into the world according to his father. In the *Masnavi*, Rumi draws a naturalistic scene of a mother and father quarreling over sending their son to school. The mother wants her child to stay home:

> *That anxious mother complains to her husband,*
> *"My child has grown thin from going to school."*

The disciplinarian father forces him to school, his tough love identified with the intellect:

Stay away from that mother and her worries
A father's slaps are better than her sweet pastries.
The mother is impulsive, the father, noble reason,
At first, difficult, but finally a hundred times easier.

While still living in the harem with his mother when he began classes, and alert to the world of women—as indicated by his close observation of the plight of their female neighbor during the siege—Rumi aspired mostly to become a man exactly like his father.

Traits of Rumi as a boy in school for the first time among other boys included many of the qualities to be expected, though with some surprises. He was a natural student and focused on his teachers, as might be expected of the son of a serious imam. He was also predictably precocious. The boy whose playmates were convinced he had disappeared to tour other realms with angels stood out in a classroom setting. More surprising was a suggestion from the adult Rumi that he had been a bit of an unwilling student, perhaps even a prankster, and preferred his imaginative realms to the studious.

When he was later teaching his own students, Rumi occasionally summoned his *maktab* memories for examples of model teachers. Rumi's father was a disciplinarian and a great believer in strict observance of protocol. Yet Rumi from an early age was drawn to kindness as the most effective teaching tool. Second only to Quranic recitation in elementary school had been handwriting lessons, a subtle skill with Arabic cursive script, and he recalled most fondly one penmanship teacher, clearly gentle in his pedagogy:

At first, when the child shows his handwriting to the teacher, the letters are all slanted and wrong. But the teacher, patiently and skillfully, says to the child, "All the letters are good! You have written them very well. Very good! Very good! You have only written this letter the wrong way. You should write it like this. And also that letter is incorrect. It's like this."

Rumi never bragged of any exceptional signs of adolescent intellectual power, yet he did allow himself to etch a portrait of a boy in the third person that might well be understood as a self-portrait, a tactic he coyly used several times in the *Masnavi*. In a slight detour, while writing a scene set in a school, he meditated on gifted children, arguing the Sunni philosophical position that all minds are created different, against the claim of some philosophers that all minds are created equal and that differences occur later because of education, a sort of nurture over nature argument. Rumi brings to life, as his example, a young prodigy, already wise beyond his years, self-possessed, with a knowing manner:

> *The opinions of a young boy*
> *Without much experience in life,*
> *May arise from thoughts that an old man,*
> *Full of years, might never comprehend.*

Rumi's vignette has a knowing ring, and the boy he describes is recognizable in the anecdote passed down from Sharaf of the pupil refuting the "cleverly subtle" scholars.

In one of the funniest tales in the *Masnavi*, a group of boys in a *maktab*—hardly seeming to be entertaining thoughts beyond their years—plot how to escape the grind of work being assigned by a demanding teacher. One cunning pupil decides to use the power of suggestion to convince the instructor of an illness during the core *maktab* class of recitation of the verses of the Quran to learn to give each letter and vowel its due:

The cleverest boy in the class made a plan
To tell the teacher, "You look so pale.
I hope you are well, but you've lost all color.
I'm wondering if it's the weather, or fever."
The teacher began to have his doubts.
Then the clever boy told another, "Do the same."

After all thirty students express concern, the teacher hurries home and stays abed, shivering. Rumi's glee in the prank obviously came from siding with the students and made believable an even more direct confession of his younger self resisting classwork:

Your love of mother's milk didn't last
Your hatred of going to school didn't last

The heart of this education, though, for Rumi, both young and old, was the Quran, the sacred text of Islam, recited by the Prophet Mohammad in Mecca and Medina in the seventh century, as holy verses memorized and transcribed in mostly rhymed Arabic prose. The Quran was divided into suras, or chapters, eventually arranged in order from longest to shortest. While Rumi could be comical or even rebellious about *maktab* lessons, he was never ironic about the Quran. Everything about the temperament and family of this sensitive child primed a mesmerized reader and listener. If his ears burned hearing the tales of jackals or lions in *Kalile and Demne*, the accounts in the Quran were narrative "husks" that included moral "kernels." Later in life, he grew even more fascinated by the model of Mohammad, the ordinary merchant chosen as the messenger of the words of God put down in the Quran, whose personal qualities were nearly erased by divine inspiration—"A window through which we see the Creator."

Over and over, the young Rumi heard the stories of prophets from the Quran that would form the raw material of his prayers, talks, and certainly poetry. Among his favorites were: Abraham, surviving Nimrod's fiery furnace without being burned; Noah, whose restive son dies in the flood; Joseph, so handsome some Egyptian women slice their hands with their dinner knives while distractedly staring at him; Moses, whose rod turns into a serpent and swallows the magician's wands; Mary, giving birth beneath a palm tree that showers her with ripe dates; the baby Jesus, gifted with speech in his cradle, and able to give life to clay birds with his breath; David, fashioning armor from iron chain-links; King Solomon, with his magic ring, like Rumi's father in his dream, understanding the language of birds:

> *The flames were obedient to Abraham,*
> *The waves bore Noah on their backs,*
> *Iron obeyed David, and melted like wax*
> *While winds were the slaves of Solomon.*

Rumi later imagined the Quran as a rich fabric brocade woven on two sides—"Some enjoy the one side, some the other. Both are true." And he saw these two complementary sides as a woman, both a mother and a wife, supplying different needs:

Her baby's pleasure comes from her breasts and her milk, that of the husband from enjoying intimacy with her. Some are children on the path and drink milk—these enjoy the external meaning of the Quran—unlike those who have become mature and understand in a different way.

The *Masnavi* unfolds with long stretches of probing philosophical questions raised by the Quran, in sermonic style, and in parsed couplets. Rumi could be precise and legal in his musings on free will or determinism. But other parts of the poem reveal a more immediate, childlike response to the Quran as a boyhood book of wonder. In one such story of the Blind Man and the Quran, a visiting sheikh is confused by the prominence of the scripture on a shelf in the home of a blind man. At night he hears him reciting verses, and rushes out to catch him in the act, and to demand some explanation:

> *"Amazing, with your blind eyes*
> *You recite as if you see the lines*
> *You have touched what you are reading*
> *You put your finger on the very word!"*

The blind man explains that when he went blind he prayed to be able to read the Quran, as he was not a *hafez*, who had memorized the entire book. God granted him sight for the sluices of time when he read verses, and then—like magic—his eyes snapped shut again:

> *"That peerless King restores for me my sight*
> *Like a lantern that brightens the dark night!"*

❖

During the decade between 1212 and 1221, most probably in 1216, when Rumi was nine or ten years old, the camel caravan of the family of Baha Valad set out again, this time in the direction of Mecca, the birthplace of the Prophet Mohammad and holy city of Islam, a required pilgrimage destination for every Muslim in reasonable health at least once in a lifetime. Theirs was a journey with no certain plan of return. All the accounts record their point of embarkation from Khorasan as Balkh—likely enough, given the family history. To travel from Samarkand to Balkh, they simply would have needed to double back alongside the Oxus River.

A natural crossing point to the Balkh side of the river was the fortress town of Termez, hometown of Rumi's tutor Borhan, who had decided to remain there. In his midforties, Borhan was Rumi's *lale*, a tutor assigned the special task of looking out for his well-being and spiritual education, and so was a warm and important figure in Rumi's boyhood, surpassed in influence only by his father. Borhan was later fondly remembered for "always lifting Khodavandgar on his shoulders and carrying him around." Rumi spoke of this tutor in the same glowing terms as he spoke of his father: "Go! Turn into pure light like Borhan-e Mohaqqeq!" And he remarked on his "ability to argue fine points well from his reading the masters."

Borhan had become one of an intimate group of acolytes around Baha Valad, devoted to studying mystical practices in a sort of advanced seminar in prayers, visions, and dreams, which was not shared publicly. Of these practices, Borhan was particularly fanatic about fasting as a technique for self-discipline. In imitation of Baha Valad, he kept his own spiritual diary, where he wrote of the benefits of abstinence, so that his body might become "just like a glass through which the light of faith shines." Rumi quickly absorbed these cues. By age six, he was supposedly able to sustain a fast as long as three or four days. So this sudden, absolute separation from his *lale* was not easy for the boy.

Other separations caused by his father's decision to embark were equally difficult. Staying behind, most likely in Balkh, were his grandmother "Mami," in her seventies, too aged for the rigorous and uncertain trip; his older half-brother Hosayn; his half-sister Fateme, who stayed with her husband; and, along with Borhan, the other figure Rumi missed most, looking back, his dear nanny, Nosob. When he wished to stress the need to count solely on God, he evoked the loss of this nurturing pair from his young life:

> *Closeness to anyone but God's untrue,*
> *Where now is the love of your nanny and your tutor?*
> *Only God is your true supporter*

His eminent family friend, and another mentor in his young life, Sharaf Samarqandi, had recently died—another separation. Since Sharaf had been a man of means, his widow used the remaining family resources to travel on the pilgrimage, too, with her daughter Gowhar. Both mother and daughter would grow in importance to the family over the course of this journey. Baha Valad later said of the widowed "perfect saint," "My spiritual level and her spiritual level are the same." By the time they neared the end of their travels, nearly a decade later, Gowhar had become Rumi's first wife.

Whether paranoid or realistic, Baha Valad was always anxious about the risky politics of the region. While they were still living in Vakhsh, he feared that he would be imprisoned for his political opinions in an area far removed from his family and his followers, where no one could help him. During his time in Samarkand, the power of Khwarazmshah had grown, and his influence was everywhere. On the eastern borders, the first threats from Mongols had been felt as early as 1211, as this Asiatic power made border skirmishes from China. So the practical concerns of Baha Valad interlocked well with the requirements of his religion to make a trip to Mecca.

Baha Valad often wrote in his journal of yearning for quest and for movement—"When God is taking your body and your soul from East to West." He would not have been disappointed in the larger caravan they now joined. In the first leg of their journey, as they trekked along the borders of Central Asia, countless other long trains of double-hump Bactrian, or single-hump dromedary camels and donkeys, were making their way across the deserts and plains ringed by snowcapped mountains, stopping in oasis towns surrounded by subtropical palm trees. Busy markets were crowded with merchants peddling melons or horses to travelers from a wide swathe of the known world—as Rumi would write when reaching to express geographical expanse, "from Rome to Khorasan."

As a boy, Rumi absorbed the rhythm of these camels as they traced their shuffling lines in grass and sand, dutifully following the lead of their drivers, who steered with pegs of wood inserted in the camels' noses, through which loops of rope were strung. He would later come to imagine himself as just such a camel, guided by reins held by love's hand, "Drunkenly pulling your load, in ecstasy." And he came to know by heart the tunes permeating everywhere on the trip, sung to pass the time or quicken the pace. Accompanied at each stride by the jingle of silver bells fastened near their camels' ears, the drivers spontaneously broke into traditional songs—often love songs—only interrupted for the call to prayer. Most pronounced in these melodies was the *nay*, or reed flute, an almost mournful Persian instrument that became for Rumi an image of his art and soul.

Spaced a day's journey apart along the way were the caravanserai, outfitted with a well and stables for animals, a prayer room, a small bazaar, and a gallery of guest rooms around a central courtyard. In the colder mountains, these inns were built of stone, with roofed courtyards to keep out rain and snow. On the warmer plains, they were constructed of compacted earth or brick with open courtyards. Such inns always evoked for Rumi transience rather than comfort, as he passed through so many growing up. Yet the tenor of his writing about this juvenile time of traveling was positive. He was moving farther from any *maktab* school, being taught by his father or others. And images of flutes and camels, caravans and inns, crescent moons and desert sands, along with the constant change would eventually be compressed into his great theme of nonattachment:

> *Our voices like the bells of a caravan*
> *Or thunder when the clouds are full*
> *Traveler, don't leave your heart in the inn.*

CHAPTER 3

On the Silk Road

IN the early stretches of their travels, Rumi's family followed simple roads that traced the shortest distance between two points. Yet as their destinations became more distant, they joined into an elaborate network of trade routes that connected China, India, and Persia to the Mediterranean Sea. This well-kept system of major roads, inherited by the Arabs from the earlier Persian kingdom, radiated out of Baghdad and served both trade and religious purposes. Known in later centuries as the "Silk Road," the route was actually neither: "silk" was just one of its transported goods, which included everything from spices and fine glass to ammonium chloride for treating saddles; and the "road," in outlying regions, broke into unmarked paths over deserts or steep mountains.

Like other travelers from Balkh, Rumi's family would have followed a southern route that linked to the most trafficked of the trunk roads, the Great Khorasan Road, to Baghdad and Mecca, passing through Khorasan, and continuing westward, with the Great Desert to their south and the Tabaristan Mountains to their north. Eventually they would have descended from the highlands of Persia to cross the Tigris River and enter Baghdad through its eastern Khorasan Gate. From western Baghdad, the main Pilgrim Road then led on toward Mecca and Medina, crossing over the vast Arabian Desert in a direct line.

This journey, though, was as much inward as outward, even if Rumi was still such a young boy and much of its impact not fully realized for some time. He was seeing many fantastic sights by touring through the great Islamic cities of the day, yet he was even more crucially coming into contact with important clues to his poetic, cultural, and spiritual lineage, especially in Nishapur, Baghdad, and Mecca. Nishapur was the center of a vibrant scene of devotional poetry and mystics trading in scandal as a spiritual practice; Baghdad, the very nervous system of both Islamic university life and Sufism from its beginings, as well as the seat of the caliph, both pope and king; in Mecca, Muslims of all ages came to reflect, once in a lifetime, on the relation of their souls to God, a matter of early concern to Rumi as it was to his family. The man Rumi became would have been inconceivable without the pieces of his identity he discovered in this decade-long trip.

Their first stop would have been Nishapur, near the northeast border of present-day Iran, where they likely arrived sometime in 1216, when Rumi was about ten years old. Nishapur was the fourth of the large capitals of Khorasan, the most populous, and the most western in location, a final outpost of the land of Rumi's birth. It was also a welcome respite on such a trip, as branch roads from Balkh were among the more meandering kind, less well kept than the broader routes leading into Baghdad, and so the family had just passed through long stretches of dusty badlands, a forbidding hideout for outlaws, with endless plains enlivened in spring only by a fuzz of green grass dotted with red poppies, domed adobe houses, and the tent camps of nomad shepherds. The resolve, and health, of Baha Valad would have been tested with such a rocky beginning, and the relative comforts of home and the *maktab* schools set in high contrast for the boy Rumi.

In Nishapur in 1216 was the geographer and travel writer Yaqut, who visited many of the same cities as Rumi and his family, and often in the same year. He described the capital in the phase that would have been witnessed by the family of Baha Valad as still distressed in spots from the great earthquakes of 1145, followed, in 1153, by a siege by Oghuz Turks, who captured and carried off their grand sultan Sanjar the Seljuk. As an empire builder, Sanjar came to stand for powerful, worldly rulers in Rumi's poems:

Since I came into your shade, I am the sun in the sky
  Since I became a slave of love, I am the Khan and the Sultan Sanjar

As with many of the cities he described in the florid style of the time, Yaqut still found fine marvels to catch his eye, praising especially the turquoise mines and the swift river of Nishapur, powering dozens of mills with the snow melting from nearby mountains.

While Nishapur was not the most memorable or significant of places visited by Rumi's family, the city did offer its style of liberated, freewheeling spirituality, and an equally novel and brilliant poetry scene—with both of which Rumi eventually revealed an affinity. Nishapuri mystics were distinctive enough to become labeled the "School of Khorasan." Their most notorious members were followers of the "*malamatiyya*," or "path of blame." Camouflaging their actual piety so as not to be deemed saintly, these brazen types walked the streets barefoot, appeared to drink wine, wore finely embroidered silks, and behaved as if sinful or crazy. Having witnessed urban frivolity in the squares of Samarkand at twilight, which may have been extreme for a boy from Vakhsh, Rumi was likely exposed in Nishapur to these fools for God, behaving just as wildly but as a spiritual practice.

The Nishapuri poets, too, traded in scandal. Their most famous practicing master, Attar, was by then well into his eighties or even nineties, his finest works behind him, especially *The Conference of the Birds,* an inventive and vividly imagined tale of a flock of birds embarked on a quest in search of the divine, fantastically plumed Simorgh, perched atop the highest peak of the Alborz mountain range in northern Iran. Such a work was made-to-order for a boy such as Rumi. Its moral tale involved talking animals, like his favorite *Kalile and Demne,* and the Simorgh had first appeared in all her majesty in the *Shahname.* Rumi responded to its simple Arabic meter, which he later used in his own *Masnavi.* And the poem reflected much that was rich and captivating in the sensibility of Nishapur at this peak moment.

During the family's stay, Baha Valad, with his son in tow, was said to have found his way to the apothecary shop run by Attar inside a crowded bazaar. ("Attar" was a pen name signifying an herbal druggist, apothecary, or even a perfume seller, as in "attar of roses.") Such a meeting was indeed possible, though Rumi never spoke in public of such a fateful audience with the great poet, arguably his favorite. Attar was apparently in Nishapur during the year of the family's visit; an arranged conversation between a visiting religious leader, traveling from the eastern lands, and versed in the language of dreams and visions, would seem possible. The focus, though, should have been the elder dignitary, Baha Valad, not his little boy.

As the story was told, flatteringly, by others, Attar, however, was more taken with Baha Valad's sensitive son. With great prescience, the poet intuited the future of the child standing before him and predicted to Baha Valad, "Your son will soon be kindling fire in all the world's lovers of God." As a gift, he handed the boy a copy of his *masnavi* in couplets, his *Book of Secrets.* In this abstract reverie, with a sage theme, Attar reveals that the secrets of the world are hidden near the throne of God, and discovery of these eternal verities is available only to those willing "to lose their heads" and drink the divine rosewater of "meaning." With blessings bestowed, both father and son then walked off.

This story clung to Rumi's reputation in later years because whether or not it actually occurred in the bazaar in Nishapur, it occurred in a realm of "meaning," important to him and his followers. Rumi claimed in Attar a sort of father figure, a poet father, and came to venerate "the unique Attar," always comparing himself diminutively, or inventing puns playing on "the scent of Attar," or on his small perfume and apothecary shop:

Whatever you want, you will find in Attar
His is the shop of the world, and there is no other

Rumi not only looked up to Attar as a poet, but he also accepted the poetic lineage Attar fashioned for himself. Like many poets in defense of their style, Attar found inspiration and a model to emulate in the past, and contrary poets to reject for following an unsatisfying muse. He chose as his own father figure poet Sanai, a poet of the previous generation from Ghazna, in present-day Afghanistan, the first court poet credited with giving up writing fawning odes for his patron so he could practice devotional poetry. Sanai's *Garden of Truth,* in ten chapters, was the first spiritual *masnavi,* a template for those to come, including Rumi's, its flat, deliberate rhymed couplets recited throughout Khorasan. (Rumi's tutor Borhan had loved to pepper his conversations with its proverbs: "The Royal Road leading your soul to God is nothing but the cleansing of the heart's mirror.")

Attar, following the later Sanai, bragged of never having written a panegyric for hire, and both freely mixed their spirituality with scandal, in the mode of the flamboyant mystics of Nishapur.

Sanai's most notorious poem, "Satan's Lament"—parodied once by Rumi—turned on the tricky notion of Satan as the true lover of God, impossibly jealous of Adam. In *The Conference of the Birds,* Attar's flock exchanges tales of unconventional passions, between, for example, a Muslim sheikh and a Christian lady, or Sultan Mahmud of Ghazna and his Turk male slave Ayaz. Rumi was definite about his deep literary and spiritual debt to these poets, and his son Sultan Valad later ascribed to his father the line:

Attar was the soul and Sanai the eyes of the heart
I follow in the footsteps of Sanai and Attar

Rumi said as much when making clear his poetic and spiritual lineage for his students:

Whoever deeply reads the words of Attar will understand the secrets of Sanai, and whoever reads the words of Sanai, with belief, will better comprehend my own words and will benefit from and enjoy them.

The poet of the previous generation dismissed by Attar, and by Rumi, or at least by his friend Shams of Tabriz, was Omar Khayyam, buried beside a garden wall a few miles outside Nishapur, where pear and peach trees scattered petals on his tomb. Celebrated as a mathematician and astronomer while alive, Khayyam also wrote seductive, four-line quatrains, compatible with short, pithy observations about life: "Whether at Nishapur or Babylon . . . The leaves of life keep falling one by one." Yet the bracing wind of doubt and pessimism—including questioning whether an afterlife existed—that sweeps through these *robais* disturbed the mystical Attar. In his *Book of the Divine,* Attar imagined a clairvoyant, standing at Khayyam's grave, seeing the great intellectual "bathing in his sweat for shame and confusion," having to admit his error. No story was ever told of Baha Valad and Rumi visiting the grave of Omar Khayyam.

❖

Nishapur was known not only as the "Gate to the East"—the entrance to Khorasan—but also as the "Gate to the West." Having passed through that gate, as two roads diverged just west of Nishapur, travelers such as Rumi's family would have then taken the more northern caravan route rather than the southern post road. This route led past Rey, near modern-day Tehran, and on to Baghdad. Along the way, Persian tunes gradually gave way to Arabic love songs as the caravans left behind the Persian towns, where Farsi was spoken, and headed toward the Arabic-speaking regions of the Middle East and the Arabian Peninsula. Of a life spent toggling between these two languages, Rumi wrote:

> *Speak Persian, though Arabic is more beautiful*
> *Love speaks a hundred different languages*

When they passed beyond the outskirts of Persian-speaking Nishapur, Rumi's family forever departed Khorasan. He never again saw the "beauties" of his native homeland.

As they were on pilgrimage to Mecca, the family was also traveling to the center of the Muslim religious world. As important as land geography for thirteenth-century Muslims were religious quadrants, the location of these places within latitudes and longitudes of spiritual significance. All prayer rugs during ritual prayer were pointed in the direction, or *qibla,* of Mecca. In Muslim cemeteries, usually located, as in Baghdad, just outside the city gates, the deceased were often buried facing toward

Mecca. A carved wall niche in all mosques indicated the align-
ment with the holy city—this *qibla* later reimagined with roman-
tic devotion by Rumi as the *"qibla* of the friend's face."

Baghdad was constructed as a main entranceway to Mecca,
the entire city roughly oriented toward the *qibla,* as its Kufa Gate
was calibrated southwest in the direction of the holy city, leading
to a pilgrim road. As with a succession of capitals, its geography
also marked its political destiny. Mohammad's flight from Mecca
to the hamlet of Medina signaled his shift from a lone prophet
to a political leader, the beginnings of an Arabian theocracy.
The first purely Arab Umayyad Caliphate ruled from Damascus,
in Syria, backed by the Arabian Desert, the homeland of their
best soldiers and nomadic kin—the caliph, meaning "deputy"
or "successor," was the ruling descendent of the Prophet Mo-
hammad. The succeeding Abbasid Caliphate built Baghdad—a
Persian name, meaning "Given by God"—on the banks of the
Tigris, in the eighth century, near the old Persian capital Cte-
siphon, closer to Central Asia and accessible to the non-Arab
Muslims of Khorasan.

Probably arriving in Baghdad in January or February of 1217,
Rumi's family had missed the golden age of the Abbasid Caliphs
in Baghdad. Its glamour had been at its most radiant during the
reign of Harun al-Rashid in the ninth century, the prosperity of
his capital city opulently conveyed in the *Arabian Nights.* Harun
set up a court in the Persian imperial style and encouraged intel-
lectual projects—primitive Bedouin songs were transcribed, and
Greek scientific texts translated by Nestorian monks. The gar-
dens of his Golden Gate palace were plotted about a tree made
of silver with mechanical singing birds, and beyond stretched a
cosmopolitan city that included three pontoon bridges, anchored
by iron chains to either bank of the Tigris, plus thousands of ferry
skiffs; a Christian district with churches and monasteries; public

parks for horse racing and polo (a Persian sport); and a wild beast park, with Indian peacocks.

During the winter of 1217 Baghdad was a less coherent show-place of urban planning, with travel across town for Rumi's family probably made more difficult by a great flood. The caliph al-Nasir had been ruling for nearly forty years, striving to maintain the glories of the Baghdad of Harun but without unified military power. The caliph remained checked by Khwarazmshah to the east and Seljuk Turks to the west. Yet he dealt effectively, while cultivating his gardens and moving the palaces from Harun's round city to the eastern banks of the Tigris. The poet Khaqani, as he passed through Baghdad, swooned over the gardens as a paradise, comparing the Tigris to the Virgin Mary's tears.

Medieval Baghdad was widely diverse and tolerant, with a few restrictions. Some caliphs decreed that non-Muslim women wear yellow or blue clothing and red shoes. Yet Christian neighborhoods were among the most popular in Baghdad, partly explained by the unofficial role of monks as bootleggers for abstaining Muslims, as they brewed and dispensed wine from their cloisters. "On a rainy day, what a pleasure it is to drink wine with a priest," wrote one chronicler. Around the time of Rumi's visit, the geographer and travel writer Yaqut was quite taken with a Greek Nestorian church, in the Dayr al-Rum quarter, where he said crowds of Muslims came on festival days to stare at "the young deacons and monks, with their handsome faces" and enjoy "dancing, drinking, and pleasure-making."

Rumi accumulated a personal geography, a poetic version of Yaqut's *Dictionary of Countries,* where these cities he visited were consistently pegged. Samarkand and Damascus were forever sweetness and light, Bukhara forever tied to the suspect "logic" of Greek sciences on display in its renowned library, where the texts, stored in chests rather than on shelves, were delivered on request by the staff. "Bukhara is a mine of knowledge," he wrote, adding a warning against just such knowledge elsewhere:

> *Give up art and logic for amazement*
> *Go towards humility, not Bukhara*

As the center of the caliphate, Baghdad remained, for him, a symbol of justice and power:

> *Your Baghdad is full of justice*
> *Your Samarkand is full of sweetness*

In one tale of Baghdad in the *Masnavi*, the ambitious wife of a Bedouin nomad convinces her husband to advance their fortunes by petitioning the caliph, and bringing to him as a tribute the greatest and scarcest treasure in the desert, a jug of rainwater:

> *The Bedouin's wife was not aware*
> *The Tigris, sweet as sugar, flows there,*
> *Flowing through Baghdad, like a sea,*
> *Full of boats, with nets full of fish . . .*
> *All our senses, and perceptions*
> *Are like a drop in that pure river.*

The joke was about the comic limits of human understanding of the unknown, especially the divinely ordained unknown. Rumi was impressed with the "hot sun of Iraq," and the Tigris and Euphrates from then on joined the mighty Oxus on the map of his imagination:

> *The Euphrates, Tigris, and Oxus would be bitter*
> *As the salty sea, if they were not flowing*

The family likely stayed in Baghdad for a month. By the thirteenth century, the city was full of *khaneqahs,* or Sufi lodges, often built next to cemeteries, appropriate for otherworldly yearning. Yet Rumi's father was said to have chosen instead to reside in one of the *madrases,* or colleges. On the western side of Baghdad, the terminus for caravans from Khorasan, at least thirty such religious colleges were located. He never publicly identified with Sufi lodges, and the college setting was deemed more appropriate for a jurist and preacher, traveling with his family. In an important moment in his life, an emissary of the Seljuk sultan of Konya supposedly heard a weekday sermon given by Baha Valad in a Baghdad mosque, and reported back his favorable impression.

If not in residence at Nezamiyye College, Baha Valad would at least have toured this most magnificent university in the Islamic world, founded by the Vizier Nezam al-Molk in 1065, over a century before Oxford or the Sorbonne. Providing free education in the Shafiite branch of Sharia law, this institute, with branches for research, known as the "Mother of Madrases," was located near a wharf on the banks of the Tigris River—alongside the great Tuesday Market street of East Baghdad that led in a serpentine route around the walls of the palaces of the caliphs—and was funded by the state with generous stipends for professors, as well as for building and grounds maintenance. Babylonian willow trees provided shade, while date and dried fruit sellers plied their trades nearby.

Even a casual stroll through Nezamiyye College offered a sampling of the textures of academic life that would become familiar to Rumi during the studious years of his young adulthood. Following a student riot and fire years earlier, the college had been rebuilt and was again stirring with activity. The long, open-fronted robes of the scholars debating one another in the porticos were often dusty and frayed, while more celebrated jurists, in the manner of Baha Valad's imagined rival Razi, were elegantly dressed and perfumed, their sharp beards trimmed, and their large turbans tightly wound. (In the *Masnavi*, Rumi pokes fun at one such scholar stuffing his academic turban with rags to make it appear bigger.) The universal language of students bustling in the courtyards was Arabic—like Latin in Europe, the lingua franca for all scholarly discourse and writing.

Most famously at Nezamiyye, nearly two hundred years earlier, in the eleventh century, the renowned scholar Mohammad al-Ghazali lectured in halls that were crowded with hundreds of students, for four years, then apparently suffered a nervous breakdown and left Baghdad to wander the deserts of the Hejaz, near Mecca and Syria. Haunted by doubts about Aristotelian logic, he eventually entered a Sufi lodge, where he wrote his widely influential treatise on "inner" science, *The Revival of the Religious Sciences*. In his lifetime—and Rumi's—*The Revival of the Religious Sciences* was akin to a best seller.

Rumi would refer to al-Ghazali with respect, but his true passion was al-Ghazali's more radical and outrageous poet brother, Ahmad, sometimes credited with the dramatic turnaround of the older philosopher from logical analysis toward his more therapeutic religion of the heart. Ahmad had always been a highly visible Sufi in Baghdad, espousing mystical love in aphorisms in his well-known book, *Savaneh,* or *Flashes,* and rather notorious for meditating on the eternal while gazing on the face of a beautiful boy, known as *shahed-bazi,* a controversial practice in Sufism. Ahmad liked to lay a rose before a comely face and contemplate the lovely pair alternately. Yet Rumi remarked on the diminution of Mohammad's intellect next to Ahmad's hot passion: "Had he possessed just one atom of love like Ahmad, it would have been better."

If Baghdad had lost a degree of its caliphal splendor by the time Rumi's family visited, the city was still a great laboratory of developing Sufism, as it had been for over the previous four centuries. While the plain woolen robes of the earliest Sufis—their name probably derived from *suf,* or wool, for this near-uniform—associated them with Christian desert monks, the label "Sufiyya," rooted in the Arabic word *tasawwuf,* from which the English word "Sufism" is derived, was first applied to a mostly urban movement in eighth-century Baghdad. As one modern scholar of Sufism has speculated: "The term 'Sufi' had a certain 'avant-garde' or 'cutting-edge' resonance among both renunciants and others . . . this 'hip' quality facilitated its application to the new movement."

Starting from simple notions of clean living and exile from the luxuries of civilization—following the example of Ebrahim ebn Adham, the "Buddha of Balkh"—Sufism exfoliated into a subtle theology, emphasizing a more intimate relation with God and the possibility of inner union, or reunion, with the divine. Sufis favored verses of the Quran that emphasized closeness and accessibility over the sheer transcendence of God. Especially beloved was the fifteenth verse of Sura 50: "We indeed created man; and We know what his soul whispers within him, and we are nearer to him than the jugular vein."

A chronicler of these early Sufis, appropriately enough, was Attar. Uninterested in writing yet another *Lives of the Poets,* he had retooled the genre, as Sanai had lyric poetry, by compiling a Persian *Lives of the Saints*—such compilations of popular stories about holy figures had long been popular in Arabic. There he told of Rabia, the woman mystic of Basra, said to have torn through the streets with a torch in one hand and a jug of water in the other to burn down Paradise and douse the fires of Hell, so no one would love God solely for reward or punishment. He profiled Jonayd, the glass seller, who promoted a "sober" School of Baghdad, advising speaking in code, and his foil Bayazid Bestami, who inspired a "drunken" school of Sufism similar to the

School of Khorasan, full of music and ecstasy. These stories were lore the boy Rumi either already knew or was now discovering.

The climax to Attar's seventy-two life sketches was Mansur al-Hallaj, a larger-than-life "drunken" Sufi, brutally executed in Baghdad in 922. Attar blamed his death on his famed utterance, "I am the Truth." Since Truth was one of the ninety-nine names of God in Islam, the claim was judged heretical. (For his supporters, the statement indicated a complete annihilation of ego.) The sister of Hallaj also caused a minor stir by walking the streets of Baghdad without wearing a proper veil. Attar told a gruesome tale of the martyrdom of Hallaj—the merciful saint was led to the gallows, where his hands and feet were cut off, while he smiled and prayed. His body was then burned and his ashes tossed into the Tigris. Rumi's Baghdad was a city of power, but sometimes that power was harshly wielded:

In the world of Baghdad I cried out, "I am the Truth!"
While that world was busy debating the words of Hallaj

❖

Traveling to Mecca in 1217, Rumi's family would have needed to depart Baghdad by February, at the latest. That year, on the Muslim lunar calendar, the final month of the year, or *Dhul-Hijja*, named as the month for the pilgrimage, or *hajj*, to Mecca—the birthplace of Mohammad—began on March 11. The official ceremonies in Mecca took place during the first two weeks of this month; Muslims could make a "little" pilgrimage to the holy city at any time throughout the year, though without fulfilling the commandment to participate in the *hajj* at least once in a lifetime. Incumbent on Hanafites departing from Baghdad, such as

Baha Valad, was to first visit the grave of Abu Hanifa, the founder of the Hanafi School. His shrine was marked with a white dome, where a charitable station was set up for feeding the poor. The first phase of their trip was then the hundred-mile journey to join with pilgrim caravans departing from the squat brick city of Kufa.

Caravans leaving Kufa took nearly a month to arrive in Mecca, a journey of over a thousand miles across the Arabian Peninsula, through much of modern-day Saudi Arabia, which included forbidding territories troubled by stifling heat, deadly winds, and clouds of black flies. The desert road stretching from Kufa to Mecca offered only water in wells, or cisterns, and an occasional underground canal. Absent were the caravanserai stationed along the Khorasan Road. Pilgrims remained in caravans at night, without the protection of walls, or they continued traveling in the dark. As Rumi later embroidered:

> A man traveling with a caravan on a dark, overcast night does not know where he is, how far he has traveled, or what he has passed. At daybreak, he sees the results of the journey, that is, he will have arrived at some place. Likewise, whoever labors for the glory of God is never lost, though he shut both his eyes.

While Rumi had many experiences with caravans to draw on, his more extreme memories of fears faced during travel were consistent with tales told of going on *hajj* in medieval times. He spoke of travelers attacked in one spot, "piling a few stones on top of each other as a marker, as if to say, 'This is a dangerous place.'" And his evocation of caravans in desolate terrain conveyed the menace for a child of many imaginary threats:

Say there is someone in a caravan on a dark night. He is so afraid that he constantly imagines that bandits are attacking the caravan. He wants to hear and recognize his fellow travelers' voices. When he hears their voices, he feels safe.

The greatest threat was marauding Bedouin tribes that raided caravans. By day these Bedouins tried to sell hungry travelers meat, milk, and cheese. Yet even in daylight the journey was filled with the potential for accidents and sudden catastrophe. The Spanish geographer Ibn Jubayr, traveling to Mecca thirty years before Rumi's family, witnessed a roadside stop where seven pilgrims had been trampled to death in a rush on a water tank used by men and camels. Rumi compared these travails to spiritual efforts:

> *The glory of the Kaaba and its gathering is proved*
> *When pilgrims brave Bedouins and travel the wide desert*

Once within the sacred zone of Mecca, the basic rituals of *hajj* had remained constant over the centuries, though political control of the region shifted. (One local ruler during this period mistreated pilgrims from Baghdad to display his power in a feud with the caliph.) While the majority of pilgrims were males, their families and single women also took part. Men and boys wore the pilgrim's robe—two sheets of white cloth, secured by a white sash, with sandals. Women wore modest dress and *hijab*. The core event was walking seven times counterclockwise around the Kaaba, the granite cube that stood at the center of the Islamic world, the vanishing point of *qibla*, so that, as Rumi wrote: "When you're inside the Kaaba, you don't need to face in any direction." Especially cherished was the Black Stone, affixed by Mohammad in the Kaaba wall. Other rituals included running between the hills of Al-Safa and Al-Marwah, drinking from the Zamzam Well, standing vigil at Mount Arafat, and the symbolic Stoning of the Devil.

While the meaning of *hajj* centered on communal worship at the Grand Mosque, and the final animal sacrifice in the nearby village of Mina, marketplaces thrived, even if officially discouraged. Ibn Jubayr noted, between the hilltops of al-Safa and al-Marwa, a "market full of fruits" set up such that pious runners could "hardly free themselves from the great crowd." He described the exhalation after the two weeks, when the Grand Mosque, the sanctuary of the Kaaba, "became a great market in which were sold commodities ranging from flour to agates, and from wheat to pearls." Poor Yemenis bartered wheat, raisins, or butter for "women's veils or strong quilts," worn by Bedouins.

Rumi once told his students that the true place of the Kaaba in Islam was to fulfill the recorded saying of Mohammad that "cohesion is a mercy, and isolation torment." Visiting the Kaaba was made obligatory so that people from many cities and climes of the world might gather there. Yet most often he transposed Mecca to the spiritual plane, never commenting on his personal experience of *hajj*. He even pitied a poor pilgrim, lost in the surrounding desert:

> *Oh you who've gone on* hajj—
> *Where, oh where, are you?*
> *Here, here is the Beloved!*
> *Oh come now, come, oh come!*
> *You, lost in the desert—*
> *What air of love is this?*
> *You are the house, the master,*
> *You are the Kaaba, you!*

Such sentiments reflected the attitudes he shared with, and may even have learned from, Attar and the Sufis of Baghdad: in his

Lives of the Saints, Attar told a story of Rabia on her way to Mecca being met and welcomed on the road by the Kaaba, rather than proceeding as a pilgrim to pay her respects at the shrine. "I need the Lord of the house," she said. "What am I to do with the house?"

Within a week of the conclusion of these sacred ceremonies, all pilgrim caravans once again departed for Yemen, Syria, Egypt, Iraq, and points beyond as Mecca and Medina reverted to quiet and sleepy towns until the following year. And the Black Stone of the Kaaba, for Rumi in his later poetry, like the *qibla,* resolved into a human face:

> *The pilgrim kisses the Black Stone of the Kaaba*
> *As if he were kissing the red lips of the beloved*

CHAPTER 4

"Fire fell into the world"

As a gathering place for pilgrims from throughout the wider Muslim world, Mecca also served as a center of news and information, where Rumi and his family would have heard the latest in eyewitness reports, or twice-told rumors from various corners of the map. In 1217, the urgent talk among travelers from Central Asia concerned the threat of the Mongols. Since the time of the departure of Rumi's family from Khorasan, tensions had only increased between Genghis Khan and Khwarazmshah, with word spreading of an onslaught that was taking place along the easternmost borders, nearer to Vakhsh and other outlying regions. The fate of those on *hajj* was unclear, and the decision open of whether to return to endangered cities such as Balkh or Samarkand.

After Mecca, Rumi's family next appeared in Damascus, which required taking a route from Mecca back to Baghdad, and connecting near its Syria Gate with a western road, the entire journey lasting about two months. Not knowing whether war was imminent, Baha Valad would have been pushed to clarify his decisions about the future. A teaching post in Damascus, one of the core cities for Islamic intellectual life, along with Cairo and Baghdad, was desirable, but Baha Valad's imperfect spoken Arabic may have been an impediment, as seamless eloquence was expected from public speakers. Damascus itself was also volatile. While the Crusades, launched by the Latin Catholic Church, were according to one historian a "sideshow" compared to the destruction about to be inflicted by Tatar armies, Syria was still checkered by this conflict—the ruler of Damascus at the time was al-Moazzam, whose father was off fighting the Fifth Crusade.

Baha Valad moved with his family, once again, this time from Syria to Anatolia—the Asian, or Asia Minor, section of modern-day Turkey—probably during the summer of 1217. Until this move, Rumi, about ten or eleven years old, had been exposed to diverse religious groups, but always in Muslim-controlled areas and with clear Muslim majorities. Anatolia was territory defined in the imagination of Muslims as the outer limits of their civilization, the borderlands of Christian Rome, or Rum. (The term "Rumi" was used sometimes as a synonym for "Christian," this shadow meaning still clinging to the name when used for Rumi after his death.) From now on they would be living in cities where they were greatly outnumbered by mostly Greek-speaking or Armenian Christians, with Muslims in Anatolia estimated at just 10 percent of the population.

The city where they first alighted, Malatya, in southeast Anatolia near a juncture of the Euphrates River, was a garrison town attached to an eighth-century fortress, the first square of defense in a line of fortresses against the Byzantines extending to the Mediterranean. Yaqut described the town as part of Greek territories when he traveled through, yet the Seljuk Turks were apparently in charge when the family of Baha Valad resided there briefly. The climate of the large town wavered—between desert aridity and northerly precipitation—as did its religious persuasions between Christian and Muslim.

While in Malatya the boy Rumi had the second of his reputed meetings with remarkable men. Also living in town at the time was the Spanish-born Arab mystic Ibn Arabi, the grandest and most sublime thinker of the era, his speculations concerning the merging of Creator and Creation sometimes accused of being a pantheistic, heretical bending of the theology of a transcendent deity in Islam. Picking up pieces left behind in the writings of al-Ghazali a century earlier, Ibn Arabi created a synthesis of mystical thinking, an intellectual Sufism in hundreds of volumes, where he developed ruminations on abstruse matters such as a "science of letters" of God's name, which had absorbed Sufi thinkers since at least the eleventh century. Although he taught in Damascus, Syria was enough of a war zone that he passed the years from 1216 to 1220 in Malatya.

As the story was told, a conversation had been arranged between the newly arrived Baha Valad and the greatest living master of Sufi theology. He brought along his son, yet when they departed, as with Attar, it was the boy who drew the attention of the great mystic. Watching young Rumi trail his father down the street, Ibn Arabi remarked, "Glory be to God! An ocean is following a lake!" Again, Rumi never spoke of such a meeting. Yet unlike his supposed encounter with Attar, Rumi as an adult had more ambivalent feelings about Ibn Arabi, as about all things highly intellectual or abstruse, and later in life even made a small joke at Ibn Arabi's expense. He had walked into a hall where his disciples were discussing Ibn Arabi's esoteric *Meccan Revelations*. Suddenly Zaki the Singer entered and broke into a joyful song. Rumi exclaimed, "Well now the *Zaki Revelations* are even finer than the *Meccan Revelations!*" And he began to whirl. His point was that music, poetry, and dance were more important than abstract ideas.

The first solid patron of Baha Valad in Anatolia was Bahramshah, the prince of Erzincan, and his wife, the princess Esmati. Their capital was located at the upper end of the Euphrates Valley, where Rumi's family soon undertook yet another journey, of two hundred miles, to northeast Anatolia. Erzincan was a large and primarily Armenian Christian town. Such towns often provoked the ire of visiting Muslims, who expressed indignation at all the wine, pork, and religious processions. Wishing to avoid these alien practices, Baha Valad insisted that his own school be established nearby in the more sober town of Aqshahr, and there he apparently was set up in the winter of 1218, in "Esmati-yye," named after his royal patroness, teaching general classes, rather than a strict Hanafi law curriculum, with a soft edge of Sufi mysticism.

This minor shah of Erzincan was already accustomed to patronizing Persian cultural figures such as Baha Valad. He had earlier supported the production of a long didactic poem, *Treasury of Secrets,* written in the style of Sanai, by Nezami. A court poet of Azerbaijan, Nezami had also written the most famous romance in *masnavi* couplets, *Layli and Majnun,* a classic tale of the unrequited love of Majnun, a Bedouin youth, his name meaning "Crazy," driven insane by his intense devotion for the delicate Layli. This star-crossed pair remained in Rumi's imagination as his favorite fictional lovers, and he later sainted suffering Majnun as the quintessential Sufi "martyr of love" for God:

> *Majnun, embrace the Layli of night*
> *Night is the time for divine solitude.*
> *Layli is night, and the day is ahead, Majnun.*
> *At dawn, wisdom will light the curls of her hair.*

About a year had passed since Rumi and his family had been on *hajj* in Mecca. During this time Baha Valad, and anyone else from Khorasan, was anxiously looking and listening to discover recent news of the situation there. No one was truly settled anywhere. Yet the reports brought by travelers were increasingly dire, and any future plans of Baha Valado eventually to

return were quickly demolished, their sojourn in Anatolia look-
ing more permanent. If Rumi's family set out on their quest as
pilgrims, or even as emigrants, within the next few years they
wound up as displaced refugees. Rumi later brought to life the
feelings aroused by hearing of the chaos caused by this greatest
of historical disruptions:

> *Day and night I'm thinking of you*
> *In these bloody days and nights, how do you feel?*
> *As this fire fell into the world*
> *In this smoke of the Tatar army, how do you feel?*

❖

By the time Baha Valad was finally settled in his new school in
Aqshahr, the Khorasan region, where he had left behind his aged
mother, as well as oldest son and daughter, was registering serious
activity, sparked by a small border incident. Rumi later told this
history, with accuracy, as he knew the terrain and players inti-
mately. As a boy, he had seen the Asiatic faces of the traders in
Chinese silk and camel cloth, silver and jade, and his father had
early identified the unreliable character of the Khwarazmshah:

> Some of them who used to come as traders into the terri-
> tories of the Khwarazmshah would buy muslin to clothe
> themselves. The Khwarazmshah prohibited them and or-
> dered their traders killed. He also taxed them and barred
> his own merchants from traveling to their lands. The
> Tatars went humbly before their king, wailing, "We have
> been destroyed." The king sought ten days to consider the
> matter and went into a deep cave, where he fasted the ten
> days, and he beseeched and prayed. A cry came from God,

saying, "I have heard your plea. Come forth and be victorious wherever you go." They came out and under God's command they were victorious and conquered the world.

This provocation, retold by Rumi, occurred in 1217, when Genghis Khan, eyeing Khwarazm as a lucrative trading partner, sent his ambassadors to negotiate a trade agreement and followed them with a caravan of 450 merchants carrying luxury goods. As the caravan crossed into present-day Kazakhstan, just north of Rumi's childhood home, its governor, a relative of the Khwarazmshah, seized the goods and killed the merchants, as spies. Genghis Khan sent envoys to demand retribution. Instead, Khwarazmshah beheaded one envoy and returned the others, their beards insultingly shaved. Verifying Rumi's account, the contemporary Persian historian Jovayni reported that Genghis Khan ascended a mountaintop to pray, and descended, "ready for war." He dramatically added that the rash acts would wind up having "laid waste a whole world."

The ensuing, punishing invasion lasted four years, until Genghis Khan, in his sixties, returned home to Mongolia, leaving behind in ruins the grand cities that Rumi had known as a boy—Bukhara, Samarkand, Balkh, Herat, Merv, and Nishapur. As Jovayni described the vanguard of the descent of the Mongol forces on Bukhara—a signature display of sound and fury—the townspeople "beheld the surrounding countryside choked with horsemen and the air black as night with the dust of cavalry, and fright and panic overcame them." Genghis Khan himself rode into the town that for Rumi "stands for the true source of knowledge," halting to ask if the mosque, the biggest edifice, were the sultan's palace. He ordered imams to feed his horses, using the libraries as stables, and Quran stands as mangers for straw. One survivor succinctly reported, "They came, they sapped, they burnt, they slew, they plundered, and they departed."

From Bukhara, the Mongol armies proceeded through the fertile Zarafshan valley to attack Samarkand, an operation far more brutal than the siege Rumi had witnessed as a boy, just eight years earlier. Mongol numbers were augmented by a forced march of prisoners, the weakest dropping from exhaustion. Outside the walls of the city, these prisoners were disguised as soldiers, with every tenth one holding a flag, so that the citizens of Samarkand imagined a force many times larger. Genghis Khan entered by the northwest gate, dividing thirty thousand of the skilled artisans among his sons and kinsmen, and then killing a sizable portion of the population. The lustrous new Cathedral Mosque, built by Khwarazmshah after his own siege, was bombarded with hurled pots of flaming tar.

The cavalry then retraced the same route from Samarkand to Balkh that had likely been traveled by Rumi's family. Termez—where Rumi's tutor Borhan stayed behind—was shown no mercy. Jovayni recorded that "all the people, both men and women, were driven out onto the plain and divided proportionately among the soldiers in accordance with their usual custom; then they were all slain, none being spared." In Balkh, where members of Baha Valad's family were perhaps still living, any fortifications and walls, as well as mansions and palaces, were obliterated, and the killing fields of Termez were replicated: "Wild beasts feasted on their flesh, and lions consorted without contention with wolves, and vultures ate without quarreling from the same table with eagles."

Nishapur suffered the most numbing treatment of all the cities in this prolonged exercise in bloody revenge and tactical empire building. An arrow shot from the city ramparts during its defense killed Tokuchar, the son-in-law of Genghis Khan. The conqueror allowed his widowed and pregnant daughter to exact the revenge. In April 1221 she decreed death for all except four hundred craftsmen, including dogs, cats, and any living animals, and ordered the skulls of the corpses to be piled into three pyramids—for men, women, and children. A few accounts numbered Attar among these dead, seemingly fitting for this subtle and melancholy poet who described himself as "the voice of pain."

For the three years leading up to the Mongol invasion, the geographer Yaqut had been staying happily in Merv, where he was researching his travel books in its many libraries. "But for the Mongols I would have stayed there and lived and died there," he wrote, "and hardly could I tear myself away." When the Mongol attack was imminent, Yaqut fled to Mosul. Soon afterward the invaders burned down all of its libraries, and smashed the dams and dikes so that the oasis reverted to a desert swamp.

Yaqut then joined an exodus of displaced Persians on the clogged roads heading west toward Mesopotamia, Syria, and Anatolia. Caravans now included escapees from Khorasan, crossing paths with returning *hajj* pilgrims. In Baghdad, lodging was in short supply, and housing difficult to rent, as the displaced attempted to find places to stay. In a letter penned shortly after his escape, Yaqut, in an effusive, elegiac court style, mourned the palaces he had witnessed "effaced from off the earth as lines of writing are effaced from paper, and those abodes become a dwelling for the owl and the raven; in those places the screech-owls answer each other's cries, and in those halls the winds moan."

The numbers of dead were wildly exaggerated at the time, with suggestions of casualties in the hundreds of millions, far beyond the population of any cities in Central Asia. (Even some modern scholars, though, have confirmed the possibility of a 90 percent extermination rate among the Persian population in Khorasan, constituting racial genocide.) If a percentage of the victims were spared for deportation as skilled slaves, Genghis Khan was uncompromising in his systematic destruction of cities, as well as lead piping and irrigation systems, turning farms and orchards back to grazing lands for his herds. Voicing a general pessimism in the society, one contemporary historian opined that the Mongols were "the announcement of the death-blow of Islam and the Muslims."

Yet as Genghis Khan was establishing his brutish militarist state in Central Asia—an absolute threat to the religion of Islam—curiously resilient were the mystical practices of Sufism, already established in the western provinces and revivified by these Khorasani immigrants, including Baha Valad and his family. Sufi lodges became welcome cultural outposts of refinement, where sheikhs, or spiritual leaders, offered messages of hope and transcendence, friendship and love, as well as musical concerts, poetry, and dance, evoking rapture. Sufi orders, loosely similar to Western religious orders, were beginning to multiply and would become more formalized in the next decades and centuries. As the German Middle East scholar Annemarie Schimmel summed up the contrast: "This period of the most terrible political disaster was, at the same time, a period of highest religious and mystical activity."

The full force of the Mongol campaigns would be concentrated in two aggressive phases—the first, the conquest of Central Asia, and the second, commandeered by the grandsons of Genghis Khan, marked by incursions into the Middle East and Anatolia in the 1250s. A newly configured world map spread contiguous Mongol-controlled territories from Korea to Hungary. From the age of ten until his death, Rumi coped with the turmoil caused by this churning realpolitik of the Mongols. Yet either ignoring, or because of, the pain and suffering caused to his family and community, as an adult, Rumi stuck resolutely to his surety of an "invisible hand" in these dark historical events:

While everyone flees from the Tatars
We serve the Creator of the Tatars

He framed the issue even more starkly for his circle, often im-
migrants from Khorasan, writing, "If you're afraid of the Tatars,
you don't believe in God."

❖

In the final phase of his life, Baha Valad—now nearly seventy
years old—found the acceptance, even acclaim, which had
eluded him during his earlier years. He might well have dis-
cerned divine providence at work—and communicated to his
son this understanding of otherwise tragic events. His choice of
location in Asia Minor was not random, as he moved as an itiner-
ant preacher from city to city, and patron to patron, working his
way always closer to Konya, the capital of the Seljuk Sultanate of
Rum, ruled by Sultan Alaoddin Kayqobad I, which he may have
first visited as early as 1221. And of course the timing of this
late-life migration had allowed his family to escape possible ex-
ecution by the world conqueror known, by then, simply as "The
Accursed." He and his family spent the next seven years in the
center of Anatolia before finally arriving in Konya, and Rumi
passed from a boyhood spent traveling to young manhood.

Within four years of arriving in Erzincan, by 1222, Baha
Valad was finally on his way, with his family, to the more cen-
tral city of Larande, well inside the realm of the Seljuk sultan-
ate. The daughter of the shah of Erzincan had been married to
Kaykaus I, the Seljuk king, and may have smoothed the way for
Baha Valad with members of the royal family. Originally one
of dozens of nomadic Turkic clans in Central Asia, the Seljuks

were nearing the apogee of a two-century hold on power in the central Islamic lands. In 1055, the Great Seljuks had taken control as "protector" of the Abbasid Caliphate; in 1077, the Seljuks in Anatolia defeated the Byzantines, at the Battle of Manzikert near Erzincan, almost to their own surprise, giving them sway over much of Asia Minor.

Arriving when he was about fifteen years old, Rumi truly came of age in Larande, or modern-day Karaman, sixty miles southeast of Konya. The hilltop town was full of gardens, fountains, and sweet peaches, which he later said could set a whole town smiling:

Today a hundred beautiful faces are smiling in Konya
Today a hundred peaches are arriving from Larande

This pleasant association fit the experience of his family, particularly his father. Baha Valad's patron was the local governor, who built him an entire school on the main square in town. Baha's orientation as a Sunni Hanafite with Sufi leanings fit with the broader agenda of the Seljuks, as they had been part of the military force behind a "Sunni Revival" of the Abbasid Caliphate, and had originally been converted to Islam by the heartwarming preaching of the Sufis. This formula worked especially well in trying to win over the local Greek Christians, rather than a hardline legalism. (Larande also included many Christian Turks, who were writing Turkish using a Greek alphabet.)

Most of Rumi's adolescent education took place in these learned settings arranged for his father in such Anatolian towns. In spite of any juvenile resistance to primary school lessons, he had grown into an avid pupil, curious and studying widely, absorbing all manner of religious, scientific, and literary texts. The basics of his classwork were meant to prepare him for a life of preaching, teaching, and judging. He studied Arabic grammar and prosody; commentaries on the Quran; accounts of the life and sayings of the Prophet Mohammad; and Sharia, or religious law. He also studied history, philosophy, mathematics, and a favorite Persian science, astronomy, its scientific instruments for precise measuring and stargazing recurring in many of his later lyrics:

> *The sky is an astrolabe, while the truth is love*
> *When I speak, spin your ear towards my meaning*

Turning seventeen in Larande, Rumi was wed, in 1224, to Gowhar, in a ceremony that bore all the marks of a traditionally arranged marriage. As the daughter of Sharaf of Samarkand, the deceased patron and disciple of Baha Valad, and his widow, the matriarch now known as the Great Kerra, Gowhar had been close to Rumi since they were both learning their alphabets. She had traveled with her mother in the harem of the caravan all the way from Samarkand, and, like Rumi, had grown from a child into a young adult over the course of the eventful decade—rare memories, which they shared. Almost immediately, they had two sons: Bahaoddin Mohammad, later known as Sultan Valad, born in 1226, and named with his grandfather's full name, and Alaoddin Mohammad, named for Rumi's older brother, who possibly died during the long journey.

Rumi was keenly observant of the process of giving birth, and the transformation of a wife into a mother, his empathy palpable in the *Masnavi*, where he writes of pregnant women trembling at each spasm, or chewing on clay lumps to help ease their birth pangs:

> *In childbirth every mother suffers aches*
> *As her baby tries to break out of prison.*

The mother cries, "Where is my refuge?"
The baby laughs, "Salvation is here!"

He graphically rendered the first demanding phases of child rearing, when he devised an analogy for his students about God's transformative patience with spiritual immaturity:

> God is able to do all things. . . . When a child is newly born he is worse than a donkey. He puts his hand in his filth and then his hand in his mouth to lick. His mother slaps him to prevent it. When he pisses, he spreads his legs so that the pee doesn't drip on his leg. . . . Yet God is able to turn a baby into a human being.

And he tenderly recalled a mother's breastfeeding moments at the side of a baby's crib:

Unless the baby in the cradle cries and weeps
How does the anxious mother know to feed him milk?

From earliest childhood, Rumi's two sons were a tumble of conflicts. Even the order of their births has never firmly been established. Sultan Valad was named after his grandfather, a distinction signaling a firstborn, especially as Rumi's father was about seventy-five years old at his birth. Yet one contemporary biographer recorded that Alaoddin was one year older. Less ambiguous would be Sultan Valad's place as his father's favorite, not only his child but also his disciple, revering his father as Rumi had revered and tried to emulate Baha Valad. So sibling rivalry was ever roiling between these brothers—a source of pain for their father, who sketched all boys' games as combative:

Wars are like the fights of children,
Meaningless, thoughtless, and petty
They aim at each other with wooden swords
But their goals and purposes are futile.

In Larande, Rumi, now a married young adult, stepped into
the position of preacher, occasionally taking his father's place
on the steps of the pulpit, where sermons were delivered in
mosques, or in the seat of honor, in a college. In the medieval
Muslim world, preaching was an art and a pillar of moral teach-
ing, both entertainment and instruction. Rumi's father's deliv-
ery was fiery, a popular timbre. His grandson Sultan Valad told
of him once throttling three sturdy camel drivers on the road
to Baghdad. "They repented and begged forgiveness," he said,
comparing his grandfather to a lion. Such force came through
in his sermons. He was saturated in the preaching culture of
Khorasan, where sermons often ended on shrill warnings about
judgment on the Last Day as weeping listeners, revival-style,
came forward to repent of sins by having their heads shaved.

Rumi's tone was already more dulcet and controlled. He
did not preach fire and brimstone, yet he adhered to the basic
model. His early sermons were traditional and fairly standard,
opening with a benediction in Arabic rhymed prose, in the style
of the Quran, praising God, His Messenger Mohammad, and
Abu Bakr, the first of the four "Rightly Guided" caliphs vener-
ated by Sunni Muslims. He then prayed for God's intercession
in a lyrical Persian that was full of crescendos—the language
was understood in Anatolia by the many Persian immigrants as
well as being generally used as the universal court language for
business and ceremonies. In one sermon evidently delivered in
Larande, he prayed for his father and mother, and for his "in-
structor," another figure clearly involved in his sophisticated re-
ligious education. He then repeated, in Arabic, a saying of the

Prophet—the text of his sermon—after which he switched back into Persian.

In periodic flashes, the later mystic and poet Rumi can be glimpsed in some of these early sermons—otherwise they were the works of a young man trying to conform to his father's pattern. In one of seven surviving sermons, he borrows a metaphor from a long poem attributed to Attar, *The Book of the Camel,* but common enough in mystical literature—a Turkish puppeteer performs with seven veils, and at the end of the night, like the cosmic creator, breaks all of his puppets and stores their pieces again in the dark box of Unity. In his opening prayer, Rumi makes enchanting theology from this material:

> The magician of the skies, from behind the curtain of imagination, brings forth a play of shimmering stars and gorgeous planets. We crowd around this theatrical spectacle, mesmerized, passing away the night. In the morning, death will arrive, and the performance of these shadow players will grow cold, and the night of our life will vanish. Oh Lord! Before the morning of death dawns, let our hearts grow cold towards this play so that we might escape in time from this crowd, and not fall behind those who have been traveling through the night. When morning dawns, may we find ourselves arriving within the wider precinct of Your acceptance.

Around 1229, Baha Valad finally received his invitation from the Sultan Alaoddin Kayqobad I to travel to Konya to teach and to live, with his family, at the Altunpa Madrase, the only *madrase* operating at the time in the capital. If Baha Valad hoped to realize his wish to be preaching in one of the more "glorious cities," he was fortunate. The sultan was gathering together a court unequalled in the Anatolian Seljuk dynasty, with many

Persian-speaking poets, artisans, administrators, and scholars, even if the atmosphere included wine drinking and harp playing, which Baha Valad abhorred.

Others were not so fortunate. Uprooted scholars, poets, and religious leaders, bereft of their former university posts or courtly sinecures, were arriving in Anatolia daily, and the court of Kayqobad I was murmured among them to be the most supportive refuge as they tried to recoup their livelihoods in the aftermath of extreme trauma. Just one example of a suddenly needy fellow scholar was Najmoddin Razi, a leading Sufi thinker, a generation younger than Baha Valad, who fled the Mongols to Kayseri in East Anatolia and quickly dispatched inscribed copies of his well-known writings to the Seljuk sultan, without the desired result of a royal invitation to Konya. Yet Baha Valad had luckily managed to salvage, even improve, life for himself and his uprooted family.

Before the Valad family departed for Konya, Rumi's mother died and was buried in Larande. (The burial place of Momene, known as "Madar Sultan" by the Mevlevis, became a much-visited shrine.) By the time Rumi—now a young father and preacher—left Larande he had experienced not only a panoply of traveling, but he had also seen the stages of life played out, with the deaths of his mother and older brother, his marriage to a childhood friend, and the births of their two sons, who took their names from the older generations. Rumi would discover in birth, and the constant metamorphoses of the life cycle, his favorite metaphor for the inner life:

> *Like a baby in the womb, I am nourished with blood.*
> *Everyone is born once. I have been born many times.*

CHAPTER 5

Konya

THICK stone walls, one hundred and forty watchtowers, and twelve gates rose from the central plateau of Anatolia with all the force and stature of the ramparts of Samarkand, Bukhara, Balkh, or Nishapur, as Rumi's family made their way to settle in the city where he would spend most of his adult life. The difference between Konya and these classic cities—by then, mostly razed to the ground—was its relative newness. In 1229 Konya was still a buzzing construction project rather than a monument to the past, the Seljuk capital intended as a living replication of these former capitals of Khorasan. The Sultan Alaoddin Kayqobad I had attempted to consolidate and add legitimacy to his raw power by creating a Turco-Persian axis, and coopting Persian literature, religion, art, and architecture, as well as statecraft and pageantry. Baha Valad and his family would have felt some sense of familiarity and even homecoming as they relocated to the capital, a kinship that resonated in warm tones in Rumi's later poetry:

> Come into my house beloved—a short while!
> Freshen my soul, beloved—a short while! . . .
> So that the light of love radiates from Konya
> To Samarkand and Bukhara—a short while!

Even in its layout, Konya more closely resembled the cities of Central Asia than those of Asia Minor. Houses were spread out between markets and flower gardens. Streets and wide alleys were lined with terra-cotta gullies of running water. Fountains were inset into the walls of public buildings in arch-shaped enclosures. Public baths were centrally located, with sections for men and women, and fresh water spilling continuously from a spout into a basin—all the water was drawn from a reservoir pool beneath a marble dome at one of the city gates. The three miles of city walls were arranged as a rectangle with rounded corners, while the Citadel hill was freestanding in the center of town, in a pentagonal shape, with its own wall and towers constituting a second inner ring of protection. None of this conventional scheme, or its social significance, was lost on Rumi, who later delineated its rigid hierarchy for his son from a celestial perspective:

> Bahaoddin, in this city of Konya notice how many thousands of houses, villas and mansions belong to commanders, noblemen and the wealthy. And notice how the houses of the gentlemen and administrators are grander than the houses of the artisans, and the mansions of the commanders are grander than the houses of the gentlemen. Likewise, the arches and palaces of the sultans and rulers are a hundred times grander and more splendid than the others. But the height and splendor of the heavens compared with these mansions turns out to be far more lofty, mighty, and splendid, and indeed many times more so.

Having drawn on Persian mythology to enhance his status in the capital, Sultan Alaoddin Kayqobad I lent himself an invented pedigree distinct from his nomadic Turkic ancestors, beginning with his name. Like his brother, Kaykaus I, and his father, Kaykhosrow I, the sultan took his royal name from the great fictional kings of the seminal epic of Rumi's boyhood in Khorasan, the *Shahname,* or *The Book of Kings.* The sultan likewise had chiseled onto the towers of the two main entrances to Konya's Citadel sculptural figures and quotations, in tall gold lettering, from the *Shahname,* and, throughout the palaces were set statues of dragons, a symbol in the epic poem of a Turk warrior, whom Ferdowsi, in the *Shahname,* describes as "a dangerous dragon whose breath is as fire." The sultan's glorification of all things Persian, combined with the status of the Seljuks as latecomers to Islam, helped create the perfect milieu for welcoming Rumi's family to Konya, as well as the later crucial tolerance and protection for Rumi by the sultan's descendants.

Kayqobad I was the single most important force in the reversal of fortune for Rumi's family and was generally convincing in fulfilling the heroic ideal of his glorious fictional namesake. His reign was the bright center of the comparatively brief two-century arc of imperial Seljuk Rum. Having ascended to power in 1219, after surviving imprisonment by his older brother Kaykaus I, he was a mostly wise ruler, evidently charismatic, though considered overly haughty by some of his emirs. He was also an able administrator, bringing into his treasury annual revenue of 3,300,000 gold dinars, from trade with Europe, and according to one historian, "embellishing Konya beyond all recognition." During his fifteen-year reign, his armies secured the whole of Asia Minor from the Black Sea to the Mediterranean, transforming Anatolia into a maritime power.

A patron of architecture, a devout Muslim, and an ambitious ruler with a talent for stagecraft, Kayqobad I chose as his legacy project the reconstruction of the Great Mosque on the Citadel hill, adjacent to the royal palaces and overlooking the plains. (When Konya was the classical Roman city of Iconium, Paul, from coastal Tarsus, preached Christianity on this Acropolis.)

Built by a Syrian architect, the mosque retained the floor plan of the Great Mosque of Damascus, with a flat roof. The main prayer room held four thousand worshipers, with an atmosphere of awe created by forty-two marble columns, like a stone forest. Including an intricate ebony pulpit, the congregational mosque was used for noon sermons, and Rumi would kneel many Fridays on its woolen prayer rugs:

> *I prayed so much that I turned into prayer*
> *Whoever looks into my face remembers to pray*

The imaginative creatures chiseled on walls and gates surrounding these ceremonial buildings, including the palace, which stretched from the main gate to the wall of the mosque, would filter into Rumi's imagination, too. Two pairs of winged angels guarded entrances to the Citadel. Over twenty lions, and several double-headed eagles, were carved in relief, as well as a caparisoned elephant pierced by a rhinoceros's horn:

> *If you turn into a lion, Love turns into a lion hunter*
> *If you turn into an elephant, Love turns into a rhinoceros*

Built as well at the command of Kayqobad I, in 1229—the probable year of the arrival of Rumi's family in Konya—was Sultan Han, a traveler's caravanserai, on the road from Kayseri to Konya, in a region of flat Anatolian grasslands broken only by clumps of mountains, much like the steppes of Central Asia. In the first decades of the thirteenth century the main Seljuk construction project was to repair the old Roman stone roads, making them safer for merchants, and positioning rest houses at distances of nine hours travel by camel, or every eighteen miles. The largest of these inns provided mosques and fountains, camel and horse stables, kitchens and bathhouses. The

Sultan Han even kept a band of musicians for entertainment. Near the outside gates, water usually gushed from stone animal fountains—decorative, yet for Rumi, also symbolic:

> On all the roads they have built caravanserais with stone birds and other figures set around the edges of pools. Water flows from their mouths and spills into the pools. Any intelligent person knows that the water is not flowing from the beaks of the stone birds but from some other place.

His analogy was to God's force behind "whatever words, voices, or languages He wills."

These government-funded inns and reinforced roadways were crucial in Anatolia during the severe winters, when heavy snowdrifts inundated the highlands, five thousand feet above sea level, forcing travelers to remain indoors for days until the roads were cleared:

> *At night Easterners and Westerners and Transoxanians*
> *Stay together inside the same caravanersai*
> *Small and great remain together for days*
> *At the inn, because of the frost and the snow*
> *As soon as the road is opened and the obstacles removed,*
> *They separate, and go in their different directions.*

Prime time for traveling was spring—the season the family of Baha Valad would have chosen in the absence of any pressing issues—when the roads leading into Konya from the Salt Lake to the north were lined with camels bearing salt, as well as grass, straw, or wood. On other passes into town, fields of cotton and corn gave way to gardens of yellow plums, or the famous Konya *Qamar al-Din*, or Moon of Faith apricots. On mornings following thunderstorms, more roses opened, more greenery filled in, and the scent of silverberry trees, hanging like willows, with yellow blossoms, pervaded. Spring is the favorite season in Rumi's poems, his springtime vignettes often vividly Anatolian:

The rose garden, and sweet basil, all shades of peonies
A violet bed among the dirt, and wind and water and fire, O heart!

Baha Valad was reportedly given a royal welcome to Konya. His great-grandson, Rumi's grandson Aref Chelebi, about ninety years later, commissioned his disciple Aflaki to gather memories of these times from survivors, and collect them in an often romanticized history titled *The Acts of the Mystics.* According to Aflaki, the Sultan Alaoddin Kayqobad I personally greeted Baha Valad, and offered him residence, if he preferred, in a room in the palace used for storing vessels, or hand washing, as well as for sleeping quarters. In declining health, Baha Valad, now an old man of Khorasan, spoke of the traditional divisions of society, perhaps not quite as set in the still evolving Seljuk Rum. "Religious teachers belong in schools," he said. "Sufis in lodges, commanders and princes in palaces, merchants in inns, artisans in guilds, and foreigners in guesthouses."

The extravagant gestures credited to the sultan were extraordinary for a king—such as kissing the knee of Baha Valad—but not entirely out of character. Sultan Kayqobad I was always at pains to display his reverence, especially toward mystical teachers from the spiritual homeland of Khorasan, considered a repository of ancient Persian wisdom as well as known territory to the Turkic clans. As Asia Minor was set off from the Arabian mainland, and its population was mostly Greek and Armenian Christian, Islam was being allowed to develop under these Seljuks in a fashion more attuned to the universalism of Ibn Arabi. (While living in Malayta, Ibn Arabi had served as an adviser and a spiritual father for the sultan's older brother, Kaykaus I.) The Seljuk sultans also believed that prayers for prosperity from saintly old men, such as Baha Valad, were especially potent.

❖

Fitting Baha Valad's sense of propriety, as in Baghdad, he and his family then set up residence at a school, rather than in a Sufi lodge or palace room. The Altunpa Madrase and Mosque had been built for the sultan's commander Shamsoddin Altunbey in 1202, in the sober and restrained style of early Seljuk architecture, and was located near the main market square in the more populous district of Konya. Such Seljuk schools tended to be rectangular, two-story buildings, with lecture halls and study rooms on the first floor and student bedrooms with fireplaces and cupboards on the second floor, set around a central courtyard and fountain, much like a medieval cloister. Baha Valad paid retainers of a thousand dinars each to two of his new disciples, a baker and a butcher, described as "pleasant and polite young men," to tend to the kitchen and to the meals.

Baha Valad rapidly attracted a number of other disciples, both men and women. Rather than a drawback, his advanced age of nearly eighty was considered desirable in a religious teacher. In a manual for students written a few decades earlier, in Khorasan, one Hanafi jurist advised selecting as a teacher the "most learned, the most pious and the most advanced in years." With his livelihood secured by the sultan, Baha Valad, as in Aqshahr and Larande, began teaching a mixture of law, ethics, and mystical Islam, and drawing students from different social classes. He shared his learning not only with a weaver, and with someone identifying himself as a "simple-hearted" Turk, but also with the courtiers.

An early disciple of Baha Valad from among the governing elite was Amir Badroddin Gowhartash, also known as the fortress commander, one of the chief stewards of the palace. Gowhartash took responsibility for building a new *madrase* for Baha Valad and his family that eventually came to be known during Rumi's lifetime as the Madrase Khodavandgar, and to establish the village of Kara Arslan as its endowment—a financial practice designating a portion of the village income from farming to the *madrase*. While closer to the ceremonial main gate of entrance to the Citadel and the palace, this *madrase* was located in the same general neighborhood as the Madrase Altunpa, a merchant and artisan district of earthen houses with red tile roofs set among cypresses, maples, and thick oak trees, the sound of water flowing in its gutters always faintly audible. The *madrase* included an adjoining harem for Rumi's wife and mother-in-law, as well as his two young boys, who remained, as he had, living in the harem until age ten or eleven.

Baha Valad's decision to live near the markets made his teaching available to a wider following, as the Citadel was a much more elite and self-contained gated town-within-a-town. Only about nine hundred of the hundred thousand residents of Konya lived and worked in the defended Citadel. They were mostly administrators, palace servants, translators, often Jewish doctors, and, as Rumi observed, commanders living in houses just to the north that were visible from the two-story, blue-tiled imperial palace, its balconies facing in three directions atop an outer wall. The entire complex included a harem, bakery, treasury, bathhouse, stables, wine cellar, gardens, and—about fifty yards from the Great Mosque—the Church of St. Amphilochios, a chapel used by the many Christian mothers, wives, and daughters-in-law of the sultans. (One of the wives of Kayqobad I, Mahpari, was a Greek Christian; she was the mother of his eldest son and successor, Kaykhosrow II.) This nearly accidental religious diversity—a matter of indifference as much as design among these governing sultans—eventually helped to create the conditions for Rumi's being able to inspire, teach, and learn lessons from all of these different faith communities at once.

Baha Valad did preach regularly at the Great Mosque in the Citadel complex. Indeed, Gowhartash first approached him at the mosque of the sultan, following a sermon that he found powerful. Yet Baha Valad mostly moved among the merchants and craftsmen, following a routine similar to his life in Vakhsh. In the style of the Sufis, he liked to wander about the Konya cemetery, reciting the Quran in a low voice. One day he had a pulpit set up outside the cemetery and preached to both men and women about the Day of Resurrection, reminding them of the stark terrors of the final judgment. He continued delivering legal judgments, many as strict as ever, especially on drinking wine, with his son Rumi always beside him, increasingly serving as his "tongue" and "walking stick."

After two years, Baha Valad's health began to fail. Most of his teeth were now missing, his voice quavering, and he was receiving his followers, including the sultan, at home. "Wait until I pass away and you see how my son Jalaloddin Mohammad turns out!" he said of his son, then twenty-three years old. "He will take my place and become more elevated than I." Late one morning, in February 1231, at about eighty years of age, Baha Valad died. Having led his family thousands of miles, escaping possible extinction, and achieving recognition for wise leadership, he died as a patriarch and hero for his community. Kayqobad I donated the grounds in his rose gardens, beyond the Horse Bazaar Gate, where Baha Valad was buried. When his grandson Sultan Valad later wrote of the widely attended funeral, he emphasized the passing of authority next to his father: "After the mourning was complete all the people, young and old, gathered around, and looked to his son, saying, 'You are like him in beauty. From now on we will hold to the hem of your robe. We will follow you wherever you go. From now on you are our king.'"

Rumi had always been a highly sensitive and emotional boy. So he remained as a young and mature man, with no event so far in his life shaking and challenging him as much as the death of the father he idolized and emulated. He would return, full of both sorrow and need, to the grave of Baha Valad, near a marble fountain, whenever he wished to gather his thoughts or solve problems. Faced with crises, he was often spotted striding out through the Horse Bazaar Gate to visit his father's tomb. "He clearly heard the correct answer from the garden of his father's tomb," said one of the townspeople.

Rumi also began carrying pages of his father's writings tucked into the inner sleeve pocket of his long robes. Although Baha Valad was outwardly strict, and stressed the wages of sin, his private journal was filled with intimate meditations on divine love expressed in passionate language that allowed Rumi to hear the voice of his dear father once again, filling him with warmth and purpose, and informing his ideas about love and God. "The most effective and the strongest creation of God is love," wrote Baha Valad. "Nothing created by God is as strong and as marvelous as love. Without love, life lacks its true power. I am constantly remembering God and I am always occupied with Him."

❖

Following the death of his father, Rumi traveled to Larande, where his mother was buried and many of his father's students from his former school were living. He obviously felt a need to reconnect with family and homeland. One day during this visit, the grieving son received a startling message. His mentor from Khorasan, Borhan, had not only survived the Mongol devastation in Termez but had arrived in Konya, and was staying at the Senjari Mosque. Rumi had not seen his tutor in fifteen years, since Borhan carried him on his shoulders during childhood, so he quickly returned home. Borhan, now over sixty years old, rushed through the front door of the mosque and the two embraced again.

The timing of Borhan's appearance, around 1232, was uncanny. Borhan attributed his arrival to the prodding of Baha Valad in a dream. As Borhan was mourning the news of his passing, Baha Valad angrily rebuked him: "Borhanoddin, why is it that you are not attending upon our Khodavandgar but have left him alone? This is not the behavior of a guardian and a tutor. What explanation do you give for this shortcoming?" According to a different report, Borhan was on pilgrimage in Mecca when he learned from either the sheikhs of Syria or the pilgrims of Rum of the whereabouts of Baha Valad, but not of his death. The result either way was fortunate for Rumi, who was not yet quite ready to assume leadership of the school, the age of wisdom in Islam being considered about forty. So he invited Borhan to move into his room, and to take over his father's place as preacher and teacher.

Borhan in turn invited Rumi to learn more of the "secret" knowledge he had received from Baha Valad. The psychological subtleties of the matters they needed to discuss could only be understood, he explained, in intimate encounters between a teacher and his student. On their reunion, Borhan told Rumi, "Your father mastered both knowledge of words and knowledge of spiritual states." Encouraging him to expand his knowledge

of such states, Borhan became Rumi's sheikh, or spiritual direc-
tor. Over the next decade, he plotted the course of his spiritual
higher education. Listening to Borhan was like listening to his
father. He trusted him and regarded him with filial tenderness.

At the *madrase*, Borhan took flight with Sufi notions of the mys-
tical life. He was less circumspect than Baha Valad, though he
likewise rarely used the term "Sufi," preferring to speak of mys-
tics, or of "dervishes," the Turkish version of a Persian word for
those who had renounced the world and served God in poverty.
He loved poetry more than Baha Valad and recited favorite lines
from the poems of Sanai and Attar. Yet his presence gave the fol-
lowers of Baha Valad a sense of continuity, as he was an aging, dig-
nified preacher, scholar, ascetic, and Quranic commentator. With
his Khorasani accent and bearing, he carried with him echoes of
the vanished worlds of Samarkand and Balkh.

Borhan was always trying to impart esoteric ideas he described
as "secrets," which essentially conveyed an understanding of di-
vinity as present in everyone. The "science" he was teaching was
a science of the soul. But such a science was not easily put into
language and presented perils if the line between human and
divine appeared to have been crossed. Most of the Sufis' dou-
bling of language and use of elliptical and poetic words was in-
tended to, or subtly resulted in, the intertwining of the divine
and the human, either through transformation by knowledge,
a vision of light, or ecstatic immolation in love. Borhan used
many of the standard Sufi images for these experiences, such as
discovering a pearl, reflecting light in a mirror, or burning like
a moth in a flame. With students, perhaps even Rumi, taking
notes, he explained, "You are your own pearl. . . . If you don't
know anything else, but know yourself, then you are a scholar
and a mystic. If you don't know yourself, then all the science and
knowledge that you possess is useless."

Such messages of self-knowledge were not unfamiliar to the

Greeks of Anatolia, either. From the inscription "Know Thyself" (*"gnothi seauton"*) on the Temple of Apollo at Delphi, knowledge, or *gnosis,* had been aligned for the classical Greeks with religion. Neoplatonic thought emphasizing knowledge as a mystical path was alive in the Anatolian region, and Plato was an almost magical figure, treated as a saint by both Greeks and Turks. Near Konya bubbled "Aflatun Pinari," or "Plato's Spring," where he was believed to have lived. (*Aflatun* was a translation of *Plato.*) Some said Plato was buried in the chapel on the Citadel. Rumi often visited the monks in the Eflatun Monastery near Konya, and he made Plato a symbol of great wisdom in his *Masnavi*:

> *God's seal on the eyes and ears of the intelligence*
> *Turns an intelligent man into an animal, even if he is a Plato*

Sometimes he spoke of Plato in the tones he usually reserved for a Sufi spiritual master:

> *Whatever the Plato of the age advises you to do,*
> *Give up your self-will and act according to his counsel*

This resonance may have helped the warm reception given Khorasani mystics in town.

Yet not all his students immediately took to Borhan. Baha Valad had kept a judicial, scholarly tone, while Borhan was more openly (rather than covertly) mystical and poetical. Rumi often needed to come to his defense. Some of the infighting was stinging enough that Rumi could still relate the heated debates to his own students, decades after Borhan's death, especially concerning the mixing of poetry with theology:

> They said, "Sayyed Borhanoddin speaks very well, but he quotes Sanai's poetry too often." This is like saying the

sun is good but it gives off too much light. Is that a fault? Quoting Sanai's words casts more light on the discussion. Sunlight casts light on things!

Once a student interrupted Borhan to protest his overuse of analogies, as a frivolous tool for scholars to use. As Rumi told the story, Borhan was not shy in defending his methods:

> Sayyed Borhanoddin was giving a lecture. A fool broke in and said, "We need words without analogies." Sayyed answered, "Let him who seeks to hear words without analogies, draw closer. For you are actually an analogy yourself. You are not this thing. Your self is only your shadow. When someone dies, people say that he has departed. If he were this thing, where has he gone? It is clear that your appearance is only an analogy of your true self, from which your true self can be deduced."

Others adored Borhan in the manner a dervish did toward his sheikh, looking for guidance on a path deemed dangerous without direction from a mature teacher—a path envisioned by Borhan as an expansive journey, like the flight of Attar's birds. "The path of reunion has no end," he told them, "God is the goal and destination." His most excited recent follower on this spiritual quest was a humble, unlearned goldsmith—Salahoddin Zarkub—a Turk from one of the nearby fishing villages on the Konya plains—who arrived in the capital in the 1230s to set up a small shop in the goldsmiths' bazaar. He was fervent about Borhan's emphasis on fasting and purification, and became important enough to Rumi later in life for him to describe Salah as his "root of spiritual joy."

Rumi spent a year or so in the growing circle of Borhan,

learning more of the basics of Sufi thought. He was highly receptive to all of Borhan's mystical language and concepts. Borhan imparted to Rumi his passion for Hallaj, also known as Mansur. He liked to make a contrast between the "I" of the villain Pharaoh in the Quran, proudly refusing to bend to God's will in the liberation of the Hebrew slaves, with the egoless "I" in the "I am the Truth!" of Hallaj, which reportedly got him executed in Baghdad. "Pharaoh, God's curse upon him, said, 'I am your Lord,'" preached Borhan. "His use of the word 'I' brought God's curse upon him. Mansur said 'I am the Truth' and his use of the word 'I' was a mercy from God." In his *Masnavi,* years later, Rumi neatly set this thought of Borhan:

"I am the Truth," shone from Mansur's lips like light
"I am the Lord," fell from Pharaoh's lips like a threat

Borhan eventually decided on a plan to prepare Rumi to manage the school established by his father and evolve into a religious jurist and guider of souls. To accomplish this ambition, Borhan resolved that his young charge travel to the most respected colleges in Aleppo and Damascus and study with elevated scholars in a curriculum combining readings in law and religion with a glass-bead game of esoteric knowledge. Borhan would take responsibility for caretaking the *madrase,* and their grandmother, the Great Kerra, would serve as spiritual mother for Rumi's boys, then about six years old. She was considered another beneficiary of Baha Valad's higher "secrets."

From the seat of honor one day, Borhan singled out Rumi and addressed him directly, charging him with his imminent mission: "God the Almighty, elevate you to the rank of your father. No one is at a higher rank than him, or I would have

prayed, 'God, let him surpass him.' But that is the ultimate."
Rumi's son painted the farewell as even more luminous, remembering Borhan as extravagantly and emotionally blessing Rumi at his departure, with the glorious prediction: "And like the sun you'll scatter light worldwide."

CHAPTER 6

"I kept hearing my own name"

ARRIVING in Aleppo in northern Syria to begin his studies at about the age of twenty-five, and moving on eventually to Damascus, Rumi took his place in an entitled "turbaned class" of scholars and their chosen students. This selective gathering of the religious elite was made all the more lively and competitive as Syria in the early decades of the thirteenth century was widely considered the heart of Muslim culture in the Arabic language. Here he could see once again the learned society of debaters with clipped beards, trailing turban tassels, and green academic robes with wide, long sleeves, which he first might have glimpsed as a boy in the courtyards of Nezamiyye College in Baghdad.

Yet education in Rumi's time was also intimate and personal, a matter of a student being taken in hand by a teacher, or a small circle of teachers, and imitating their *adab*, or manners and style, as much as mastering a single field of apprenticeship. Dispatching his charge to Aleppo, Borhan was entrusting him with cosmopolitan choices, not only in interpreting religious law, but also in comportment, intellectual tastes, and moral conduct. With his disciple Salah, he accompanied Rumi as far as Kayseri, midway between Konya and Aleppo, where they stayed briefly with the governor, who was building Borhan his own *madrase*. Kayseri was the second most important city in Rum, as Sultan Alaoddin Kayqobad I had built his ornate Qobadiyye Palace on its lakefront.

As a married student, with an ascetic practice encouraged by Borhan, Rumi lived a circumscribed life, in a traditional student cell in the most famous of the colleges of Aleppo, the Halaviyye, which was converted into a mosque from a Byzantine cathedral a century earlier as revenge against the Franks for pillaging during the First Crusade. While Rumi was in Aleppo, around 1233, the Halaviyye was sliding into disrepair and barely used as a teaching facility. Such schools were as much dormitories, with charitable endowments for supporting residential students, as academies granting certificates. The situation was fluid as mosques evolved into schools, then changed back again, and Rumi was free to follow lectures at the Shadbakht Madrase or reading circles at the Great Mosque.

Much like Konya, Aleppo was flourishing in a rare phase of peace and prosperity. The previous Ayyubid sultan al-Zahir, a son of the famed commander Saladin who had founded an Ayyubid dynasty in both Egypt and Syria, had reinforced the oval Citadel in the center of town, added a grand entranceway, repaired the canal system, and built a palace, upgrading Aleppo into one of the most beautiful cities in the Middle East. His son al-Aziz, who ruled during Rumi's school years, capitalized on the advantages of the city's trading location on caravan routes linking China with Europe, bringing in revenues second only to Egypt. The wood-roofed bazaar was its trading floor, offering local specialties such as pistachios and the glassware that glimmered in Rumi's later poems:

> *I'm the slave of hopeless time, until that time*
> *The wine of unity shines in a chalice of Aleppo glass*

Like the interlocking patterns displayed on its stone and marble walls and portals, Aleppo was a complex mesh of East and West, Christian and Muslim. Much of its prosperity came from shrewd trading agreements with Venice that allowed Venetian merchants to establish a colony in Aleppo, with their own trading post, baths, and church. In 1219 Francis of Assisi met in Egypt with the Ayyubid sultan and won an agreement for his "Monks of the Rope" to wander the Holy Land. During the time of Rumi's stay, the first Franciscan friars began arriving in Aleppo to minister to Crusader princes and soldiers held prisoner in the Citadel. They swept through the streets in their rough, woolen robes, much like the robes worn by Sufis, with similar vows of poverty, and may have imprinted on Rumi the affinities between these two expressions of spirituality.

Rumi's main teacher in Aleppo was Ibn al-Adim, a quick-witted and urbane scholar, historian, legal expert, diplomat, and calligrapher in his midforties, with a post at Shadbakht Madrase. Five members of his eminent Hanafi "old family"—including his father—had served in the powerful post of chief justice, or *qadi*, in Aleppo, since the tenth century. Ibn al-Adim was best known as a historian of Aleppo, and as a biographer of its leading citizens in his *Biographical Dictionary*, a massive, forty-volume who's who of short vignettes, written by him in penmanship so fine that the sultan once summoned him to the palace to praise its beauty. He also wrote treatises on preparing perfumes, and on handwriting (practices, pens, and papers), as Arab intellectuals of his time were given to such encyclopedic "boundless compilation." He did most of his writing on diplomatic missions for the sultan, when he traveled on a palanquin rigged between two mules.

Ibn al-Adim was a master of the basic sciences, explaining his quick ascent in the academic ranks, and was equipped to

instruct Rumi in most areas of knowledge required for an ad-
vanced religious scholar: Arabic linguistics and grammar; dia-
lectic reason and legal conflict; and the Quranic sciences. He
gave indications of being a fellow traveler of Sufism, though he
was too shrewdly political to proclaim such sympathies openly.
(In the early years of his reign, al-Aziz had executed the Sufi
leader Sohravardi for heresy.) Yet his father had called on his
deathbed for the prayer beads of a Sufi saint, and Ibn al-Adim
reserved a room in his own tomb for a Sufi, perhaps as a hedge
against divine judgment. He espoused, if not always fully prac-
ticed, the virtues of poverty, solitude, and self-reliance.

While Rumi never absorbed his teacher's passion for his-
tory, he was delighted by his exposure in Aleppo to the intri-
cate joys of Arabic poetry. Ibn al-Adim was a minor poet. He
wrote clever lines on slight topics, such as sighting the first white
hairs in his beard. Yet he idolized those with "innate poetic abil-
ity," and championed the poetry of the premier Arabic poet al-
Mutanabbi, whose verses remained a lifelong pleasure for Rumi.
During the eleventh century al-Mutanabbi had lived in the quar-
ter of Aleppo where Ibn al-Adim's family's marble compound
was located. Rumi's favorites were al-Mutanabbi's *qasidas,* often
odes of praise for a patron, known for their technical virtuosity,
though a surprising choice perhaps given their standard use of
the tradition of braggadocio and praise of wine, power, and bat-
tlefield glory. Al-Mutanabbi wrote zestfully of "the play of swords
and lances" and "the clash of armies at my command." Rumi
later scattered lines of al-Mutanabbi in his talks, and one of the
Arab poet's more famous openings—"A heart that wine cannot
console"—entwined for Rumi with memories of school years in
Syria, he transposed as a closing for a poem on spiritual wine:

> *We can look for the answer in Mutanabbi:*
> *"A heart that wine cannot console"*

In Aleppo, Rumi was also introduced to an active Shia com-
munity, especially visible during the festivals of the family of
Ali, the son-in-law and cousin of the Prophet Mohammad,
whose heirs are believed by Shia to be the rightful holders of
the leadership of all Muslims. The Sunni rulers observed these
festivals warily, while Rumi's teacher, Ibn al-Adim, a member
of the establishment, was described by his biographer as a "sen-
tinel of the Sunni state." On the Day of Ashura, mourning the
death of Ali's son Hosayn at the Battle of Karbala in 680, Rumi
witnessed pious Shia weeping and beating themselves at An-
tioch Gate, the main fortress gate at the entrance of Aleppo.
Thinly disguising himself as "A poet," Rumi recorded this
memory in *Masnavi*:

> *On the day of Ashura, all the people of Aleppo*
>   *Gather from day until night at the Antioch Gate . . .*
> *One day a stranger, who was a poet, came along*
>   *On this day of Ashura, and heard their lamentations . . .*
> *He went along, asking questions gently on his way,*
>   *"What is this sorrow? Whose death are they mourning?"*

Though Rumi may not have been previously aware of this ritual,
as Persians were mostly Sunni during his lifetime, his naïveté in
rendering the experience was exaggerated, as he feigned dis-
covering that the martyrdom being mourned had taken place
centuries earlier:

> *Have you been asleep all this time?*
>   *You are only now tearing your garments in sorrow?*

Rumi may have felt some shock as a young man, but revisiting
the event, in his maturity, he was more intent on questioning
sorrow as a response to death rather than joy:

Mourn for your own broken faith and religion
If your faith doesn't see beyond this old earth

❖

The second phase of Rumi's advanced education took place in Damascus, where he likely traveled about a year later and had previously visited with his family during their original journey from Central Asia. While Aleppo was known as a trading and mercantile city, Damascus, in southern Syria, in the midst of a desert oasis, was both a commercial center and a holy city, the capital of the former Umayyad Caliphate, and one of the important departure points for *hajj*, especially for pilgrims traveling from points west. Because of the city's religious history and geography, students of the Quran were welcomed and treated respectfully. The magnificent Umayyad Mosque, still enshrining the reputed head of John Baptist from its previous days as a Christian basilica, hummed all day with groups of students listening to their sheikhs read aloud. As Damascenes were not encouraged to read books silently or alone, the murmur of these many study circles was a kind of spoken music filling the courtyards daily from dawn until dusk.

Over about four years, in his midtwenties, Rumi studied in Damascus in one of the Hanafi seminaries, probably the Moqaddamiyye Madrase, near the Bab al-Firdaws, or Gate of Paradise, where he could stay in an outer building, free of the nighttime regulations overseeing entrances and exits that were enforced on younger students in the inner buildings. Of his studies of one important Hanafi text, he later recalled, "In my youth I had a friend in Damascus who was a companion with me in studying the *Hedaya*." He also seems to have attended sessions of a famed Hanafi scholar from Bukhara, who was teaching at Nuriyye Madrase. All public classes were highly formal, modeled on behavior in a mosque, with a nearly sacred space cleared about the lecturer, so his rug and cushion were left untouched. As one manual prescribed proper student etiquette: "Do not look at anything but the teacher, and do not turn around to investigate any sound, especially during discussion. Do not shake your sleeve. The student should not uncover his arm, nor should he fiddle with his hands or feet or any part of his body parts, nor should he place his hand on his beard. . . . Nor should he try to say anything funny or offensive; and he should not laugh except out of surprise. If something overcomes him, he should smile without giving voice."

Though student life was rigorous, Rumi loved his time in Damascus. He often called Damascus the "City of Love," punning on the word for love, "*eshq*," tucked into its Arabic name, "Dameshq." He even wrote his single example of an ode to a city for Damascus, not only as homage to the capital, but also to Arabic poetry, where such love poems to cities abound, especially to Baghdad. Only Samarkand comes across in his writings with such verve and close observation. He exuberantly opens his city poem:

> *I'm madly in love, and crazy for Damascus*
> *Damascus, where I left my heart and soul*

Rumi catalogs the most prominent of the thirteen gates to the medieval city:

> *Separated from friends, I stand alone at the Barid Gate*
> *Beyond the Lovers' Mosque, in the green fields of Damascus . . .*
> *Far from the Gate of Joy and the Gate of Paradise*
> *You'll never know what visions I'm seeking in Damascus.*

His references are often built on inside jokes that only other visitors to Damascus at the time would fully understand. The

Ayyubid sultan, during his stays in town, liked to play polo in the Verdant Field hippodrome, where Rumi imagined his own head as a swerving ball:

I want to roll through her Verdant Field, like a polo ball
  Struck by polo sticks, towards the main square of Damascus

A large Quran commissioned by Caliph Uthman was kept veiled as a relic in the mosque:

Let me swear an oath on Uthman's holy book
  The pearl of that beloved, shining in Damascus

The soft border between Muslims and Christians was nowhere more evident than in Damascus, even in these waning days of the Crusades. Many Christians and Jews lived in the capital, though neighborhoods were segregated by religion, with gates clanged shut at the dusk curfew, and beliefs worn on the sleeve: under a legal dress code, Christians wore crosses, and Jews a yellow or red shoulder rope. Syria was the historical center of monasticism, and Rumi was said to have come across a group of forty desert fathers, or hermit monks, on his way from Aleppo. The Quran was understood to say that Jesus stayed on the hill of nearby Rebva, and Damascenes hoped to witness his resurrection at their Eastern Gate:

Let's climb Rebva, as if we're in the time of Christ
  Like monks, drunk on the dark red wines of Damascus

The Bab al-Faraj, or Gate of Joy, evoked by Rumi stood just east of the Salehiyye, or the Righteous District, outside the walls of the old city at the foot of prominent Mount Qasiyun.

This neighborhood had grown in the past few decades and was crowded with mostly Sufi hostels and learning centers, explaining Rumi's exclamation "On the Mount of Righteousness is a mine of pearls!" The most illustrious of those pearls, of course, was Ibn Arabi—who Rumi may or may not have met in Malatya a decade earlier. Ibn Arabi lived the final phase of his life in Damascus and was buried in a tomb in Salehiyye. Whether Rumi was included in his reading circles, he was certainly aware of the famous mystic. Definitely in attendance at readings of his voluminous texts, as Ibn Arabi was still producing them, though, was his godson Qonavi, with whom Rumi had a gradually evolving friendship later in Konya. Some of Ibn Arabi's readings aloud were meant for Qonavi's ears alone. Rumi saw venerated in the person of Ibn Arabi a sublime and knowledgeable approach to spirituality as an elite science available only to initiates with rarefied experience. Though tempted by Ibn Arabi's approach, he was never entirely committed.

Along with dazzling verbal performances and abstruse examinations of religious thought, Rumi was surrounded in Damascus by a scholarly culture that valued rank and fame. Books were stacked according to importance, with the Quran on top of any pile. Seating at lectures radiated out from the sheikh in decreasing order of status, as he was faced with his most eminent guest, judged by knowledge, age, piety, or fame. Of these qualities, fame weighed most strongly, the making of a name, especially a name beyond Damascus or, even better, Syria. Sources of the time noted that one young scholar "flashed his merit like a bright star rising on the horizon," and, of another, "his name flew to fill the regions"—values far from Rumi's later yearning for a nameless sort of oblivion.

❖

Following nearly five years of study in Aleppo and Damascus, having saturated himself in steep and difficult texts, and having been exposed to some of the most renowned religious scholars of the day, Rumi, about thirty years old, returned to his teacher of teachers, Borhan. Rumi sought to integrate the last and most important missing piece in his education, held out by Borhan as the ultimate achievement—advanced lessons in spiritual practice designed to unlock interior practices even more demanding and essential for his future responsibilities than the academic exercises mastered in Syria.

Their meeting likely took place in Kayseri. The sultan's governor had constructed by then the *madrase* where Borhan was based, though he still made the trip of about two hundred miles to Konya regularly. When Rumi arrived, the governor invited him to stay in his palace, but Borhan, channeling the words of Baha Valad, warned Rumi that schools were the proper place for scholars to reside. The name of the town reflected its grand past history as a Roman capital, and Rumi punned on the naming of Kayseri, or Caesarea, after the Roman emperor Caesar Augustus, when alluding to Borhan:

> *When our Caesar is in Kayseri—*
> *Don't keep us waiting in Elbistan*

The brunt of Rumi's joke, Elbistan, was a smaller Anatolian city on the road to Syria.

But their reunion might have taken place anywhere, as Borhan was now stressing the inner world with his pupil. In the tradition of the historical Sufi movement, Borhan trained Rumi in exercises of asceticism, especially fasting. Borhan had been dedicated to fasting all his life. During this period, he wrote in his notes of the exemplary effects of fasting on the soul: "The thinner the shell of the walnut, the fuller is its nut, and the same for the almond and pistachio." He had advised his disciple Salah that even if he found himself unable to perform other devotions, he should never neglect fasting. Such self-denial was meant to instill martial discipline, as well as to wean the practitioner off the ordinary values of the world. The ultimate "fasting of the elite" meant the desire for God alone.

From this intensive season in Kayseri, Rumi never relaxed his stance on fasting, a habit he pursued with passion, almost thrilled, becoming as identified as Borhan with the practice. In Book V of the *Masnavi*, he would lift off in an inspired hymn to fasting:

> *Don't eat straw and barley, like donkeys:*
> *Graze on flowers of the Judas tree, like musk deer in Khotan*
> *Only graze on clove, jasmine, or roses,*
> *In Khotan, with your beloved companion . . .*
> *The stomach of the body pulls towards the straw-barn*
> *The spiritual stomach pulls towards fields of sweet basil.*

If spring is the favorite season in Rumi's poems, Ramadan, the month of fasting from dawn to sunset, obligatory for able Muslims, became his cherished religious observance:

> *Congratulations! The month of fasting is here!*
> *Have a good journey, my companion in fasting.*
> *I climbed to the roof, to see the moon,*
> *With my heart and soul, I longed for fasting.*
> *When I looked up, my hat fell off,*
> *My head was set spinning by the king of fasting!*

Fasting became a reminder for Rumi of memories of Borhan, as few anecdotes about the displaced mystic of Khorasan failed to link him with his habitual practice. Fasting was also Rumi's introduction to the consolations of "tightening the belt." He was learning that things were not what they seemed, and that empty stomachs held "hidden sweetness."

Like the scholars of Damascus, the mystics and Sufis had their own ranks and an organized ladder of mystical practices that indicated status in the spiritual world. More extreme than regular fasting but essential was the completion of a forty-day trial in sealed isolation from the world known as *chelle*—from *chehel*, Persian for "forty." This period of solitude and subsisting on bread and water was a sort of vision quest, conceived as an inward *hajj*, or desert experience, owing its origins perhaps to the Syrian hermit monks, such as those Rumi met on his way to Damascus. Borhan arranged Rumi's retreat, sealing him into total seclusion, and then helping him with interpreting his insights afterward.

A chip of remembrance, likely from this retreat, appears in Book V of the *Masnavi*. This time, rather than "a poet," Rumi casts his younger self as "a certain man," but his exact recording of one disorienting nightmare was quite personal, nearly surreal:

> *During the* chelle, *a certain man*
> *Dreamed he saw a pregnant dog on a road*
> *Suddenly he heard the cries of her puppies*
> *Though they were in the womb, invisible . . .*
> *Puppies howling in a womb, he thought*
> *"Has anyone ever heard of such a thing?" . . .*

Interpreting dreams was a problematic challenge—for medieval Muslims especially, a religious problem. Isolation only exacerbated Rumi's confusion, blurring his waking:

When he woke from his dream and came to himself,
His astonishment grew greater at every moment.
During the chelle, *there is no other solution to problems,*
Except for being present to God the Almighty.

So he began to pray, and heard a wise voice interpreting his bizarre dream imagery:

At that moment, he heard a mysterious voice,
Saying, "That is a symbol of the yelping of the ignorant,
Those who have not pierced the veil and curtain,
But with blind eyes are speaking aimlessly."

Rumi emerged from his *chelle* with a personal experience of having heard a voice that he felt was available to him for guidance. He could hear wisdom, not just in reading circles, or from lecturers, but also in meditation, and he could copy down the words, as in dictation. In trying to measure the gap between human and divine, such an encounter was revelatory.

After instructing Rumi in the wisdom tradition shared with him by Baha Valad, and encouraging him even more insistently to study his father's notebooks, Borhan began to decline. During his last few years Borhan was sometimes in Konya, but he kept returning to Kayseri, possibly wishing to withdraw so that his charge could take on a leadership position alone. In Kayseri, Borhan showed poignant signs of loss of the strength, mental focus, and near athletic prowess in self-discipline that marked his prime years, though his behavior was also taken as evidence of saintliness, of having moved beyond the ordinary restraints of religion. When he led prayers in the mosque he spent long stretches of time—rather than minutes—in bowing or standing poses. When some members of the congregation complained,

he apologized, "Some madness continually overwhelms me. I
am not fit to be your prayer leader." The plea only made him
more revered and followed, as he was now understood to be as
humble as he was wise.

Most striking was the transformation of the rigid ascetic into
a corpulent gentleman as he relaxed his tight regimen. Borhan
once heard a voice commanding, "Undergo no further hard-
ship!" He now obeyed this voice. A grand lady, who had become
his disciple, teasingly asked why he had given up fasting and was
not practicing his five daily prayers. "Oh child, I am like a load-
bearing camel," he replied, comparing himself to an emaciated
camel at journey's end being fed a few grains of barley. When
his patron, the governor, grew concerned about his unkempt
appearance, he snapped, "So I came into the world for the sake
of doing my laundry? Leave me alone!" Rather than feats of fast-
ing, Borhan focused on his love of pickled turnips for indiges-
tion. In old age, he began behaving with some of the carefree
joy of the holy fools for God of Nishapur.

Borhan died in Kayseri in 1240 or 1241, in his midseventies.
Following a conventional mourning period of forty days, a letter
was sent notifying Rumi in Konya. A decade after the death of
his father, this news had a similar impact. Rumi collapsed into
the knowledge that he was again without fatherly support. He
set out quickly with a band of disciples on a road he traveled
regularly enough during those years to recall later all the stops
on the way, while illustrating the difference between ritual and
true spiritual progress:

> The stages on the road from Konya to Kayseri are fixed
> and defined. They are Kaymaz, Uprukh, Sultan, and so
> forth. But the stages on the sea between Antalya and Al-
> exandria are not fixed and defined. A ship's captain may

know them, but he won't tell them to land dwellers because they would not understand.

Rumi visited the grave of his mentor and held a funeral banquet in his honor. Borhan's books and notes were spread out for him to choose whatever he wished. He cherished these words and found in rereading them the connection so important in his growth over the past decade. As with his father's writings, Borhan left Rumi not only hard ascetic rules, but also messages of love that were the soft core of his discipline of curbing impulses: "If you prick your foot on a thorn, you would leave all the important things aside, and wholly attend to it. You ought then to do the same for your brother."

❖

In his midthirties Rumi, finally, if inevitably, ascended to the leadership of his community. At the Madrase Khodavandgar, he was looked upon as the living embodiment of Baha Valad and Borhan. He walked the streets of Konya in the official garb of a religious scholar—wearing a cumbersome wide-sleeve cloak and a large turban, wound with one band unraveleld and hanging down his back. Although he never served in Konya as chief justice, or *qadi*, he held academic appointments at four separate colleges, all respected, including the Cotton Sellers Madrase, endowed by the guild of cotton merchants, and located on their street in the market district. His name appeared on lists of the most prominent doctors of the law belonging to the Hanafi School.

At about the same time as the death of Borhan, Rumi's wife, Gowhar, also mysteriously died, with no record of the cause. Again, Rumi experienced the loss of an intimate link to his childhood in Central Asia as well as, most crucially, the mother of his two sons. Yet Gowhar's mother continued to live in the harem and take special interest in her grandsons. Rumi soon afterward married a widow, Kerra, from a Roman-Turkish family in Konya, whose deceased husband Mohammad Shah had been an aristocratic Persian speaker from Iran. Like Rumi, Kerra brought two children to their marriage—a boy, Shamsoddin Yahya, and a girl, Kimiya. Over the next few years Rumi and Kerra had their own son, Mozaffaroddin Amir Alem Chelebi—Rumi's third— and a daughter, Maleke. With these four young children, the harem grew even more crowded and busier.

Unlike his father, Rumi never kept multiple wives, and the widower and his widowed bride remained together for the rest of his life. Kerra was more vividly remembered than Gowhar, as theirs was not an arranged marriage, and she lived with Rumi during the period of his growing fame. Though he never wrote about Kerra directly, she was remembered by those in his inner circle and was later the source of some of the more magical and fantastical tales about her husband. Her choice to leave the aristocratic household of her deceased husband to marry a cleric pointed to spiritual leanings, underlined in Aflaki's description of her as "a second Virgin Mary." She was certainly superstitious, and was forever seeing *jinn,* or invisible, mischievous spirits. Early in their marriage, Rumi used to stand by a tall lamp stand at night, reading his father's pages. She told him that the *jinn* complained to her of the bright light. Rumi smiled and three days later tried to mollify her. "After today do not worry. The *jinn* are my disciples and they are devoted to me. They will not cause any harm to come to our children or friends."

Rumi's bemused smile to Kerra, on news of the *jinn,* either patronizing, loving, or both, expressed some of the enigma of his attitude toward women and marriage, as well as the general ambivalence toward women in medieval society. Rumi often fell into a traditional classifying of men as strong and rational, and women as mercurial and emotional. He once even painted wives as purifying tests for their coarse husbands:

> God showed the Prophet a narrow and hidden way to refine himself, and that was the path of marrying women, and enduring their tyranny, and listening to their complaints, and letting them order him around. . . . Character would only become purer through such patient forbearance.

In other moods, he could be more sympathetic, as in his ode in the *Masnavi* to women:

> *A woman is a ray of God, heavenly and beloved*
> *She is a creator, uncreated, from above*

Rumi later argued against imposing veils on women and had many female disciples, whose Friday evening gatherings in one lady's garden he was criticized for attending.

When his two older sons reached adolescence, Rumi sent them both to study in Damascus, a decision that distressed their maternal grandmother, the Great Kerra, as she would miss them greatly. He evidently thought highly enough of Damascus as the standard for religious education. Overseeing them on this trip was their tutor and guardian, Sharafoddin. Yet as both boys were now in their midteens, the combativeness of their childhood conflicts was only magnified. When they were younger, Rumi himself had mostly been away in Syria, leaving his first wife, Gowhar, with the problem of their bad behavior. Now the target of their rebelliousness in Damascus quickly became their tutor, and Rumi was upset at needing to write them a pointed letter, advising them to be more respectful to their elders:

Dear son Bahaoddin, and dear son Alaoddin. Don't forget to be polite to this father, the father of your education and training, Sharafoddin. Don't be rude, or judgmental, or abusive, and treat him as a father. I am indebted to this dear father Sharafoddin. I am hoping that my dear children will be patient and kind and generous with him, and talk to him in a very kind way, and when this father is angry, I want my children to make themselves busy with other matters, or go to sleep. I am waiting to receive some news, and I pray for my children to become more kind and hopefully very soon you will return home and make us happy.

Rumi was now flourishing in Konya, where he had become known for the power and popularity of his eloquent preaching. By the time he was seventeen and had returned from Syria, his son Bahaoddin, later known as Sultan Valad, would sit next to his father during these sermons, just as Rumi sat next to his father, Baha Valad. However, Rumi had such a youthful appearance that when the two appeared together in public they were often mistaken for brothers. Rumi was satisfying his patrons, the Sunni Seljuk rulers, as his public speeches displayed enough emotion and beauty to convert Greeks and Armenians, a desired outcome for the regime. He could later still summon the fervent emotion that his sermons had stirred among local Greek speakers, who did not understand much of their content:

I was speaking one day to a crowd that included non-Muslims, and during my talk they were weeping and going into ecstatic states. "What do they understand? What do they know?" someone asked. "Not one out of a thousand Muslims can understand this sort of talk. What have they comprehended that they can weep so?" It was not necessary for them to understand the words. What they understood was the essence of the speech . . . the oneness of God.

Seeing the response of audiences from the viewpoint of his father, as he sat beside him, Sultan Valad, too, recalled the excitement stirred by his gifted and warmhearted oratory: "Now that he stood alone, his greatness became more visible, in the eyes of the old, and the eyes of the young. Even among those who had kept their distance from him before."

Yet Rumi was not wholly satisfied by this early success. Ironically he had achieved everything his father and tutor desired for him, and attained the goals and station considered most lofty by his society at a relatively young age. Ever since childhood he had been a bit of a prodigy, and always had a graceful power over those around him. These indicators of success were borne out by his talents as a teacher, preacher, jurist, and spiritual counselor. He traveled both outward and inward paths of education, yet he was feeling incomplete, inauthentic, not yet arrived at his destination.

Now in his late thirties, Rumi particularly puzzled over the limits of the learning he had accumulated with such exertion in Aleppo and Damascus—expending great effort was another virtue of the scholarly culture. He struggled, as well, with fame, the sort of important status recognized by the scholars. By his combination of the authority of learning with youthful charm and charisma, he attracted an eager retinue—if not quite the "ten thousand more" newly minted followers counted by Sultan Valad. His pleasure in this easy adulation was authentic, but so was a jagged shadow of doubt. Rumi began to feel uneasy about expectations being laid on him. He distrusted his need for notice of an identity he could not comfortably fit—a discomfort made worse by having no one to talk with about these unexpected doubts, no confidant. The vehemence of Rumi's later attacks on intellectual preening and the traps of fame grew from experiences during this unexpectedly conflicted moment in his life. He admitted as much in a reflective *robai*:

> *For some time, like everyone, I adored myself,*
> *Blind to others, I kept hearing my own name.*

PART II

CHAPTER 7

"The face of the sun is Shams of Tabriz"

A stranger appeared in Konya on November 29, 1244. About sixty years old, dressed in a cloak fashioned from coarse black felt, and wearing a simple traveler's cap, he checked into one of the inns managed by the sugar confectioners or the rice sellers within the market district, not far from Rumi's school. His name was Shamsoddin, or Shams of Tabriz, and he was a singular outlier mystic in a period of history crowded with extreme religious seekers, especially active in the wake of the Mongol invasions. From decades of restless travel throughout all the religious capitals of the Muslim world, he had earned the nickname "Parande," or "The Flier."

Ignoring the social etiquette that Baha Valad had followed so strictly, Shams bypassed the Sufi lodges, where he could easily have found subsidized room and board. Instead he chose to remain incognito in a merchant inn, disguising himself as a commercial businessman, even putting a giant lock on his door to insinuate that he was carrying valuable wares that needed to be safeguarded, though inside was nothing but a straw mat. In conversations with Rumi later written down by students, including Sultan Valad, Shams remembered being asked, "Aren't you coming to the *madrase?*" and answering, "I'm not a debater. I'm a stranger. The inn is the right place for strangers."

Most likely during the first week of December, Shams and Rumi suddenly met. At the crest of his prominence as a religious teacher and jurist, Rumi was on his way from one of his teaching appointments at the Cotton Sellers Madrase and was passing by the inn where Shams was staying. He was riding a mule and surrounded by a posse of students, walking on foot, holding his stirrups, adding an aura of celebrity similar to the retinue of Razi in Herat during Rumi's childhood, though on a smaller scale. In place were the symbols of his scholarly status he wrote about later in a self-deprecating tone:

> *My turban, my robe, and my head*
> *Are worth less than a single penny*

Slicing through all the jostling, his black cloak wrapped tightly about him, Shams grabbed the reins of Rumi's mount. The conversation that ensued was a hasty theological exchange. As Shams later recalled:

> The first words I spoke to Mowlana were: "Why didn't Bayazid follow the example of the Prophet and say, 'Glory be to You!' or 'We have not fully worshipped You?'" Mowlana perfectly understood the full implications of the problem, and where it came from, and where it was leading. It made him ecstatic because his spirit was so pure and clean, and shone in his face. I realized the sweetness of my question only from his ecstasy. Before then I had been unaware of its sweetness.

The issue that Shams was raising pivoted on Bayazid Bestami, an Eastern Iranian Sufi mystic of the "drunken" school, who exclaimed, "Glory Be to Me! How great is My Majesty!" Like Hallaj's "I am the Truth!" Bayazid's unorthodox hymn of praise, seemingly to himself, could be interpreted as evidence of a mystic having lost all sense of self. To ordinary ears, he was risking blasphemy by merging his human identity with the divine. Shams was asking Rumi how such a high state of rapture should be compared with the Prophet Mohammad, who had spoken of being raised to the highest heavens, and yet, more humbly, prayed, "We have not known You as You should be rightly known."

"Was Bayazid greater or Mohammad?" pressed Shams.

"Bayazid's thirst was quenched by a single mouthful, and he was satisfied, and claimed he was no longer thirsty," answered Rumi. "The water jug of his understanding was filled with a single sip. His house received light that fit the size of its single window. But Mohammad's quest for water was immense, consisting of thirst upon thirst."

Some reported that Shams "fell in a swoon" at Rumi's response, though it was fairly standard in the Muslim catechism: Mohammad was the greatest of all men. Yet Shams and Rumi had gazed at each other, and this exchange was far more disruptive. A recurring theme in the literature of romantic love and Sufi mystical love was this deep gaze. Not only Layli and Majnun exchanged amorous looks, so did Sufi masters and their true disciples behold each other. Writing of this extraordinary meeting, Sultan Valad used all the rich language and imagery of ecstatic love to describe his father's first glimpse of Shams. Rumi "saw the veil pulled away from his face" and "fell in love with him."

Describing their meeting months later, among a circle of interested students, Shams did not spell out Rumi's parsing of his leading question. Rather he simply remembered responding to his pure spirit, shining face, joy at finding a kindred soul, and a tenor of sweetness. A through-line in Rumi's poetry, too— following from this flash of a meeting—was the certainty that recognition occurs beyond speech, language, and thought:

For lovers, the beauty of the beloved is their teacher
His face is their syllabus, lesson, and book

❖

Whether in a faint or awake, Shams was led immediately afterward by Rumi to the Madrase Khodavandgar. In seclusion, the two spoke more openly, and their intimate discussion was compelling enough for Rumi to decide that he wished to follow its thread even further. He also realized such an exploration would be impossible in the burgeoning school that was doubling as his home and a busy harem for his wife, children, and extended family. So he decided that same day to decamp. As Aflaki described the next of the startling developments: "After that Mowlana grasped his hand and they departed."

Rumi took Shams back into the market district, to the street of the goldsmiths, to the shop of Salah, who had been such a devoted follower of his tutor Borhan. After the death of Borhan, four years earlier, Salah returned to his fishing village, married, had several children, and then moved back to the capital city to set up his permanent home and shop. Though an illiterate workman, he had an enthusiastic spirit that Rumi trusted, as had Borhan. In the past few years, whenever Rumi delivered one of his celebrated public sermons, Salah was said to have shouted fervent yells of assent. Rumi's intuition proved correct, as Salah responded warmly to the unusual newcomer from Tabriz.

Rumi and Shams lived together in near seclusion in a room of Salah's house for at least the next three months. The rapidness of their bonding was shocking, but not without foreshadowing, as the vehemence of Rumi's seizing at an escape from his daily round, as well as his future eviscerating of his former way of life, all indicate that he was ready for a major change. He later claimed to have had some premonition of a figure like Shams. Since *shams* is the Arabic word for *sun*, Rumi used imagery of the sun to express his feelings for the man. His poems would be saturated with this sunlight, as he revealed:

> *I already held a sweet image of you in my heart*
> *When at that dawn, I first truly felt the sun*

While Rumi may have had some inkling, Shams claimed the two had actually met once. The place was Damascus; the time, sixteen years earlier. Shams later spoke in his talks of remembering Rumi, as a student, a sort of prodigy, talking in public about the unity of souls: "I remember Mowlana sixteen years ago. He was saying that creatures are like clusters of grapes. If you squeeze them into a bowl, no difference remains." He greeted him with "Salam," in a public square. Rumi did not pay much attention, yet Shams, older and wiser, quickly perceived the glimmer of Rumi's true potential: "From the first day that I saw your beauty, attraction and kindness towards you filled my heart."

The friendship between Rumi and Shams was intense from the start, and often difficult to define. Shams did not fit the pattern of a traditional sheikh, as he never received a cloak from a Sufi master, the standard ceremony of commitment, and so was not part of an established lineage. (He claimed to have received a cloak in a dream directly from Mohammad, as Attar claimed to have received his cloak in a dream from Hallaj.) With Shams, who was nearly twenty years his senior, Rumi's attitude was that of a pupil. Yet Rumi was already a spiritual director and teacher. Shams complained once about this lack of clarity: "I need it to be clear how our life is going to be—brotherhood, friendship, or sheikh and disciple. I don't like not knowing. Is it teacher and pupil?"

During the period of withdrawal in Salah's house—a sort of *chelle,* for two rather than one—Shams was directing Rumi toward a new way of being in the world, and he followed. "Before me, as he listens to me," said Shams, "he considers himself—I am ashamed to even say it—like a two-year-old before his father or a new convert to Islam who knows nothing. Such submission!" While Shams refused labels, he was well within the *malamatiyya* tradition of the fools of God—his mission, to free Rumi from the weight of his own dignity. So he devised tasks such as dispatching him to the Jewish neighborhood to buy wine and carry the pitcher through the streets. Konya had a tavern frequented by Armenian Christians, and Shams said: "Let's go see the women in the tavern. Let's go to church, too, and look in." Such neighborhoods became romantically spiritual for Rumi:

> *The tavern keeper became my heart's companion*
> *Love turned my blood into wine and burned my heart*

Shams grew keen to dismantle Rumi's reliance on his talent for using words to spin arguments and spellbind audiences. "Where's your own?" he demanded, if Rumi was quoting too many proverbs, or poems and tales. "Come on, answer!" Like Kerra, irked by the incessant lamplight while he read, Shams was bothered by Rumi's poring over pages of his father's manuscripts. He once barged in while Rumi was reading, and shouted, "Don't read! Don't read! Don't read!" Aged disciples informed his biographer Aflaki that Rumi told them, "He firmly commanded me, 'Don't read the words of your father any longer!' Following his instruction, I stopped reading them for some time."

Shams also disapproved of the fashionable poetry of Rumi's favorite Arabic poet from his schooldays in Aleppo, al-Mutanabbi. Besides his father's writing, Rumi loved to read verses of al-Mutanabbi in the evening. Shams said to him, "That is not worthwhile. Never read that again." Rumi ignored his warning until, one night, falling asleep reading the poet, he had a nightmare in which Shams grabbed al-Mutanabbi by the beard and dragged him forward, saying, "This is the man whose words you are reading!" Al-Mutanabbi, scrawny with a tiny voice, begged, "Please release me from the hands of Shams and never read my book again!'" Another dubious poet read by Rumi was al-Maarri, a blind Syrian, melancholy—like Khayyam—about life's quick passing: "How sad that man, after wandering freely through the world, is told by fate, 'Go into the grave.'" (Even Shams was known to recite a line or two of al-Maarri now and then, but he thoroughly disliked Khayyam for speaking "mixed-up, immoderate, and dark words.")

Rumi and Shams were not entirely isolated during their stay at Salah's home, just insulated from conventional responsibilities. Both Rumi's wife and Sultan Valad visited, and were drawn into some extreme tests of loyalty, obedience, and liberation, sprung by Shams. Rumi allowed his wife to be unveiled in front of Shams, an exposure reserved for family members, which would have been a difficult transgression for her. When Shams asked for a beautiful boy to serve him, Rumi presented Sultan Valad, though Shams thoughtfully declined, saying that the young man was more like a son to him. Missing was Alaoddin, Rumi's second son, who was following an orthodox path, with plans to become an esteemed religious figure like his father. Shams posed a threat to his ambitions to carry on the family name, and Alaoddin was appalled by his influence. These dynamics among family members—lining up in response to Shams's presence—remained set from that first encounter, with Alaoddin always sorely judging from outside.

The only other intimate allowed into the charmed circle was Hosamoddin Chelebi, a nineteen-year-old from a good middle-class Konya family of Kurdish origin, from Urmia in Azerbaijan, who had grown enamored with Rumi's way of teaching. Hosam's recently deceased father was Akhi Tork, his name indicating that he had been a leader of an *akhavan* organization, a fellowship of craftsmen, laborers, and merchants, like early guilds. This brotherhood (*akhi* could mean "my brother") overlapped with a wider *fotovvat* movement to which even the caliph belonged, combining chivalric morals with Sufi mysticism and a touch of vigilante power, as its members wore uniform vests and trousers. At the time, the streets of Konya were full of such young men, often long-haired, with glinting daggers slipped into their ceremonial belts, protective yet intimidating.

Hosam was welcome because of his mild temperament. He was intuitive and empathetic, as he was said to feel the pains of his friends in his own body. He was considered a handsome paragon of decent behavior and, like Salah, was drawn to asceticism from an early age. Most importantly, for Rumi, Shams expressed great fondness for the young man. Shams's judgments of character became Rumi's judgments, and the circle forming around Shams would remain the nucleus of his own world. Decades later, Rumi described Hosam, in an affectionate letter to him, as "both father and son to me, both light and sight." With the death of his father, Hosam was looked upon as the leader of the group of workingmen, and key in aligning these new followers with Rumi, just as Alaoddin, and other traditional pupils of Baha Valad, were growing disgruntled.

Shams had an aggressive, domineering manner that could seem extreme to many. Unlike Rumi, a public speaker practiced in politic turns of phrase and graced with the ability to charm, Shams was guileless. He avoided small talk: "I rarely speak with people." His speech was spare, yet musical and expressive in its rhythms and its simple, moving imagery, occasionally like Rumi's mature poetry. He disapproved of the gap between Rumi's speaking in public and the voice he heard when they were alone. "He has a beautiful manner and speaks beautiful words, but don't be satisfied with those," he warned a group of students. "Beyond them is something else. Seek that from him." He claimed, "He has two ways of speaking, one is circumspect, and the other, honest."

During these intensive first three months together, the range of conversation between the two men was wide, and Shams did not hold back from exposing Rumi to all his beliefs and practices, acting as if these moments together might never be repeated. Shams especially encouraged the honest, heartfelt Rumi. His was entirely a religion of the heart. "Practice is practice of the heart, service is service of the heart, and devotion is devotion of the heart," he told him. To illuminate Rumi's heart, he felt the need to shake him loose not only from his father's writings and al-Mutanabbi's poetry but also from all the language and philosophy that had been his support and the basis of his fame in early adulthood. Consistent with some strains of Sufi thought, Shams saw words and logic as "veils," hiding Rumi from the truth. Of the Greek philosophers, he preferred Plato because he "laid claim to love." As Rumi would write of this radical reorientation:

> When your love enflamed my heart
> All I had was burned to ashes, except your love.
> I put logic and learning and books on the shelf.

To replace thinking in words, especially the words of others, Shams rapidly introduced music, sung poetry, and dance into Rumi's life, through the practice of *sama*. Technically meaning "listening," *sama* applied to listening in the scholarly reading groups that Rumi had attended in Damascus, when a certificate, or *ijazat al-sama*, was granted for having heard a book read aloud. In many Sufi circles, though, *sama* came to mean a session of listening to music and poetry, sometimes accompanied

by a whirling dance. The Great Kerra had taught Rumi as a boy
to sway his arms to music. Shams, within weeks of their having
first met, instructed him more fully in whirling—teaching him
to literally spin loose of language and logic, while opening and
warming his heart:

> *When all the particles of the air*
> *Are filled with the glow of the sun*
> *They all enter the dance, the dance,*
> *And never complain of the whirling!*

❖

Shut away in private with Rumi, Shams soon became a compul-
sive topic of gossip throughout Konya, much of it malevolent and
suspicious. The result of their sequester at the home of Salah
was chaos and anxiety for Rumi's family and seminary students.
Both groups relied on Rumi, not just for moral guidance but
also for their livelihood and support as the patronage for his *ma-
drase* trickled down. As Sultan Valad dramatized the passing of
the staff of leadership, his father's pupils had sworn allegiance
to Rumi, saying, "We will seek wealth and gain from you." So
Shams was disparaged as a bewitching sorcerer, casting a spell
on their local saint, or an unlearned "Towrizi" from Tabriz.
("Towrizi" was another term for "Tabrizi," in a local spoken dia-
lect of Persian.)

Actually Shams was neither a sorcerer nor uneducated, yet
he was not in the habit of sharing many of the details of his ec-
centric and extraordinary life. In their three-month period of
intimacy, though, shut away in Salah's home, Rumi did begin to
learn his life story, as Shams told of decades passed as a lonely
sojourner, seeking the truth, but often confronted with the pain

of being misunderstood. While on the surface the conditions of their two lives contrasted highly, like Rumi, Shams had been driven by a longing rarely satisfied. The revelation of this shared quest and mutual dissatisfaction only ignited further their spiritual and intellectual romanticism, and sealed Rumi's final commitment.

Like many others in this era of chaos and high mobility, Shams traveled long distances before arriving in Konya, having grown up in Tabriz, in eastern Azerbaijan, where he was born sometime around 1180. Similar to Balkh or Samarkand, though farther west, situated in a fertile province between modern-day Turkey and the former Russian Transcaucasia, Tabriz was an important Persian market on the main trade routes between India and Constantinople. The city was also pinpointed in lore as the location of the Garden of Eden. Rivers to its north and south flowed into the Caspian Sea; nearby was the salt lake of Urmia, and the hometown of Hosam's family. Rumi never visited, though he spoke knowingly of "the rose-garden district" of the "glorious imperial city."

Like most commercial cities of the era, Tabriz was constantly changing hands, a contested chip in power struggles. When Shams was a boy, the Turkic ruler was Atabeg Abu Bakr, described by him as "towering over everybody, and surrounded by armed guards an entire arrow's flight around." Similar to the Seljuks, the Atabegs favored Persian as their primary language, and art and culture flourished. Tabriz, too, was culturally closer to the cities of Central Asia. In 1220, the unchecked Mongol invasions of Khorasan reached the city. For urging resistance to the non-Muslim Mongols, Shams praised its ruler as the "greatest of the age," though by the time Shams arrived in Konya to meet Rumi, Tabriz was securely part of the Il-Khan Dynasty of the Mongol Empire.

Both Rumi and Shams wrestled with the authority of father

figures, but in opposite manners. Rumi had tried to imitate and
please his revered father, while Shams, apparently an only child,
from early on struggled with his own father, Ali ebn Malekdad,
for lack of understanding and for being pampering and over-
protective. "The fault is that of my father and mother for they
brought me up with too much kindness," Shams oddly com-
plained. Shams's father worried over signs of spiritual zeal in his
unusual son, who had not yet reached puberty yet was already
hearing preaching whenever he could, and fasting for at least a
month at a time. "You're not crazy," his father said, "but I don't
understand your ways." Shams felt as if he were a duck egg laid
by a common hen. Like Rumi, at the same age, he was sure he
saw "angels and higher and lower worlds. I assumed that every-
body saw what I saw. Then I found out that they could not see it."

His father's "spoiling" was partly a response to the exceed-
ingly sensitive spirit that he recognized in his introverted son. In
Tabriz, stray cats often jumped in windows to swipe food from
cloths on the floor, and were duly beaten off with sticks. Even
if one of these cats broke a dish of milk, Shams's father spared
it because of his son's delicate sensibility. Instead he would say,
"This is destiny! This is a good omen!" In the fifteenth century,
Dowlatshah, writing a *Lives of the Poets* in the Timurid court in
Herat, recorded for the first time stories that had been passed
down of Shams as a beautiful boy, with a temperament consid-
ered by some "effeminate," supposedly proved by his skill as an
embroiderer in gold, a handicraft learned from tarrying with
the women in the harem.

Shams told Rumi of a search for kindred spirits that led him
first to the lively Sufi neighborhoods of Tabriz—the Sorkhab
quarter to the north, where many Sufis were buried in tombs at
the foot of Valienkuh, or Saints' Mountain, and, to the south,
the Charandab quarter. The density of Sufis in these neighbor-
hoods was so high that the souls of saints in the cemeteries were

said to rise on Friday nights, form groups of red and green doves, and fly to Mecca to encircle the Kaaba. Nearly seventy Sufis were clustered about one charismatic leader, who built a Sufi lodge in the Sorkhab district and taught a popular form of devotion based on mystical states rather than on studying books. Many Sufis in Tabriz favored this simple, unlettered approach, of the type described by Rumi:

> *The Sufi's book is not made of words*
> *It's nothing but a heart, as white as snow*

Shams said to Rumi, of these inspiring local figures, stimulating so much excitement and growth, "There were people there in comparison to whom I am nothing, as if the sea cast me up, like waves tossing up driftwood. If I am like this, imagine what they were like!"

He told of gravitating, while still a teenager, toward Sheikh Abu Bakr Sallebaf of Tabriz, who headed a Sufi lodge in the Charandab district. A maker of wicker baskets by trade, his followers tended to be drawn from the working-class *fotovvat* movement and were often threateningly more loyal to him than to the rulers. "There were dervishes staying with Sheikh Abu Bakr," remembered Shams. "When one of the assistants of the vizier would come to see him, the dervishes would show reverence to the sheikh a hundred times more than they had before the official arrived." Sallebaf did not bother with all the Sufi trappings, such as bestowing cloaks. Either from this sheikh, or another passionate local Sufi, Shams learned the whirling practice that he was teaching to Rumi: "With such a love, the passionate companion seized me in the *sama*. He was turning me around like a little bird. Like a husky young man who hasn't eaten for three days and suddenly finds bread—he grabs it, and breaks it apart hastily. I was like that in his hands."

As with most of his mentors, though, Shams finally felt mis-
understood, or underestimated, and stepped back from uncondi-
tional loyalty. He later confided to Sultan Valad, "I used to have
a sheikh by the name of Abu Bakr in the city of Tabriz and he
was a basket weaver by trade. I learned much about godly friend-
ship from him, but there was something in me that my sheikh
could not see and that nobody ever saw. Only Mowlana has seen
it." Unlike Baha Valad when Rumi had visions of angels, Abu Bakr
cautiously forbade Shams to talk about his visions. In turn, Shams
was suspicious of the practice of Tabrizi Sufis of begging for a
living. So he set out from home on a protracted quest that lasted
four decades and took him on a scribbling route through the
Middle East. A highly motivated seeker, he traveled to Baghdad,
Mecca, Damascus, Aleppo, and many Anatolian cities, meeting
on his journey with most of the prominent Sufis of his day.

Shams supported himself on the road by working odd con-
struction jobs, teaching the Quran to children, or weaving trou-
ser ties. Due to the frail look that came from his indefatigable
fasting, he was often passed over for hard labor crews, to his
disappointment. "They chose everybody else but left me stand-
ing there," he recalled. He was more successful as an elementary
school instructor and appreciated the humility of the position.
He recognized one of Rumi's disciples as having once seen him
as a teacher and not acknowledged his presence. "You used
to come to the school and saw me as a mere teacher," accused
Shams. "But how often an unknown person does us a service."
He was proud of having taught a stubborn boy to memorize the
Quran in three months, though he appeared to have done so
with the help of a liberal use of strict beatings.

Eventually he found his way to Baghdad, the center of Sufism,
some years before Rumi passed through with his family. Shams
belonged to the Shafii School of Islamic jurisprudence, more
common among Sufis than the Hanafi interpretation followed

by Baha Valad, Rumi, and many from Central Asia. Shafii judges based their legal decisions as much as possible solely on the blueprint of the life and practices—or *sunna*—of Mohammad, often by using analogies. Shams and Rumi discussed one of the basic Shafii legal texts, written by an early professor of the Nezami-yye College in Baghdad. Yet their slightly different legal orientations never seemed to matter overly to either of them. "If Abu Hanifa saw Shafii, he would pull his head towards him and kiss his eyes," said Shams, of the founders of the two schools. "How can God's servants disagree with God?"

Likely having stayed at the Daraje Sufi lodge on the western bank of the Tigris, Shams told of being involved briefly with the Turkish Sufi Kermani, the leader of an order in Baghdad and Damascus. Kermani was one of the more vivid and outrageous of the Sufi figures of his time. Very much in the school of Ahmad al-Ghazali, who glimpsed flashes of divinity in the faces of beautiful boys, Kermani was notorious for tearing open the cloaks of beardless young men during *sama* dancing and pressing his chest against theirs. He was also rumored to have undone some of their turbans in the heat of whirling.

Although Kermani was decades older, Shams was not intimidated. One evening he came across the mystic staring into a bowl of water, and asked what he was doing. "I'm looking at the reflection of the moon in a bowl of water." "Unless you have a boil in your neck, why not look at the sky?" Shams questioned, sarcastically. "Maybe you should see your doctor to be cured so that you can see the real thing." His intent was to refute the practice of looking for divinity reflected in human beauty rather than directly in God. Nevertheless, Kermani invited Shams to become one of his close companions. Shams insisted that he first "drink wine with me in the middle of the bazaar of Baghdad." Unlike Rumi, who at least bought wine for him publicly, Kermani refused, and Shams moved on.

In Damascus, Shams gravitated toward the renowned Sufi Salehiyye district, at the base of Mount Qasiyum, near Rebva, its panorama evoked by Rumi in the *Masnavi* using a popular Arabic proverb, which counseled maintaining perspective on life's trials:

> *When you see grief, embrace it lovingly:*
> *Look on Damascus from the top of Rebva*

According to Shams's own dating of his first passing encounter with Rumi, he was in Damascus around 1230, if not before or after. While Rumi may have had some contact with the circle around Ibn Arabi, Shams appears to have become a serious student. He spoke of a "Sheikh Mohammad," who is thought to have been the visionary Andalusian Sheikh Ibn Arabi, to whom he had likely been referred by Ibn Arabi's friend Kermani. "He was a mountain, a true mountain!" praised Shams. "He was such an exalted scholar, and he was more knowledgeable than me in every single way . . . a seeker of God."

Yet Shams's warm praise of Ibn Arabi's scholarly knowledge was not the entire story. As with all his teachers, relations were occasionally contentious due to Shams's defiant attitude. The two of them discussed many intricacies of prophetic sayings and related Quranic passages, a sort of Muslim version of the Talmudic scholarship of Jewish rabbis. Shams, though, was disappointed that they did not engage in more extended sparring. "Sheikh Mohammad used to give in to me, and not debate," grumbled Shams. "Yet if he had debated, there would have been more benefit. I needed for him to debate with me!" He would accuse Rumi, too, of refusing to debate with him satisfactorily. Obviously tireless, Shams wore down his debating partners. "You crack a powerful whip!" wryly joked Sheikh Mohammad, yet he always referred to Shams endearingly as his "son."

Off-putting for Shams was his opinion that Sheikh Moham-mad did not "follow," or imitate the Prophet Mohammad faith-fully enough. "He was compassionate, a good friend. He was a unique human being, Sheikh Mohammad, but he did not follow." This "following" was a charged issue in debates among the Sufis of Anatolia. Shams's original question to Rumi when they met had pointed toward it. Wherever Rumi fell in this argu-ment, his odes to Mohammad were certainly inspired by heights of adoring passion, which would have been shared by Shams. Rumi wrote of Mohammad in the mode of love, often return-ing to the account in Sura 54 of the Quran on his splitting the moon:

> *Our caravan leader, Mohammad, the pride of the world*
> *The moon was split in two, by seeing the beauty of his face,*
> *The moon, with its good fortune, gazed on his humility . . .*
> *Look into my heart, split, like the moon, at every moment.*

For such tender logic, Rumi became a "pearl" to Shams, and Ibn Arabi a mere "pebble."

Shams also grew close in Damascus with Shehab Harive, a materialist philosopher from Herat, where he had been a prize student of Razi. Shehab relied on logic, analysis, and reason, and dismissed revelation, miracles like the splitting of the moon, or bodily resurrection as fables for common folk. Theirs was an unusual friendship that should never have been if the logic that Shehab found so irrefutable were applied. In the scholastic fer-ment of Damascus, Shehab was sought after for his brilliant ar-guing that God has no free will, backed up by the certainty that "intellect makes no mistakes." "For me, death is as if a weak man has been loaded down with a sack tied to the neck," he said. "Someone cuts the rope, the heavy load falls, and he is released."

Years later in Konya, Shams was still arguing in his mind with his old friend Shehab. He told Rumi, "I would say, 'I don't want that God. I want a God who has free will. I seek that God. I would tell him to destroy that God of whom he spoke. . . . If the whole world were to accept that from Shehab, I still wouldn't!'" Yet Shams and Shehab were brought together by their aloof dispositions, their sharp misanthropy and stubbornness, and each other's appetite for ceaseless debating. "This man is congenial," said Shehab. Likewise Shams said, "I felt at ease when sitting with him. I found ease there." He wittily added, "Though Shehab spoke blasphemy, he was pure and spiritual." Tellingly, for Shams, their mutual affection outweighed any philosophical differences.

Contrary, difficult, and unpredictable, Shams debated and refuted his way through the emerging intellectual centers of Anatolia, as well. Traveling north from Aleppo, he spent time in Erzurum and Erzincan, where Baha Valad had taught in his "Esmatiyye" school for four years; Sivas; Kayseri, where Borhan passed the final years of life; and Aksaray, unusual in the region for having been organized by the Seljuks as a purely Muslim model town, a hundred miles northeast of Konya. Typical of Shams's arguments was a disagreement with a scholar in Sivas. Annoyed that Shams contradicted him in public on a fine point about man's knowledge of God's essence, the scholar said, "You are asking old questions." "What do you mean 'old?'" Shams snapped back. "It's aching with newness! Is this what passes for lecturing these days?" A number of eminent teachers refused to take on Shams as a private student because of his abrasive manner.

Having trouble finding his place within this well-ordered society of saints and scholars in the medieval Islamic world, Shams's individuality kept interfering. His conversation was flecked with mentions of challenging texts of law and spirituality. He resided in a *madrase* college in Aleppo for fourteen months. Yet he never felt comfortable among either the legal scholars or the Sufi dervishes. Of his ambivalence, he said to Rumi, "At first I wouldn't sit with jurists, I sat with dervishes. I used to say, 'They're strangers to dervishes.' Then I began to know what it is to be a dervish and where they were coming from, and now I would rather sit with the jurists. At least the jurists have taken some trouble to learn. The others simply brag about being dervishes."

Shams did have one trusted guide—his heart. He did not reject teachers one after another on the basis of a consistent theological stance as much as on feeling and intuition. Within his crusty exterior still beat the heart of the sensitive boy from Tabriz, which remained the source of his discernment. "Whenever you see someone whose character is expansive, speaking broadly and patiently, and blessing the whole world, so that his words open up your heart, and you forget this narrow world . . . he is an angel from paradise," he counseled Rumi. "Whenever you hear in someone's words anger and coldness and narrowness, you become chilled by his words. . . Whoever discovers this secret, and puts it into practice, pays no attention to a hundred thousand of the sheikhs."

Shams told of visiting Konya on previous occasions. On his first visit, he found three dirham coins, marked as currency of the Seljuk sultan, on the road to a main gate, leading toward the town square. Kayqobad I was the first Seljuk sultan to mint gold coins, but Shams obviously found an ordinary one. Each night he would buy a half piece of fine white flatbread and give away an amount equal of its cost to the poor. When the money was used up, he departed once again for Syria. His visit in the fall of 1244 was more intentional. He later said that he had a dream in which God promised to answer his prayers, and to make him at last the companion of one saint, "in Rum." Shams had arrived in Konya with strong hopes of reaching the end of his long and solitary road, and his meeting with Rumi clearly seemed to him the fulfillment of that prophetic dream, just as Rumi had revealed the premonition that he felt was surely being realized in Shams.

❖

Sometime in 1245 Rumi and Shams emerged from the winter of seclusion that followed their first meeting. They returned to the Madrase Khodavandgar and began to take part in a curtailed manner in the life of the community. Making short work, though, of the longings of many family members and students for a complete resumption of normalcy, the two quickly disappeared behind closed doors within the *madrase* for yet another intimate encounter that lasted six months—to the astonishment of those left again counting the days against an uncertain ending to the strange silence that had fallen over the school, without any classes or sermons being delivered by their youthful patriarch.

The dismay of those left behind was understandable. The connection between these two complicated souls could seem weird and inscrutable. Shams was acerbic at times and misanthropic, likely at any moment to reveal the sharp edges of his personality that had caused many sincere Sufi masters throughout the Middle East to keep their distance or back off entirely. Rumi was his foil, a man of great charm and affection in a position of power and influence, now risking everything to remain locked away in insulated confinement, allowing all that he and his revered father built so diligently to be endangered, family and students adrift, while he lost himself in the challenge of Shams.

Still their love was instantaneous and enduring. Shams had seen Rumi for who he was, and that look of recognition had begun to set Rumi free. No matter how many honors and accomplishments he accumulated, Rumi still felt encumbered by his position. Shams saw that Rumi was creative, a poet and a mystic, not a gatekeeper for rules. He encouraged him to find his voice, and so Rumi owed him his newfound heart. Likewise, Shams, for all his grumbled bragging about self-reliance, traveled for decades in search of someone who would recognize his own authentic self, his softer core. As Shams had told Sultan Valad, Rumi was the first to do so. The religious life for men of their day was often demanding and restrictive. Together they created a safer, lighter domain of their own. Both were old enough to know the value of their discovery, and wished it to last.

The only two visitors allowed during this time were Salah and Sultan Valad, who gained even more of his father's affection to the degree that he supported his devotion to Shams. Even Kerra was now excluded from the room, kept apart from her adored husband, who she was used to fussing over for trifles—like warning him to chew a stick of straw to ward off bad luck because he had broken his belt. Yet although her marital and family life had been greatly disrupted because of Shams, she never spoke publicly against him. Likewise Shams occasionally spoke affectionately of Kerra and seemed to understand her predicament. "Kerra Khatun is jealous," he said. "But hers is the sort of jealousy that takes you to paradise, not hell, and is truly part of the path of goodness." Belying slurs against Shams as untutored, Sultan Valad later accurately wrote of him as a man of "learning and knowledge." (Rumi likewise attested to Shams's familiarity with "alchemy, astronomy, mathematics, theology, astrology, law, logic, and debate.") Sultan Valad looked up to Shams as "beloved" and a spiritual "sultan." In turn, Shams took a guiding role, teaching him the meditative *sama* as well as counseling the adolescent young man.

While Rumi was undergoing this major change of life with Shams, and evolving in his understanding of his vocation, the Seljuk Empire of Rum, outside the wall of their cell in the Madrase Khodavandgar, was undergoing an equally major disruption, though more a devolution, a loss of power and might. The Sultan Kayqobad I, the patron of Rumi's father—having overseen an uninterrupted stretch of prosperity and cultural glister—died in 1237, while rumors circulated claiming he was poisoned by his son and successor, Kaykhosrow II. On ascending the throne, Kaykhosrow II married the daughter of a ruler of Aleppo, but soon revealed his predilection for Christian ladies by marrying his second wife, Tamara, or Gorji Khatun, a young Georgian princess who rose to the level of his consort and eventually became one of Rumi's most ardent female disciples.

Unlike his father, a paradigm of wise rule, Kaykhosrow II had a sillier disposition and delighted in nightly cups of wine while being entertained with songs and clever quatrains. Having inherited valuable territory that included most of Asia Minor, Kaykhosrow II managed during his decade of governance to diminish Seljuk Rum to a kingdom in name only, his father's empire never regaining its former grandeur. First among his challenges, caused by the populations displaced from Khorasan by the Mongols, were popular Turkoman Sufi preachers, usually called "Baba," meaning "father," by their followers, who preached against the power of the state and set rural Turks against urban Seljuks. These incendiary preachers riled both the Khorasani refugees and local peasants until Kaykhosrow II put down their insurrection with the help of Frankish mercenaries.

Even more destabilizing were Mongol forces on his eastern borders. In 1243 Kaykhosrow II assembled a large force to make a stand at the battle of Kose Dag, where the smaller Mongol army routed them. As panic spread through Anatolia, Kaykhosrow II escaped to the coast while his vizier negotiated a weak peace treaty, agreeing to payment of annual tributes of gold and silver to the Mongols in return for sparing Konya. By the time Kaykhosrow II returned to the capital, he had outlived his power, and

Konya its political independence. (Shams's praise of the Tabrizi ruler Shams Toghri for bravely standing up to the Mongols would have been heard as a putdown of Kaykhosrow II.)

Though a sense of floating anxiety that both Rumi and Shams knew well, from the encroachment of the Mongols into their native homelands, now permeated Konya, the streets into which they reemerged after their second retreat were still reasonably safe and unchanged from the earlier days of peace and prosperity before Shams's arrival. Shams tended to thrive in one of two settings—locked away in seclusion, or wandering and seeing the sights. He claimed these contraries in his state were actually one. "Be among the people, but be alone," he advised Rumi. "Don't live your life in seclusion, but be solitary." In Konya, Shams took his own advice, accepting that Rumi could not always be with him. "When I'm by myself, I'm free," said Shams, with a dose of his usual sarcasm. "I wander anywhere and sit in any shop. I cannot take him along—a well-born man, one of the muftis of the city—to look in on every seedy place." A favorite place for them to at least talk without disturbance was the rooftop of Rumi's school, where they could look down in the bright light of a full moon on neighbors on warm nights sleeping on their terraces. Rooftops became sweet reminders for Rumi of these elusive private interludes:

> Sometimes Love shone on the roof like a moon
> Sometimes like a breeze, moving from lane to lane

Rumi and Shams did go walking together through the epicenter of Konya, its thriving market district, which especially fascinated their moral imaginations with its power to lure and seduce by playing on basic desires and fantasies. As Rumi later wrote:

The world is an illusion, and we are like merchants,
Trying to buy its moonlight, measured by the yard

They paused to watch gypsies, or *lulis,* who passed through
Konya. With their music and rope dances, they excited interest
and were given money. Sugar was sold in the apothecary shops
in little brown bags, or wrapped in packets of paper, like candy.
So Rumi later wrote of Shams:

Whenever I write the name of Shams of Tabriz
I sprinkle my favorite sugar into a paper wrapper

Both men were equally drawn to the disturbing as well as the
pretty. Rumi was reminded by the butcher shops selling intes-
tines of the cruel beloved of Persian love poetry, like a butcher,
his hands bloodied with the livers of unrequited lovers. Fasci-
nated by the dark shops offering bloodletting, near the herbal-
ists, Shams reflected on its customers choosing to disappear into
the darkness while "a sun has come up, filling the world with
light!" More pointedly he suggested learned theologians would
do better to "be like the poor Russian man, cloaked in sheep-
skin, wearing a tall fur hat, and selling sulfur matches."

Just as central as the bazaar in Rumi's and Shams's life in
Konya were its many *hammam,* or bathhouses, particularly as
Seljuks were enamored of fresh flowing water and made medic-
inal use of the countless mineral springs of Anatolia. They both
frequented the *hammam,* singly and together. "I stop in every
bathhouse," reported Shams. Rumi was visceral in his fondness
for the *hammam* and dwelled on each detail, taking in the nim-
bleness of the attendant stoking heat in the stove, or the cup
for pouring water over the body, or the thick *sultani* soap. He
was most fascinated by decorative paintings on bathhouse walls,
often of heroes from the *Shahname,* and meditated on the dif-

ference between a painted heroic Rostam and a real warrior, be-
tween artifice and spirit, and the way light falling from a window
in a dome animated these static figures:

> *The world is a bathhouse, its skylight eternity*
> *Illumined by the window is the hero's beauty*

Following their freeing spell of withdrawal, Rumi did step
back, tentatively, into his former life as a religious leader in the
city, too. Remaining in his sights was Qonavi, the godson and
designated deputy of Ibn Arabi. After Ibn Arabi's death, Qonavi
had moved north to Konya and was continuing the philosophi-
cal tradition of Ibn Arabi, filling in more steps of mystical knowl-
edge in learned Arabic treatises. Rumi and Qonavi were about
the same age, and before Shams's arrival, Rumi attended his
lectures. Yet with Shams's influence, their ideas increasingly di-
verged, as Qonavi preached the path of knowledge, and Rumi
performed the path of love. They came to represent the two an-
tipodes of Sufi temperament in Konya yet remained respectful,
if wary, colleagues.

Rumi returned to teaching as well, but with Shams doing
most of the talking, or the two of them engaged in dialogue
in front of a hall of students. Many of the more conservative
disciples were horrified to find Rumi nearly silent, or deferring
to the words and opinions of the strangely rambling mystic
from Tabriz, who spoke at times in riddles or enigmatic non
sequiturs. Like Rumi, Shams was an intellectual. Yet inspired
by the "unlettered" Tabrizi mystics of his childhood, he had left
learning behind, as if he had climbed a tall ladder that he then
pushed away. Rumi likely assigned Sultan Valad to write down
these sessions, as one of the surviving transcripts appears to be
in his handwriting.

Instead of lecturing on logic and religious law, Shams

preferred to speak vulnerably and tenderly of his friendship with Rumi. These public teaching circles became love fests as much as occasions for unpacking one or another abstruse topic. Shams modeled speaking from the heart rather than the more formal double-talk, hypocritically mastered, he grumbled, by Rumi, which made him so impatient. "We've met each other in an amazing way," he exclaimed, with transparent joy. "It's been a long time since two people like us have fallen together. We're extremely open and obvious. The saints did not used to be so obvious. But we are also hidden and we do have our secrets. . . . I'm so happy to be your friend—so happy that God has given me such a good friend! My heart gives me to you—whether I exist in that world or in this world, whether I'm in the pit at the bottom of the earth or above the heavens, whether I'm up or down."

He revealed, in this open setting, the ground rules of their friendship: "The first stipulation I made was that our life should be without hypocrisy, as if I were alone." He insisted that he saw himself not as a sheikh but as a friend: "God has not yet created a human being who could be Mowlana's sheikh. Yet I am also not somebody who can be a disciple. Nothing of that remains in me." He compared his beloved Rumi to moonlight and, audaciously, to the *qibla,* pointing the direction to Mecca for prayer: "I wanted someone of my own kind so that I could make him my *qibla* and turn my face towards him. I was bored with myself. . . . Now that I have that *qibla,* he understands and grasps what I'm saying." According to Shams, Rumi was a bolt of natural energy, dislodging the dam that caused his waters to stagnate: "Now the water flows forth smoothly, freshly, and splendidly. . . . I speak eloquently and beautifully. Inside, I'm bright and luminous." He put much stress on the freeing informality between them both in public and private.

Shams not only spoke of his feelings, but he also acted them out, leaning over to stroke or take hold of Rumi's hand. "Now rub my little hand," he cajoled. "It's been awhile since you've rubbed it. Do you have something better to do? Rub just like that for a while." He rambled on in squibs of exalted poetry: "In the lane of the beloved there's a kind of hashish. People take it and lose their minds. Then they can't find the beloved's house and they fail to reach the beloved." And he testified to having finally found meaning, not in a set of ideas, but in their friendship. Truth, Shams implied, was face-to-face: "The purpose of life is for two friends to meet each other and to sit together face to face in the spirit of God, far from earthly desires. The goal is not bread or the baker, not the butcher shop or the butcher. It's simply this very hour, while I'm sitting here at ease in your company."

Shams examined theology, but his approach was untraditional, as he acidly put down the philosophers' need to prove God's existence. As Rumi recalled one incident:

> In the presence of Shamsoddin of Tabriz, someone said, "I have proven the existence of God, indisputably." The next morning Shamsoddin said, "Last night the angels came down and blessed that man, saying, 'Praise to God, he has proven our God. May God grant him long life!' . . . O poor man, God is a given fact. His existence needs no logical proof. If you must do something, then just prove your own dignity and your own rank in His presence. He exists without proof. Of this there is no doubt."

Shams ridiculed scholars for quoting sayings of the Prophet and giving the source—a "chapter and verse" approach—rather than speaking from their hearts and citing God as the source. He skirted heresy with provocative comments: "I do not revere the Quran because God spoke it. I revere it because it came out from the mouth of Mohammad."

Rumi, too, grew bolder about expressing his feelings for Shams in public. One day he was attending the inaugural ceremony for an important new *madrase*. Shams arrived late and he was sitting among the onlookers in the entranceway, where shoes were removed and stacked. Rumi sat with the prominent religious scholars, and a symposium was being conducted on a most pressing issue for them—"Which place is the seat of honor?" Echoing his father, while turning social decorum on its head, Rumi said:

> The seat of honor for the scholars is in the middle of this raised platform. The seat of honor for the mystics is in a corner of their own house. The seat of honor for Sufis is next to the raised platform. But in the practice of true lovers, the seat of honor is next to the beloved, wherever he may be.

At that moment Rumi stood up and quickly exited the stage, making his way through the press of gathered dignitaries, and shockingly sat down in the far vestibule next to Shams.

Such behavior was endured because Rumi was so cherished by the town fathers. They were not so patient with Shams, and kept trying to find ways to weaken his position or drive him away. One day a delegation of these local notables showed up at Rumi's school to raise the issue of Shams and wine drinking, which was forbidden in Islam, though famously a test case of rules and rituals among some Sufis. He was obviously at least understood to be drinking real wine, not just divine wine. So they asked Rumi the leading question, "Is wine forbidden or not?" His cutting reply was dismissive, as he showed that he refused to be intimidated by them, even using a Khorasani curse:

It depends who is drinking. If you pour a flask of wine into the ocean, the ocean would not be transformed or polluted, or darkened by the wine, and so it would be permitted to use its water for ablutions and drinking. But, without doubt, one drop of wine would make a tiny pool of water unclean. . . . My clear answer to you is that, if Shamsoddin drinks wine, for him everything is permitted, since he has the overwhelming power of the ocean. But for you—you brother of a whore—even eating a piece of barley bread should be forbidden.

Rumi appeared to acknowledge to them that Shams was indeed drinking real wine and presumably did not think of himself as a "tiny pool of water" rather than an ocean.

Shams did not help his position with the elders of Konya or with Rumi's more immediate circle inside his school. He made enemies more easily than friends, as he began to act as a kind of secretary, chamberlain, even bodyguard, interceding, blocking access, and occasionally charging a small fee for audiences with Rumi: "What have you brought and what will you give away as an offering, so that I show him to you?" One day a visitor asked Shams, who was sitting in front of the door to Rumi's private room, collecting money, "For your part, what have you brought since you ask something of us?" "I've brought myself," Shams answered, dramatically, "and I've sacrificed my life for him." To Rumi, Shams explained the taxes as a test: "One of them claims to love you from the bottom of his soul, but if I ask him for one dirham, he loses his mind, he loses his soul, and can't tell his head from his feet. I tested them so they would understand a bit about themselves. But they began to revile me saying that I discouraged your followers."

Such chafing words and deeds caused resentment to grow.

"The lovely son of Baha Valad from Balkh has become obedient to a child of Tabriz," complained one of Rumi's followers, obviously from Khorasan, and perhaps among the cadre of men who had accompanied Baha Valad and his family on their emigration. "Does the land of Khorasan take orders from the land of Tabriz?" Other Khorasanis went about saying that the people of Tabriz were all "jackasses." (These loyalists were eventually buried near Baha Valad in the imperial rose garden.) In his later biography in verse about his father, Sultan Valad recorded some of the harsher of their cascade of outraged comments to each other: "Who is this who stole our sheikh from us?" Paranoia mixed with jealousy as they accused Shams of "'hiding him away from everybody else. Of his existence there was not a trace. We no longer may see his face. We no longer may sit at his side. He must be a magician casting an evil spell, mesmerizing our sheikh with his incantations.'"

These grievances were voiced often, and openly, and Shams was just as strident in defending himself in his teaching circles, with Rumi present. He easily quashed the argument of the Khorasani by saying that if a man from Constantinople possessed grace, it would be incumbent even on a man from Mecca to follow him. He mused aloud on the difficulties that the rough edges of his personality might create for others. "Mowlana has great beauty, while I have both beauty and ugliness," he explained, perceptively enough. He recognized that his own gentleness was balanced with severity. But ugliness and severity, in Shams's assessment, were elements of absolute honesty and frankness, the absence of hypocrisy. "I'm all one color on the inside," he bragged. And he claimed to thrive on insults. "I am only troubled when someone praises me," he goaded his critics.

Rumi occasionally joined in the argument, rebuffing those who complained that Shams was "arrogant, greedy, and doesn't mix with us." He counseled understanding:

You only say so because you do not love Mowlana Shamsoddin. If you loved him, you would not see greed or anything reprehensible.

Hidden in Rumi's response was his cherished tale of Majnun and Layli. As he liked to tell the story, Layli was ordinary, her beauty only obvious in Majnun's own loving vision. He clearly knew his love for the grating and sharp-tongued Shams confused them:

> During Majnun's time there were girls more beautiful than Layli, but they were not Majnun's favorite. They said to Majnun, "There are girls more beautiful than Layli. Should we bring them to you?" He answered, "But I don't love Layli because of her face. She is not just a face. Layli is like a cup in my hand. I drink wine from that cup. So I am in love with the wine that I'm drinking from her. You look only at the cup. You are not aware of the wine. If I had a golden cup, decorated with jewels and stones, and it contained vinegar, or something besides wine, why should I use that cup? A broken old pumpkin that holds wine is worth a hundred times more."

Mostly, Rumi did not bother to argue. One time, on hearing someone begin to broach a criticism of Shams, he jumped up and shouted, "I'm not going to listen to this!" and exited the hall. At other times, he spoke so honestly of the depths of their friendship that he left little room for criticism in the wake of his blatant exhilaration and passion—articulating for them the eternal love at the core of their striking spiritual connection:

> On the Day of Resurrection, when the ranks of the prophets and the categories of the Friends of God will be drawn up, and the believers of the Muslim community, troop

after troop, will gather together, Shamsoddin and I, holding one another's hand, will walk proudly and graciously into Paradise.

Rumi was remarkably confident about the great changes caused in his life by Shams, whose bold commands helped him not only to relax from reading his father's words but also from copying the manner of life of his father, as much as he continued to respect him. He realized that he had been given an opportunity for a more expansive existence. Shams allowed Rumi to experience the heartfelt warmth that he would always associate naturally enough with the sun, from which creativity soon began to flow. As he wrote of this disruption, appropriately, ventriloquially channeling the voice of Shams:

> *You were silent and I made you a storyteller*
> *You were pious and I taught you how to sing*

CHAPTER 8

Separation

A few days before Nowruz, the Persian holiday marking the first day of spring, in March 1246—about fifteen months after appearing in Konya and upending Rumi's life—Shams abruptly disappeared. He departed Konya without any warning, leaving behind Rumi, who became startled, confused, and distraught. Influencing his quick exit was the rising volume and intensity of anger from Rumi's followers and, perhaps, Rumi's ambivalence about Shams's insistently pressing him to abandon his former life entirely.

Sultan Valad vividly recalled the agitation that had been so consuming in the days before Shams vanished. A hint of violence was in the air. Some angry men even flashed their daggers at Shams or cursed at him as he passed them in the street. "All wondered when he would quit town or come to a wrathful end," Sultan Valad wrote. Driving this wish for the eclipse of Shams was the expectation of Rumi's followers that they would have their teacher and old way of life back. Yet the opposite occurred. Rumi withdrew entirely. As Sultan Valad poetically described, "His bird of affection flew away from their houses." Realizing their situation had deteriorated—not improved—many repented.

If Shams had been devising another of his tests, Rumi passed. He found that he was not able to return to his earlier ways. He was not able to go forward, either, as his new life pivoted on Shams. In its place was an emptiness Rumi was unable to fill, and he was left feeling paralyzed and depressed. As Aflaki reported, "Because of being apart from Shamsoddin, Mowlana grew unsettled. Day and night he found no rest and did not sleep." Unknown to Rumi, Shams had traveled to Syria, either Damascus or Aleppo, or both. Yet he may have heard of Rumi's condition. Even though it took a while to travel this distance, many shuttled between these cultural capitals. So Shams relented a bit. He entrusted a note with a traveler to Konya, reassuring Rumi he was alive and thinking of him: "Please be aware this humble man is praying for you, and mixes with no one else."

Rumi's response was electric. He composed at least four letters in verse for Shams, moved by this momentous personal crisis to begin to try to find his voice as a poet. Rumi may have been experimenting earlier, since he was an aficionado of Arabic and Persian poetry, and implied in one stanza that he had begun writing poems:

> *When you're not here the* sama *is forbidden*
> *Music and dance are pelted with stones, like Satan*
> *Without you not even one* ghazal *has been written*
> *Until the clear message of your letter arrived.*

The first few of these urgent verse-letters lack the confident tone of his mature works. Tellingly, he began in Arabic, the more intellectual and formal language of the time. He did choose, though, as his form, the *ghazal*—his lifetime favorite—a rhymed poem of seven or more lines classically used as an erotic poem, sung by minstrels mostly on frivolous topics of wine, women or boys, and song, and eventually developed as a vehicle for mystical love poems. Like the English or Italian sonnet, the *ghazal* could be modulated from low to high themes, still redolent of

the roughness of the Bedouin desert chants, while expressing
the subtler Sufi sentiments.

Although Shams was so derisive of the poetry of al-Mutannabi,
these first poems Rumi wrote to him often sound like that fa-
vorite Arabic poet, both in language and in courtly convention.
Very much a poet-for-hire, al-Mutannabi had specialized in *qasi-
das,* or odes of praise, written in a heroic style for a tenth-century
ruler of Aleppo. In these paeans, the king is compared to the
sun, his perfumed scent is carried on the breezes, his power
rivals that of lions, his favor to another causes the poet painful
jealousy. Rumi simply adapted these majestic tropes for Shams,
comparing him to King Qobad, a Sassanian Persian king, or to a
great military commander bringing triumph and victory. He in-
stinctively knew that only the grandest of comparisons matched
his spiraling emotions.

If these first attempts were imitative copies of classical poems
of love and praise, like juvenile poems, some of Rumi's wit and
vulnerability are evident—that other voice Shams heard when
they were in private. A link in many *ghazals* was the *radif,* a repeat-
ing refrain of a word or phrase at the end of each line, adding a
percussive beat that made for easy group chanting, when recited
in public. For one of these verses, Rumi chose as his *radif* a sup-
plication of a command, "Come!"—an urgent refrain imploring
Shams's return:

> *Oh you, light within the heart, come!*
> *Goal of all effort and desire, come!*
> *You know my life is in your hands.*
> *Do not oppress your worshiper, come!*

Midway through the supplication, Rumi cleverly switched to
Persian, and likewise switched from the Arabic for "Come!"—
"*Taal*"—to the Persian for "Come!"—"*Biya!*":

What is "Taal" in Persian? Biya!
Either come or show mercy, Biya!

Rumi and Shams lived in a bilingual world, and this switching back and forth matched the way they spoke together and with others. When recounting to the disciples his important memory of meeting Rumi, Shams shifted to Arabic. When Rumi dictated to Hosam the precise date of Shams's departure for Syria, he segued into formal Arabic:

> The Sun of Truth and Faith, the hidden light of God in the beginning and in the end—may God lengthen his life and favor us with greeting him—departed on Thursday the 21st day of the month of Shavval in the year 643.

(A waning quarter moon on a lunar calendar, the date corresponded to March 11, 1246.)

Rumi deputized his son Sultan Valad to deliver his reply to Shams in Syria, sending with him a tribute of gold and silver coins. The offering was a subtle reminder of the tariffs that Shams had demanded of Rumi's followers to prove their love. In an accompanying prose letter, Rumi addressed the issue of these followers and assured Shams of their sincere change of heart—they were eager for Shams's return and looked forward to his renewed teachings. In his verses, though, Rumi allowed more intimate glimpses of a desperate heart, coded and camouflaged in standard poetic decor:

> *From the moment when you went away*
> *I was stripped of sweetness, turned to wax*
> *All night long I burn like a candle,*
> *Scorched with fire, but deprived of honey.*

Separated from your beauty, my body
     Lies in ruins and my soul is a night owl

He signed off with his favorite source of puns from that time on—
Shams's name, as "*shams*," lent itself, in Arabic, to the sun, as well
as to Syria (*Sham*) and, in the ancient yet still current Pahlavi Per-
sian vocabulary, to the night or early evening hours (*sham*):

May my night be turned to bright morning by you
     You, who are the pride of Syria, Armenia and Rum!

His saddlebag filled with the missive, gold and silver coins,
and the verse letters—both charming and intense—Sultan
Valad, then twenty, set off for Syria. In his writings, he spoke
of being dispatched by his father to Damascus. The biographer
Aflaki later gave more details of Rumi directing Sultan Valad
even more precisely to a well-known caravanserai located in the
Sufi Salehiyye neighborhood, where he told him to expect to
find Shams playing backgammon. Shams in his later accounting
of his time away from Rumi in Syria spoke fondly of Damascus,
and of his special love for the grand Umayyad Mosque, repeat-
ing the well-worn equation of Damascus with paradise. Mostly,
though, he spoke of having lingered in Aleppo, so that Sultan
Valad either went to both cities, the two men stopping in Aleppo
on the way from Damascus, or two separate trips were taken.

In his own mind, the high point of Shams's retreat from
Konya, and the city with the greatest pull on his spirit to remain
and never depart for Rum, was Aleppo. Shams reported having
felt the excitement of a return visitor, sitting near its grand Cit-
adel, close to the district where Rumi's tutor Ibn al-Adim lived:
"It's a wonderful city, Aleppo—the houses, the streets. I looked
around happily, seeing the tops of the battlements. I looked

down, I saw a world and a moat." Of a fortress a short distance from town, he said, "If they had said to me, 'Your father has come out of the grave and wishes to see you. He has come to Tel Bahser to see you and then die once again—come see him.' I would have said, 'Tell him to die.' I wouldn't have left Aleppo even for him." If still unsure of his feelings about Rumi, he was quite sure he had no desire to exchange Aleppo for Konya.

Shams brought between three hundred and five hundred dirhams from Konya, and paid seven dirhams a month for his room, so he did not need to seek odd jobs, as in the past. He also ate frugally. When he had been on the road in earlier days, he was so ascetic that once a day would he go to a lamb's head seller to buy bread and broth. When a shopkeeper insisted that Shams be given the best cut of lamb in his soup, Shams switched to a shop where they did not give him any such special treatment. On this trip, he was more relaxed about eating. As he later reminisced to Rumi, "I remember in Aleppo, I was saying I wished you were there. When I was eating, I would have given some to you, as well."

Apart from his absolute love for the city, though, Shams did experience mixed feelings about his motives for being there and his split with his beloved Rumi. During their first month apart he kept vacillating. He was testing Rumi's resolve. He was also testing himself, deciding whether to walk away from such a cherished friend after having spent much of his adult life looking for him. He later confided to Rumi, "Such praying I did for you in Aleppo in that caravanserai where I was staying! It was not right to show my face to the people when you were not there. So I busied myself with work or spent time at a Sufi lodge." At other times he felt ready to revert to his earlier, freer life: "When I was in Aleppo, I was busy praying for Mowlana. I prayed a hundred prayers, and only brought to mind memories that increased my affection, avoiding those that cooled the affections, but I had no intention to return." Balanced in Shams's thoughts, as well, was the mission of transformation he called "the work." He did understand their friendship as not merely emotionally charged, but also critical for releasing Rumi's potential.

Eventually Sultan Valad, with a retinue of twenty companions, discovered Shams's whereabouts: "When I found Shamsoddin, I put my forehead to the ground, and bowed." According to the account in Aflaki, Shams was touched and moved to see Sultan Valad again: "Kissing Valad several times, Shamsoddin caressed him beyond measure and asked after Mowlana." Sultan Valad duly presented the gifts, pouring all the coins into Shams's shoes, and then passed on a crucial message from his father. "All the companions of Rum have bowed their heads in complete sincerity," he reported. "Having repented, they have sought forgiveness beyond measure and regret what they did. They have resolved that from this day forward they will not show any disrespect and will not allow any envy to arise within themselves. They are all awaiting your most blessed arrival."

Shams relented—though when he later discussed their exchange that day with Sultan Valad, he insisted that he had been far from certain about his choice. He was not simply being evasive. He reminded Sultan Valad that his composure had not changed when he saw him: "When you came to Aleppo did you see any change in the color of my face? It's as if it had been the same for a hundred years." He went on to admit that he had been suffering greatly inside from the separation: "But it was so unpleasant and difficult for me that it would be bad to speak of it. Sometimes I enjoyed myself. But the unpleasantness was stronger. I preferred Mowlana." No one knew better than Rumi the hesitation that his son was likely to encounter. Shams had evidently been talking about this choice for some time. Before the group left Konya for Syria, Rumi wrote and performed for them a more lighthearted *ghazal* that warned of just that strong possibility:

> *Comrades, go, and bring back my beloved*
> *Bring back to me my runaway beloved*
> *Lure him with sweet melodies, and gifts of gold,*
> *Bring him back home, his face a beautiful moon.*
> *If he promises that he'll come along shortly*
> *He may be deceiving you. All his promises are tricks.*

Rumi's playful tone implied that he judged the worst over. Likewise playful was his toying with the romantic conventions of the *ghazal*—addressed to women in Arabic lyrics, though more often in the Persian tradition to young men, especially Turk soldiers in court, or wine stewards, with curly black hair and eyebrows. Shams was as far from that beardless ideal as from the warrior kings Rumi compared him to in his verse letters, while at the same time arousing all of the fiery love, longing, and awe that the imagery carried.

The distance from Aleppo to Konya was about four hundred miles, which would have taken a camel caravan approximately a month. Sultan Valad's contingent traveled on horseback. According to Aflaki, as they now had an extra rider, they were one horse short. Sultan Valad reasonably enough insisted that Shams ride the horse. Less reasonably, when Shams suggested their riding together, Sultan Valad refused, on the grounds of proper respect in the presence of a sheikh. Given the ancient emphasis on elaborate rituals of politeness in Persian culture, this exchange might have gone on extensively. "It is not permitted for a king and a slave to ride on one horse at the same time," demurred Sultan Valad, attending to Shams's stirrup throughout the entire journey.

Rumi and Shams's separation lasted about a year, with Shams's reentry to Konya taking place around April 1247. As Rumi was dejected for months, his happiness anticipating Shams's return was nearly manic. He saw the chance of having his life both ways—exploring the freedom, creativity, and love Shams offered, while remaining responsible to family and community. If Rumi had been more committed when the two—according to Shams—briefly met in Damascus during his student years, he might have pursued a life as a poet and mystic. He, too, could have been a "flier" like Shams, Attar, or Sanai. As his revolution occurred midlife, he needed to set responsibilities bequeathed by his father against the adventurous alternatives offered by Shams. The hope he might be able to have both made him giddy.

Rumi wishfully told his disciples of the wonderful life they would now share, as he took them at their word about leaving behind their jealousy of the provocative Shams:

> This time you will find yourselves taking more pleasure from Shamsoddin's words that faith is the sail on the ship of a man's life. When the sail is set, the wind takes it to great places. Without the sail, words are nothing but wind.

Trying to please, these disciples encouraged their teacher's excitement by reporting rumors of Shams being spotted on his way to Konya. In his playful response, Rumi scolded them for these false sightings, making a comparison between seeing Shams and having spiritual insight. Without such insight, Shams would remain invisible:

> These people say, "We saw Shamsoddin of Tabriz, Master, we did see him." You brother of a whore, where did you see him? It's like someone who can't even make out a camel on a roof saying, "I found the eye of the needle and threaded it!"

Shams's highly anticipated homecoming was treated as a civic holiday. When Sultan Valad arrived at the nearby Zanjirli Caravanserai, he sent ahead a dervish to inform Rumi of their imminent arrival. Rumi alerted his disciples, who paraded out beyond the city gates to greet Shams in a welcoming ceremony that included banging on kettledrums, waving banners, and reciting poetry. Sultan Valad then led Shams's horse to Rumi's house. Again they saw each other, and again their hearts expanded. As Sultan Valad described the event, stressing the lack of clarity, or the mutual feeling, which marked their unconventional relationship, they fell at each other's feet, "and no one knew who was the lover and who the beloved." This perceptive comment on the abandon of their greeting was circulated widely enough to find its way eventually into a quatrain of Rumi's:

> *With his beautiful face, the envy of angels,*
> *He came to me at dawn and wept on my chest*
> *He wept and I wept until the break of day*
> *"How strange," they said. "Of these two, who is the lover?"*

Rumi celebrated Shams's arrival by performing occasional poems—writing poems for special occasions would remain his lifelong practice. These lines were musical, and trancelike, designed to accompany the whirling and meditating that went on at festivals. In his rousing lyric for Shams's return, he used the same *radif*, "come," which he had used in his imploring verse letter, but in the past tense, as a wish fulfilled, making a full circle. The poem was a long exhalation of the breath Rumi had been holding for nearly a year:

> *My sun and moon has come, my sight and hearing has come*
> *My silver one has come, my mine of gold has come.*
> *My ecstasy has come; the light of my life has come*
> *Whatever you may name has come; my wish has come.*
> *My highway robber has come; my parole breaker has come*
> *That fair-skinned Joseph, suddenly by my side, has come.*

Today is better than yesterday, my dear old friend,
  Last night I was ecstatic, hearing news that he had come.
The one I was looking for last night with lantern in hand
  Today, like a basket of flowers strewn on my way, has come . . .
Now is the time to rise up, as morning rises in the world
  Now is the time to roar, because my lion has come.

❖

The peaceable community to which Shams returned held to-
gether without unraveling for several months. During the first
weeks, different members of Rumi's circle hosted parties that
included music, poetry, prayer, and *sama* dancing in their pri-
vate homes, celebrating Shams's return. Eventually he began
teaching again, speaking to the newly respectful students about
a theme close to his heart—the beauty of the world, accessible
beyond our confining minds. "The heart is wider than the heav-
ens," Shams taught them, "and subtler and brighter than the
starry skies. Why squeeze your heart with thoughts and whisper-
ing doubts? Why make this joyous world into a narrow prison?
Like a caterpillar, we weave a cocoon of thoughts, doubts, and
fantasies, slowly suffocating ourselves." He added, "I never strug-
gle with sayings of the Prophet, except 'This world is the prison
of the believer.' But I don't see any prison. I ask you, 'Where is
the prison?'"

While Shams did not pride himself on being a poet, and did
not work at the craft, he did have poetic talent and accented
these talks with couplets of his own that he recited sponta-
neously. "Tolerate me for just two or three more days—in the
book of my life, only a single page remains," he said, sighing
aloud in a rhyme one day, expressing a sentiment eerily hinting
at an imminent ending. Many of these lines show up in Rumi's

later poems, either because he memorized them, or he pored over the pages of Shams's transcribed talks, as he had pored over his father's pages—often in poems revolving around Shams:

> *In the book of my life, only a single page remains.*
> *His sweet jealousy has left my soul restless*
> *In my book, he wrote words sweeter than sugar,*
> *Words that would make the shy moon blush.*

Under no illusion about the display of newfound respect among the students of Rumi, Shams knew that much of their warmth was contrived. He was too observant not to realize that theirs was a calculated reverence, and, with his uncensored frankness, he said as much in public. "They felt jealous in the past because they supposed, 'If he were not here, Mowlana would be happy with us,'" Shams summarized the matter. "Then they experienced that things became worse, but Rumi gave them no consolation. Whatever they had in the beginning, they lost, and then even all the passion they held about the situation dissipated. So now they are happy and they honor me and they pray for me."

After his return Shams and Rumi resumed their intense companionship. According to the early biographer Sepahsalar, who presented himself as having been by Rumi's side from the earliest days, "Mowlana became even more involved with Shamsoddin, even more than the first time they met each other. They became more united than ever. Day and night they talked to each other, and they sank into each other." Yet even with the lighter atmosphere in the Madrase Khodavandgar, Shams still longed for the open road. If Rumi's ideal solution was having Shams available in Konya as he went about his duties, Shams's wish was to disappear with Rumi as his traveling companion. He wanted to show him his homeland. "I wish we could take a trip together to Mosul and—you have not seen those places—to

Tabriz," he cajoled Rumi. "You could preach in the pulpit, and then mingle with the crowds and see how they are when they get together just among themselves. Afterwards we could travel to Baghdad, and then travel on to Damascus."

Implicit in such invitations was Shams's persistent desire to depart. When he spoke with Sultan Valad of his composure when he arrived in Syria, he insinuated that Rumi was far more distraught and agitated by the sudden separation. The "work," the teaching with Rumi, was going well. Indeed the "sinking" of Rumi into Shams was the spiritual immersion that he had hoped to achieve. Yet the threat of an abrupt departure still made Rumi uneasy, while Shams's years of solitude had accustomed him to self-reliance, or at least so he claimed, though he had not been entirely sure when he was in Aleppo. "If truly you are not able to accompany me, I'm not afraid," insisted Shams. "I did not suffer when I was separated from you, nor does being together with you bring me happiness. My happiness comes from within and my suffering comes within. Now, I know living with me is diffi-cult. I know that I am complicated. I am neither this nor that."

A significant interruption in this steady pattern of com-muning followed by threats of leaving forever occurred in the early winter of 1247 when Shams, now in his sixties, surprisingly asked Rumi for permission to marry Kimiya, a young woman brought up in Rumi's harem. (As she may have shared a name with Kerra's daughter, some would surmise she was Rumi's step-daughter.) This request, with its implication of settling down, not only marked a change in the tenor between Shams and Rumi, but also a sharp break from Shams's lifetime habit of wander-ing loosely, with no family ties, though he did mention having once had children, whom he left behind to travel on his quest. Kimiya was a "pure and beautiful" young woman, and theirs was a December-May marriage. This late-life blossoming of desire on the part of Shams seemed sincere, though it clearly began as a practical transition to a more stable connection with Rumi. As marriages were arranged according to a patriarchal tradition, Kimiya's opinion may or may not have been heard.

Rumi was most pleased by this turn of events, which insured that Shams would be more committed—and nearby—as an official member of his household. On the day of the wedding, Rumi read the contract of marriage for the couple. According to the biographer Sepahsalar, "Because it was winter, Mowlana arranged special rooms with a fireplace for them to consummate their vows. That winter Shamsoddin continued to reside in those rooms." The nuptial bed was a ceremonial focus of the traditional wedding ritual, and like Rumi's father, Baha Valad, Shams emphasized the integration of his sexual relations with Kimiya and his intense religious devotion. In later years, when trying to explain to some students the meaning behind Bayazid Bestami's practice of seeking divinity in the faces of young men, Rumi told them a story about Shams from that winter:

> Shamsoddin said, "The Lord Most High loves me so much that He comes to me in whatever appearance pleases me. Just now, He came to me in the appearance of Kimiya, having taken on her form." So it was with Bayazid. The Lord Most High appeared before him in the face of a beardless youth.

On another occasion, Shams re-created a bit of bedtime conversation with his new wife for Rumi, or others gathered. "'I asked God to give me a child,'" he had apparently said to Kimiya. "'My wish to have a child is because I want you to be his mother. You are sleeping!' Then she opened her eyes. She saw me. Again she fell asleep. It's rare that I wake anybody up, but I woke her up three times. And each time she fell asleep again." On another evening, Shams took his bedding and slept alone in a corner, his head pillowed on his arm. He was as open about talking of intimacies with Kimiya as Rumi's father had been confessional in his own notebooks about sleeping with Rumi's mother.

The small heated rooms Rumi set aside for Shams and Kimiya were located off a porch leading to the women's harem. The other half of Rumi's domestic world, the harem was adjacent to the *madrase*, but entirely separate. No women were allowed to use the entrance leading to the school, and no males were allowed to pass into the small hallway, unless they were *mahram*, or religiously legal insiders, as Shams now was. Such harems often had their own courtyard, with a pool of water, gutters, and, in Konya, mulberry or plane trees, hung with icicles in winter, surrounded by mud walls, and lit at night by torches. Besides sleeping cells there was a kitchen, a bath, and an undecorated women's dining room.

If the life of the *madrase* was in constant upheaval during those years, the harem was still dominated by some of the original personalities and customary behavior, dating back to Khorasan. Holding sway as a matriarchal figure remained the Great Kerra, the mother of Rumi's first wife. A keeper of the institutional memory, she was able to tell tales of life in Balkh and Samarkand, and had been witness to the difficult period when her daughter, Rumi's first wife, Gowhar, was left to bring up their two tussling sons while her husband was off in Syria pursuing his studies. The feuding of the boys had so embroiled the harem that some said it instigated their being sent away to Damascus to school. Still living in the harem, too, was their nanny, who had been so pained when her charges were sent away that she had passed her days in her chamber, mournfully cleaning carrots and turnips. The youngest children left in the harem were

Rumi's second pair, by Kerra—his daughter, Maleke, and his third son, Mozaffaroddin.

By moving into a residence just inside the harem, Shams found himself immediately enmeshed in some difficult family politics, which were not mollified by his aggravating personality. The focus was Rumi's second son, Alaoddin, who was already antagonistic toward Shams. Among the few in Rumi's circle who did not participate in the welcoming ceremonies in honor of Shams's triumphal return, Alaoddin, now in his early twenties, had a natural talent for book learning and knowledge. In the absence of his father, many of the more traditional students in the *madrase* had begun to gather around him for orthodox teachings, as he mingled with the learned jurists in other schools. He particularly resented Shams for taking his father away from his lectures and sermons, and, now, for interjecting himself in a volatile sibling rivalry by favoring Sultan Valad. Some rumors were even circulating that Alaoddin had secretly wished to marry Kimiya. Annoying Alaoddin, too, was Shams's interfering with his favorite pastime of chess, the Persian court game, as Shams told Rumi that he should stop procuring Alaoddin's chess pieces. "This is his study time," Shams said. "He must study every day, even if only one sentence."

The incident that caused these tensions to explode was Alaoddin walking too often by Shams's and Kimiya's rooms—even though another path would have been impossible, given the layout of the harem. As Sepahsalar told the story, "The second son of Mowlana, Alaoddin, was the treasure of the world, because of his beauty, kindness, knowledge, and intellect. Every time he would come to pay his respects to his grandmother and women relatives, when he would pass through the courtyard and go by the winter house, Shamsoddin would boil with jealousy. A few times, Shamsoddin gently advised Alaoddin, 'Oh light of my eyes, even though you have wonderful manners, you need to walk by this house less often.' This rebuke humiliated Alaoddin, especially as he already resented Shamsoddin for showing more attention and kindness to Sultan Valad."

Angry words were exchanged that led to much trouble between them. "Did you see how I threatened Alaoddin, indirectly?" Shams asked around afterward, giving a fuller report of his side of the conversation. "I said, 'Your cloak is in the shop.' He said, 'Tell the merchant to bring it here for me.' 'No, I've forbidden him to come into my room because it disturbs me. I've chosen this place for my seclusion and solitude.' Likewise to the woman who brings water to the room, I said, 'Come, when I tell you to come. But otherwise don't just walk in. I may be naked or I may be clothed.'" He then quoted to Alaoddin, in Arabic, similar rebukes ascribed to Mohammad, for his followers, when they were given to walking into his private family quarters unannounced. The message Shams seemed to be sending in this conflict was of his desire to maintain his privacy—and Kimiya's—against Alaoddin's casual and frequent comings and goings.

Alaoddin spoke publicly of this perceived insult, causing more troubles in the school and the harem. According to Sepahsalar's account, "He repeated Shamsoddin's words to others. They took advantage of that opportunity to begin to rile Alaoddin even further. They said, 'What a strange thing to say! That foreigner has come and is staying in Khodavandgar's house and he doesn't allow Khodavandgar's son into his own home.' Whenever these people had a chance, they tried to challenge and embarrass Shamsoddin. Because of his great kindness and patience, Shamsoddin did not say anything to Mowlana. After awhile he spoke to Sultan Valad, as they bothered him excessively."

Although Shams swore that Kimiya's "heart was after me," she often chafed against her new regimen as the young bride of Shams. Referring to his possessiveness with Rumi, Shams admitted: "Whomever I love, I oppress. If he accepts, I roll up like a little ball in his palm. Kindness is something that you can practice with a five-year-old child, so he will believe in you and love you. But the real thing is oppression." He contrasted his harsh manner with Rumi's gentleness, a trait from childhood on. "'Someone said,' he repeated, 'Rumi is all gentleness, and Shamsoddin has both the attribute of gentleness and the attribute of severity.'" Shams added, "I become bored with gentleness." Ever the strict Quran teacher, he saw kindness as ineffectual for teaching.

Yet the wisdom that Shams accrued over long years of teaching and debating the philosophers, and praying and fasting in solitary confinement in little rooms in caravanserai across the Middle East, had not prepared him for life in the harem. Severity worked well perhaps with disciples on a chosen fiery path to self-knowledge, yet he was not entirely in control of his passions in this late-life union with a woman much younger. His traits of possessiveness and jealousy became inordinate. He grew suspicious of younger men as having potential charm for her, especially Alaoddin. After a lifetime of ascetic practice and notorious mystical feats, Shams was blindsided by domestic life.

Flashes of marital fights and conflicts began to surface in his monologues. Kimiya evidently was a free spirit and not ideal as a submissive wife. An issue was her frequent escaping to one of the gardens on the outskirts of town with other women, without his permission. Such walled gardens were located outside the city and were generally divided into orchards for cultivating figs and grapes or producing honey, and rose gardens with benches set aside for chatting and entertaining among the upper classes. Shams complained of Kimiya spending time with ladies outside of their home: "I cannot blame her. She does not know what she is doing. But why has she gone to the garden? How could she sit with this group?" He threatened to find two witnesses in front of whom he could perform the simple Muslim rite of divorce. Another time he begged Rumi to give him ten days to find a house and leave. "Stay for two months," requested Rumi. Upset, Shams responded, "It was as if he was telling me to sit still for two years."

One afternoon during that winter, the women of the harem decided to take Kimiya on an outing for fresh air. She had evidently been depressed, kept guarded in near isolation by her husband, and perhaps had been ill, too. As Aflaki told the story, "One day, without permission from Shamsoddin, the women took her with Sultan Valad's grandmother to her garden to cheer her up. Suddenly Shamsoddin returned home and asked for Kimiya. He was told, 'Sultan Valad's grandmother, with other ladies, has taken her out for a walk.' Shamsoddin let out a loud shout and became very angry. When Kimiya Khatun returned home, she immediately felt pain in her neck and she was as motionless as a dry branch. She screamed in pain, and after three days she passed away."

The sudden death of Kimiya was the darkest of Shams's many difficult challenges in Konya. However awkwardly or excessively he expressed his feelings, Shams had come to cherish Kimiya. Certainly no contemporary account accused Shams of her murder. Yet the fraught circumstances of her death, and suspicious shadow of his own violent anger over those final winter days, did not give him much confidence in his unseasonable attempt to live a settled family life, while the tragedy exacerbated the fully returned anger of Alaoddin and his emboldened cohort. Rumi would compose lines about his commitment to Shams, vow-like lines that included his refusing to listen to dissenters:

> When speaking with people, seal your lips with mud
> Keep the sugar stuck behind your teeth, and go.

Say, "'That moon is for me, the rest is for you,
I don't need a family or home," and go.
Who is that moon? The Lord Shams of Tabriz.
Step into the shadow of that king, and go.

On the subject of the death of Kimiya, however, Rumi was pub-
licly silent. Enduring his shocking loss, Shams left the harem to
return to live near the portico of the *madrase*.

Hanging over Shams was a sense of failure. While Rumi had
begun as his eager student, and Shams enjoyed the power of his
own independence—his experience as a lifelong wanderer—he
had tried in several dramatic ways to secure their valued com-
panionship. Shams changed his life more than Rumi had, and
he had sacrificed more. He never wanted to remain in Konya,
and clearly after his departure to Syria did not wish to return to
certain trouble, being constantly studied by the glaring eyes of
enemies. His marriage to Kimiya was his final attempt at making
the situation work by becoming a stable member of Rumi's ex-
tended family. Yet Shams was unsuited for domestic life. As he
left his room in the harem, having practically been banished
now from that family, he was reduced to a few moves, cornered,
and was mulling the meaning of these ominous signs of trouble.

❖

Shams's tiny cell in the school was far less secure than his pe-
ripheral room with Kimiya on the edge of the harem. Sensing
weakness, Alaoddin and his allies again tried to drive Shams
from town, as if the welcoming jubilee of nine months earlier
had never occurred. Rumi had set Shams up in a cell that he
nicknamed "The Place of Khezr," referring to the mystic friend
of Moses in the Quran, who initiated him into the secret ways

of spiritual practice. As he had with his rooms in the merchant inn, Shams padlocked the door to insure privacy and seclusion, his habit in whatever setting he found himself. Yet the protective hand of Rumi was not sufficient to guard him against unannounced nighttime local police incursions and regular threats to his security.

One incident was so distressing that Shams waited two days before informing Rumi. This confrontation at his cell was not the first, or he had been warned, because he had been awake all night in anticipation of some kind of incident. "I was restless the whole night," said Shams, when he told of the disturbing encounter. "My heart was trembling." Finally at daylight some guards arrived, under the command of Aminoddin Mikail, an important lieutenant and viceroy of the sultan, though he was not present. They claimed the emir himself ordered that the cell must be emptied and Shams must leave. They also claimed the authority of Tajoddin Armavi, a high-ranking lieutenant.

"'This cell belongs to the sweeper, and now this man puts a lock on it and says that it belongs to him.'" Shams reported the incoherent shouting of the head guard, in Turkish. "Then he said, 'We're talking to you. Why did you lock this cell? You're not a licensed instructor here. We're talking to you. They threw you out of town. What do they call you? Shams? What? Shams? What?'" Then Shams stood up silently, having not yet said a word: "Those men of Aminoddin looked at my face and thought they needed to speak Turkish to me. They didn't think I understood what they were saying. 'This is Mowlana's cell,' I said. 'It's his library. I will go and get the key from Mowlana, and I will open the door.' 'Get him,' they said. 'He's lying. He has the key. Get the key from him.'" One of them persisted, "Why are you coming here? We threw you out a few times." Shams asked whether they had really been sent by the proper authorities. "I know Tajoddin's nature," he said. "I need proof if he says that

I'm a dog and a nonbeliever." (Tajoddin, also known as "Tabrizi," was from Shams's hometown.)

Amid all the anxiety and disruption of being trapped within the surveillance of the religious military state, if only at its lower echelons, Shams in these last days persisted in his teaching, mostly meant for Rumi alone, during a period that lasted anywhere from a week to several months. He still had important themes to communicate that he felt his existence hung upon and were the core of "the work" he was intent on finishing. Essential for him was the message of love, and of the heart, which was Rumi's great inspiration. In Persian epic or spiritual poetry, *nâme* meant "book," as in the *Shahname,* the Book of Kings, or Attar's *Asrarname,* the Book of Secrets. For Shams, the Quran was the *Eshqname,* or Book of Love. He also rose to poetic utterances about the practice of whirling. "The dance of the men of God is delicate and weightless," he exulted. "They are like leaves floating on a river." That such delicate, sensitive lessons were expounded in an atmosphere increasingly unsettled and dangerous only added to their sense of urgency.

A darker and more complex theme began to emerge, as well, in Shams's teachings to Rumi during this chaotic time— separation. He revealed his departure to Syria as having been an object lesson, not an impulse, and threatened more such lessons. "If you can," Shams spelled out his intentions, "act such that I don't have to travel for the sake of your work and your best interest, so the work may be accomplished by the journey that I already took. That would be better. I am not in a position to command you to travel. I can take on the traveling for your benefit, so you may become more mature. In separation, you say, 'That degree of commandments or prohibitions was nothing. Why didn't I do it?' It was easy compared to the hardship of separation."

"I was just speaking in riddles," he went on, unpacking his

metaphor. "I should have been explicit. What's the worth of that work? For your best interest, I would make fifty journeys. Otherwise what difference does it make to me whether I am in Rum or Syria? Whether I'm at the Kaaba or in Constantinople, it makes no difference. However it is certainly the case that separation cooks and polishes. Now, is the one polished and cooked by union better, or the one polished and cooked by separation? . . . Was Mowlana ever happy from the day that I left? . . . The deeper the union, the more difficult and arduous the time of separation." This was a core lesson, a sermon, he implied, he was willing to teach with his own life.

Of all the teachings that Shams shared with Rumi, which were becoming the raw material of Rumi's poetry, he gave him perhaps his most central metaphor in these last talks: comparing the evolution of the human spirit, through the workings of separation, to cooking. This imagery—a way of explaining how a painful separation can have beneficial results, and how love, both human and divine, involves both union and separation— became a continuous motif in Rumi's poetry and talks, a familiar and homey analogy of the type that he favored. Rumi liked to tell of the chickpea transformed through suffering in the boiling water of the cook's pot. He also expressed far more personally his own suffering in the heat of separation, which was visited on him through his love for Shams:

> *My entire life has come down to three words—*
> *I was raw, I was cooked, I was burned*

He used nearly the same wording in a less precisely parsed cry from the heart in a *ghazal*:

> *My entire life has come down to three words—*
> *I burned, I burned, I burned*

Shams was emotionally riveting as he talked of separation, especially gripping for Rumi, who felt the fire in his words, yet he had motives for dwelling on separation besides the poetic and philosophical. Shams's daily life was ever more precarious in Konya, and he faced constant difficulties. The incident at his cell was not isolated, and Rumi's followers were aligning with the cohort identified with Alaoddin. Shams spared Rumi many details, though he confided his apprehensions to Sultan Valad, who later recalled Shams's ultimatum to him: "He said, to me, 'Have you seen them? Reunited again by envy with each other? They want to separate me from Mowlana, who is far wiser than anyone else. They want to separate me and take me away. After me, they want to be in charge of everything. This time, I'll leave in such a way that no one will be able to find where I am. All will fail miserably trying to find me. No one will be able to find the slightest clue. Many years will pass in this way. No one will find even a trace of my dust. When I have been gone for a long time, they will say surely they think that an enemy has killed me.' He repeated his words several times because he wished to emphasize them."

When he was feeling particularly troubled, Shams did occasionally discuss matters with Rumi. He was once accused of stealing and spoke in obviously distressed tones to Rumi. "I cannot even get a separate house," he was saying of his fragile and uncharacteristically dependent living situation. "I don't want to make you a prisoner here. But I don't want anything else from this place, just to be able to see you." He was underlining that the only attraction for him in Konya was Rumi, but that just such singleness of purpose could finally become an increasing burden for both of them. At other times, though, he blamed Rumi for not coming to his defense, and keeping him out of sight, as if embarrassed by him, or living his two lives in two discrete compartments.

One practice in Rumi's household, traditional in the Islamic culture that set Fridays apart for congregational prayer and for time spent with family, was for him to visit with the community during the dusk hours after evening prayers, following any obligations at the Citadel mosque or on the palace grounds. Customarily, the men would be seated at the top end of a long carpet, where some bread or dates were usually laid out, the women seated farther down, while Rumi listened to the concerns of the household, or told stories, or otherwise invested his charm in calming conflicts. He did not invite Shams to those Friday gatherings, and Shams was stung. "As neither Mowlana nor I like to spend time without a purpose, we tend to stay alone with each other," Shams complained. "So every Friday that he doesn't bring me with him, I become depressed. Why can't I be included in this group? I know my sadness should not be real, but it is."

Sometimes Shams's feelings of betrayal by Rumi broke through their mutually adoring banter. Rumi appeared to be trying to distance himself from Shams's disruptive presence, to keep the peace, especially following the death of Kimiya and the sharpened anger of Alaoddin, who would have been present at the Friday gatherings where Shams was excluded. "I became so upset when instead of answering them, you stayed silent," Shams said, confronting Rumi when he had not countered criticisms against him, the sorts of complaints making the attacks possible. "My whole resentment arose when they said those things and you didn't answer them. You remained silent. You know my loyalty. You know me. But when someone outside the house said something, you didn't answer."

This incident, or another similar, kept Shams awake at night. "To be able to look into my friend's eyes, I have to go through the eyes of a hundred enemies," he bemoaned. "Last night I was thinking of you, and I was picturing your face. I was saying to you, in my mind, 'Why didn't you answer those people, clearly and directly?' In my imagination, you were saying, by your expression, 'I am ashamed of them,' or 'I am shy,' or 'I don't want them to be upset.' I talked to you, and our argument took a long time within my mind." Rumi had always been averse to open conflict and had evidently reverted to trying to placate Alaoddin and Shams's many critics, doing his best to keep all parties placated, especially after the difficult events of the winter. Shams clearly felt that Rumi was not defending him sufficiently, and he was left staving off threats while feeling less certain that Rumi needed him as absolutely as he had in their early days. Yet he had not lost control of his wisdom and understanding of the events around him. His recent conversations with Rumi were profound in revealing the nature of love as including suffering and separation—a message that was about to become even more relevant.

One morning Rumi arrived at the school and, as was his custom, went to visit Shams's cell near the portico. When he entered, he found no sign of his friend other than his cap, a pair of shoes, and a few items accumulated while in Konya. Missing were the personal belongings that Shams carried when traveling, alerting Rumi to his departure. Given the dark mood and tragic events of the past months, Rumi understood that this hasty flight was not simply in keeping with Shams's elusive character but had an air of finality that even the first disappearance lacked. He realized with horror that his own attempt to live his life both ways had just collapsed. Rumi rushed into Sultan Valad's room. "Bahaoddin, why are you sleeping?" he cried out. "Get up, and seek for your sheikh. I'm not sensing his merciful presence anywhere nearby." "When Shamsoddin wasn't found after a day or two," recalled Sultan Valad, "Mowlana began crying from pain." As Sepahsalar reported, out of sorrow, "Mowlana roared like thunder."

CHAPTER 9

"*I burned, I burned, I burned*"

Rᴜᴍɪ skirted madness. Or madness was simply the only explanation those closest to him could find for his heartbreaking collapse in the wake of Shams's departure. Even five decades later, when the Arab travel writer Ibn Battuta passed through Konya, he was still hearing stories of the mad behavior of "the sheikh and pious imam" Jalaloddin Rumi following the disappearance of a Shams-like figure who sold him sugar-covered fruits, causing Rumi to abandon his college post to pursue him. "Subsequently he came back to them, after many years, but he had become demented and would speak only in Persian rhymed couplets which no one could understand," as Ibn Battuta recorded the local lore. "His disciples used to follow him and write down that poetry as it issued from him."

Rumi lost control on the morning that he discovered Shams's empty chamber, and the howling and sobbing heard throughout his school and house went on for days, not hours. When Shams had mysteriously left town two years earlier, Rumi retired to his private quarters and shut the door, allowing a recriminating silence to fill the hallways until those responsible for the rattling event repented. This time was dramatically different. He was focused only on hearing Shams's inimitable voice once again, and feeling "his merciful presence," as he said to his son, anywhere nearby. All pretense of maintaining his carefully constructed two lives that had so irked Shams was abandoned.

Their time together lasted only about two and a half years, and in that interval, Shams had disappeared for nearly a year. Yet nine of their months together were spent in near seclusion night and day as they communed, talked, and shared secrets, in a marked parenthesis that Rumi cared enough to carve out of the middle of his busy and already accomplished life. Nothing remotely resembled the intensity of the time he spent with Shams, who rightly said just weeks earlier that he and Rumi preferred each other's company to the superficiality of most other social life. Rumi knew their connection was unique. It had begun with a gaze that pierced his heart. Now he was left with the memory of those searing eyes and whatever transforming truth they had communicated to him. The memory caused Rumi to experience an unraveling between his heart and his mind.

After "a day or two," according to Sultan Valad, Rumi went even more public with his hysteria and grief, beginning a search throughout Konya for Shams. Such a wide hunt would have included all of Shams's favorite "seedy" spots, such as the taverns and Armenian churches they visited together, as well as steam baths in every district. Rumi's concerned family as well as friends and disciples tried to help. He was well connected in the government and able to involve the imperial guards and police in the action. Shams's prophecy to Sultan Valad that he would disappear without a trace appeared to have come true. "They looked for him in every alley and house," remembered Sultan Valad of the citywide pursuit, with no clues or leads turning up. "No one had any news of him. Nobody could find a hint of a scent of him. The sheikh was crazed by the separation."

Unable to find him in person, while remaining hopeful if not in full denial, Rumi tried to re-create his closeness to Shams once again in *sama*. Besides his focused final messages to Rumi on the meaning of separation, Shams, according to Sepahsalar, had encouraged him to keep practicing *sama*. "Perform *sama!*" Shams said. "Whatever you seek will be gained in abundance in the *sama*." Rumi treated this mystical dance they had performed together as a form of bonding, though now he was revolving incoherently around the absence of Shams as much as practicing enlightenment. He needed the steady rhythms to mollify his pain and was said to whirl, or turn unsteadily about a pole, while spouting some of the incomprehensible lines heard by anyone nearby.

Rumi soon invited a group of musicians to be present as well, filling in the empty spaces around his solitary dance. The traditional instruments he chose hearkened back to Central Asia, the cultural homeland of both himself and Shams. Crucial was the mournful *nay*, or reed flute, which one story credited as having first been brought to Anatolia on caravan by Rumi's family. He came to associate each instrument with the travails of love. The bold trumpet "sang" only when touched to a player's lips: "Without your lips, I'm silent." The Khorasani *rabab* was a voice heard only when stroked with a bow. Rumi imagined his heart a trembling tambourine. Included, too, in his intimate band were a harp held in the lap; drums, both large and small; a *tambura* lute; and bundled Pandean pipes. As he later wrote, "Sometimes I am a harp, sometimes a lute, night and day."

Rumi danced his repetitive spinning to music long into the night to the dismay of his exhausted musicians, who were as much drawn into the hole of his despair as they were allowed to act as a healing force. Sultan Valad recorded these frantic scenes he witnessed: "Day and night he began to dance *sama*, on the ground like a spinning wheel. His voice and his cry reached the sky. Everyone heard his lamentations, young and old. He gave gold and silver to the musicians. Whatever he had in the house, he gave away. He was continuously dancing *sama*. Day and night, he did not rest for a moment, so the musicians could not keep up. From singing so much they lost their voices. Their throats were sore from singing. Everyone hated the gold and the silver. Everyone was tired and run-down. Without wine, everyone was hungover. If that hangover had been from real wine, it would have disappeared with more wine. Everyone was tired from lack of sleep. Their hearts were cooked, not from fire, but from the pain."

Rumi's response during his first and far more benign separation had been to pivot to writing poetry to channel his pain as well as to lure Shams to return with flattery and proof of his creativity, which his beloved had encouraged and nurtured. Now Rumi turned to poetry again, but with less polished results, as stumbling in execution as his *sama* dancing. As Aflaki reported, "Mowlana was extremely agitated day and night and had no peace and no rest. He constantly walked up and down in the courtyard of the *madrase*, reciting quatrains." Sometimes he muttered broken phrases. At other times, he seemed—in painful, occasionally sinister, often roughly constructed lines—to be trying to gain a foothold onto his own sanity as much as onto the metrical terrain of poetry. The themes tended to oblivion or total annihilation in the shadow of the vanished beloved:

> *The night wears black to show us that it mourns*
> *Like the widow who wears a black dress after burying her husband*

He spoke of these desperate poems as "bloody," as they were clotted with violent images, perhaps evoking the distress caused by his menacing thoughts. He imagined in one of them Mount Sinai "covered in blood, longing for love," and elsewhere wrote:

> *This earth is not covered with dirt but blood*
> *From the blood of lovers, the wounds of a checkmated king*

Written under pressure of grief, and relying on heart and imagination rather than intellect for their rapidly flashing imagery, such lines often approached a surreal incomprehensibility.

> *When the water boiled into a wind, making mountains fly*
> *Like straw before the fierce wind, whirling and frightening*
> *Through the cracked mountains, deep mines were revealed*
> *Where you could see ruby on ruby, shining like moonlight,*
> *In that glow, you beheld him, his face porcelain, like the moon,*
> *His hands open, full of blood, like the hands of a butcher.*

Yet the "bloody" handprints in these poems may also have reflected a grim possibility that must have been playing on Rumi's mind, and certainly in his most troubled fantasies in his unsettled state, as the question spread through Konya: Was Shams murdered? The atmosphere of the past few months made such an act conceivable. Rumors of murder were swirling around Rumi, two of them—contradicting each other—finding their way into Aflaki's later accounts. In one of these dark scenarios, Shams and Rumi were seated together in the evening when a stranger came to the door and whispered for Shams to step outside. Shams rose and said, "They want to kill me," to which Rumi responded, "Perhaps it is God's will." Shams walked outside, where he was set on by seven ruffians with knives. His loud shouts caused them all to pass out in unison and when they awoke they saw nothing but a few drops of blood, with no other sign of their victim. In a second rumor, Sultan Valad, alerted by a dream, discovered Shams's corpse at the bottom of a well and buried him in the *madrase* walls. Rumi never endorsed such reports of the murder of Shams, though they were haunting his poems.

Almost as compelling as the unsolved murder mystery, though, was the distress in Konya and the Madrase Khodavandgar that allowed even the suspicion of the killing of Shams of Tabriz to have taken hold as imaginable. Somehow this unique bond between Rumi and Shams was unconventional enough to have driven those around them to irrational and outsize reactions. As Annemarie Schimmel has described their challenge: "The relationship between Mowlana and Shams was nothing like the traditional love of a mature Sufi for a very young boy in whom he saw Divine Beauty manifested, and who thus is a *shahed*, a living witness to Divine Beauty—indeed it is revealing that the term *shahed*, favored by most Persian poets, occurs only rarely in Mowlana's work. This was the meeting of two mature men." The Iranian-American scholar Janet Afary has described their connection as "a more reciprocal ethic of love." Rumi and Shams were tampering with social formalities, and their lack of clear boundaries was disturbing, as the cultural norm of "lover" and "beloved" between men and boys, or even between sheikh and disciple, required one partner to be the moth and the other the flame.

❖

Rumi next fixed on the hope that Shams was in Damascus, where he first traveled sometime between the winter of 1248 and the spring of 1249, and then on one or two other occasions, alone or with a retinue. Whatever lapses of sanity Rumi may have undergone in the first weeks and months of their jarring separation, he kept enough presence of mind to pursue with a steady logic the dwindling few chances of finding Shams, while striving to keep his spirit stitched to him through *sama* and poetry.

Even before departing Konya, Rumi seized on travelers from Damascus, hoping to hear news of Shams, his desperation making him vulnerable. As Aflaki told: "One day someone informed Rumi, 'I saw Shamsoddin in Damascus.' Rumi became more cheerful than can be expressed in words. He gave away everything he was wearing to the man as gifts—his turban, cloak, and shoes. A close companion said, 'He lied to you. He has never seen him.' Rumi replied, 'I gave him my turban and my cloak for his lie. If his news were true, instead of giving away my clothing, I would have given my life away. I would have sacrificed myself for him.'" This desire to give away, or throw away, grew extravagant.

Barely able to manage his daily existence, Rumi had easily let the business of the *madrase* fade to the margins of concern, while holding many of those in the community responsible for Shams's vanishing, especially his son Alaoddin, from whom he became estranged during this period of heightened emotion and tension. As Sepahsalar wrote, "During that time, whoever was blamed for this separation did not receive any attention from him." When he went away, Rumi put Hosam, the young leader of the local workingmen, in charge of keeping order in the day-to-day operations of the school. He instinctively only entrusted a position of authority to someone drawn from within the small, warm circle around Shams—a pattern he continued for the rest of his life.

With Syria riven by civil war, and suffering from the famine and general ruin caused by the incursions of many Crusader armies, the Damascus that Rumi confronted upon his arrival was not the paradise of brilliant intellectual debate, spirited commerce, and monumental architecture he had witnessed just a decade earlier from the removed vantage of the Sufi Salehiyye neighborhood during his student years. Yet the circles in which he had moved were still active, and so, reported Sultan Valad, he went street by street, "putting his head into every corner." He performed very public *sama* sessions, hoping to attract locals who knew Shams, or might have information. And he composed new, anxious *ghazals,* written in Arabic. As he proclaimed his mission on a third journey:

> *For the third time, I rush from Rum to Syria,*
> > *Seeking his curls as dark as night, seeking the fragrance*
> *of Damascus*
> *If my Master Shams, the Truth of Tabriz, is there*
> > *I will be the Master of Damascus, the Master of Damascus!*

The Damascus period of Rumi's search for Shams lasted about two years. After days or weeks scouring the Sufi neighborhoods, with the same disappointing results he had encountered in Konya, Rumi spent much of the rest of the time hunting down clues or listening to hearsay, waiting to talk with the pilgrims returning from Mecca, or other travelers, as travel was the main artery of communication. He was also cultivating *sama* and beginning to write poems with more intensity and frequency than ever before. The pitch of hysteria reached in Konya could not be sustained, and he began to discover in his emerging poetry and song not only expressions of pain but also inklings of love.

Rumi instinctively relied on whirling after Shams's disappearance to quell his panic and somehow stay closer to his companion by imitating him at a time when he could think of nothing or no one else. His intuition about his need at that moment for *sama* was a positive one. The philosopher Mohammad al-Ghazali, whose intellectual legacy Rumi and his father encountered, especially in Baghdad, claimed the whirling practice had pulled him back from his own period of despair, which has been construed as a nervous breakdown. Indeed, he devoted an entire volume of his monumental *Revival of the Religious Sciences* to *sama,* eloquently writing of having his spiritual life saved by such practices. His testimony helped in the spread of rooms appointed for *sama* in tenth-century Baghdad. Rumi, too, was now sensing that his sanity and spiritual revival owed much to the meditative dance.

While Shams was in Konya, he and Rumi practiced *sama* in seclusion, hidden from the eyes and ears of the legally minded, including Alaoddin. Even though Rumi's father was sympathetic with Sufis and practiced secret mystical techniques, he would never have allowed music and dance in the halls of the Madrase Khodavandgar, as such expressions were likely to be dangerous, even illegal. Just as popular as al-Ghazali's defense of *sama* in Baghdad was the treatise *The Trickery of Satan*, by an austere theologian claiming music and dance were the devil's work. Many medieval Islamic leaders—failing to find sanctions in the Quran or the teachings of the Prophet for listening to music, singing, and chanting—insisted that the only acceptable music worth listening to was Arabic Quranic recitation. As Rumi became more public and open about *sama* in Konya and Damascus, he was moving closer toward a fault line, and setting up a defining conflict of the rest of his life.

Likewise in Damascus Rumi's poems began to reveal a new lightness and to announce their true source of inspiration, Shams of Tabriz, as the messenger of love. Since the works of medieval Persian poets are arranged according to the alphabetical order of their rhyming letters—beginning with the long *a*—and within that scheme by meter, rather than chronologically, the sequence of Rumi's poems has never been clear. Yet a logic of suffering and acceptance was at work indicating their falling into loose, overlapping stages, marked by their openness in naming Shams as muse. By the time Rumi left Damascus, he had found his voice as a poet or, as he understood it, found Shams's voice through his poetry, while experiencing a midlife creative burst that was exceptional in the history of world poetry as he wrote the bulk of his lyric love poems.

Following from the verse-letters that he wrote on Shams's first
departure to Syria, over a year earlier, Rumi resumed, likely in
Damascus, rhapsodizing Shams in extravagant codes of praise.
Rather than mentioning his name, using Sufi discretion, he in-
voked his reliable symbol for fiery Shams, the "Sun of Religion,"
and "Sun of Tabriz":

> *Since I am the servant of the sun, I speak only of the sun.*
> *I do not worship the moon, nor do I speak of dreams*

Astrological houses could stand for Shams, too, such as Mars, or
Venus, or the panoply of stars. Gypsies, or *lulis,* evoked his per-
petual motion and cleverness, and the wide desert, the *sahra,* his
location beyond all places and categories, his abstraction from
daily life, his transcendence. Rumi addressed Shams as his "sov-
ereign," or, in Greek, as *afenti* or *aghapos,* honored and beloved,
and used various other glorifying terms for him:

> *I gave him so many names, perfect and imperfect,*
> *But since he is unique, he has a hundred times more*

One fixture of traditional Persian poetry that Rumi began
to experiment with in these poems, as he seemed once again
more in control of his method of composition, was the *takhal-
los,* a poetic signature, or pen name, reserved for the final line
of a *ghazal,* also romanticized as a "clasp," holding together the
strung pearls of single lines into a necklace. Rumi shied away
from using his own name as a *takhallos.* Only once, in an early,
opaque poem, did he try using his title bestowed on him by his
father as a tag in the more conventional fashion:

> *Jalaloddin, go to sleep now, and quit writing*
> *Just say: No leopards can find such a unique lion.*

Many of the poems of crisis were unruly and lacked a polished final line altogether. In some, Rumi had abruptly announced, "*Bas!*" or "Enough!" Yet he came close to an inventive *takhallos* by closing several with *"Khamush!"* or *"Silence!,"* indicating an approach to a mystical state of unknowing as well as reticence in naming his inspiration:

> *Be silent my tongue, since my heart is burning,*
> *Your heart will burn, too, if I speak of my burning heart*

A breakthrough for Rumi occurred when he was finally able to name Shams in his poems, as if the same breaking down of a wall between his inner and outer lives, which had been forced by Shams's disappearance, also needed to take place in his poetry. This transition was enacted in one crucial *ghazal* where he dramatized an imaginative vision, reminiscent of dream visions he experienced during *chelle,* including a voice of wisdom:

> *One night, I awoke at midnight, unable to find my heart*
> *I looked everywhere, around the house. Where did he go?*
> *When finally I searched every room, I found the poor thing*
> *Crying in a corner, whispering the name of God, and praying.*

As he eavesdropped on his own heart praying, Rumi heard him confessing trepidation about ever uttering the name of his beloved for fear of having his secret stolen away by someone who might be listening. A guiding voice commanded him to speak the name:

> *A voice called to the heart, "Say his name,*
> *Don't worry about others, say his name boldly*
> *His name is the key to the wishes of your soul*
> *Say his name at once, so he will open the door quickly."*

The poet's heart remained anxious, in spite of divine inter-vention, until finally at dawn the sun rose—reliable code for Shams—and the heart yelped, "Tabriz!" unraveled by these ef-forts like the woof and warp of a carpet. The poem ends with Rumi's joyful confession:

> *As I was fainting away, the name of Shamsoddin,*
>   *That ocean of generosity, was engraved upon my heart*

Having opened the door, as he described the sensation, Rumi found, within the heart of his poetry, permission to speak the name of his beloved, going against all caution and secrecy. In the Persian poetic tradition, such love poems were only written to youths, not mature men, and personal names rarely, if ever, used, except for that of the patron or the poet's own *takhallos* pen name. Rumi was explicit about the course of his evolution toward this liberation. Not only could he speak of Shams in code, but he could now also spell out Shams's name brazenly within the lines of his poems, a bold transparency he found ex-hilarating and inspiring as he made use of this new freedom rhapsodically:

> *Not alone I keep on singing, Shamsoddin and Shamsoddin*
>   *The nightingale in the garden sings, the partridge in the hills . . .*
> *Day of splendor, Shamsoddin, turning heavens, Shamsoddin*
>   *Mine of jewels, Shamsoddin, day and night, Shamsoddin.*

In the abundance of incantatory poems that followed were lines revealing Rumi's belief that chanting Shams's name freed his spirit from the guarded fear that contributed to their painful separation and gave luster and a radiant spark to his art and poetry:

Say the name of Shamsoddin every single moment
  Until your poems and songs begin to glow with beauty

Naming names was a bold personal move for Rumi, especially given his public position. His next steps, though, were even more radical, as he began writing poems that moved beyond anything dared so far in either Persian lyric poetry or Muslim devotional poetry. Novelty was immaterial to Rumi. He was not interested in becoming a poet's poet. Yet in trying to articulate his love for Shams, he was led by force of passion to breaking with tradition. His innovation in Persian lyric poetry was to begin using as his *takhallos*, or signature tag, the name of Shams of Tabriz, rather than his own. By the end of his life, he had written nearly a thousand poems mentioning Shams or ending with the flourish of his name. The most extraordinary probably date from his Damascus period, when he was away from the judgmental eyes and ears surrounding him in Konya. He had been energized by the poetic license he felt granted him by his own heart, reacting to divine prompts, and allowing him to be at once romantic and religious. As he wrote in one *ghazal* composed while the search for Shams was under way, using his special *takhallos*:

I wonder, where did the handsome beloved go?
  I wonder, where did that tall, shapely cypress tree go?
He spread his light among us like a candle
  Where did he go? So strange, where did he go without me?
All day long my heart trembles like a leaf
  All alone at midnight, where did that beloved go? . . .
Tell me clearly, Shams of Tabriz,
  Of whom it is said, "The sun never dies!"—Where did he go?

The adoption of Shams as his *takhallos* was an original solution to Rumi's quandary. He was audaciously implying that he was not the author of his own poems. Shams was writing the verses through him, and he was merely the ink pen or the paper:

> *Speak, Sun of Truth and Faith, Pride of Tabriz,*
> *For your voice is speaking through all my words!*

Rumi pushed the notion of a muse to its extreme, so that he was not merely inspired by but infused with the spoken word of Shams being dictated through him. This frame for understanding the poetry—especially these lyric love poems—remained forever affixed to them, in Rumi's understanding, and in their public reception. When the poems were later gathered in collections, or *divans,* some dating back to within a couple decades of Rumi's death, they were titled as *Divan-e Shams-e Tabrizi* ("The Collected Shams of Tabriz"), or *Kolliyat-e Shams-e Tabrizi* ("The Complete Shams of Tabriz"), or *Ghazali-yyat-e Shams-e Tabrizi* ("The Shams of Tabriz Ghazals"). (These earliest collections were helped in being judged authentic by their use of Rumi's local Khorasani spellings for Persian words, rather than Anatolian, similar to the differences between British English and American.)

Rumi then took a final step, investing Shams with prophetic or even divine powers, which was as challenging to Muslim orthodoxy as the use of music and dance in *sama.* It was as if the less chance Rumi felt of their being reunited in person, the more Shams began to merge in his heart with the source of love itself. The Rumi scholar Franklin D. Lewis has written that "there was probably no precedent for addressing any person, other than the Prophets," as Rumi in one instance praised Shams as "the light that said to Moses, 'I am God, I am God, I am God.'" Never in classical Persian poetry had the beloved been divinized as the burning bush through whom Moses heard the voice of God, or as the lover's *qibla,* for turning to prayer, or beyond the ken of the angel Gabriel, revealing the Quran to Mohammad. Such exclamations bordered on blasphemy:

> *It's not enough for me to call you a human being,*
>   *But I am afraid to call you "God."*
> *You do not allow me to remain silent*
>   *Yet you do not reveal to me the proper speech.*

Imploring Shams to forgive his own sins of pride, or heal his wounds, Rumi dared to fashion in these rhapsodic, celestial poems an audacious meld of love poem and prayer:

> *You speak for God, you see the Truth,*
>   *You save the world from drowning in an ocean of fire*
> *A king beyond compare, your majesty is eternal*
>   *You lead the soul away from harmful desires*
> *You hunt for souls on the path of self-sacrifice*
>   *Looking to discover which soul is the most worthy . . .*
> *Sun of souls! Shamsoddin, the Truth of Tabriz,*
>   *Each of your radiant beams speaks eloquently of God.*

Yet Rumi had still not accepted the difficult fact of the permanent loss of Shams in death. His last holdout of hope was Tabriz, an obviously magical point on Rumi's imaginative horizon, and a journey by land of only about seven hundred miles from either Damascus or Konya, although no record exists of Rumi actually undertaking that trip. By 1248 the Azerbaijani capital was solidly within the control of the Il Khan dynasty, under the transitional rule of a Persian ally of the Mongols, responsible for funneling taxes and tributes to its rulers. Rumi's poems of the period are dotted with mentions of Tabriz, as if the possibility of Shams's having returned home kept arising—either from reports, or because of his friend's ardent wish for them to have traveled there together. In these final poems, Tabriz remains a distant place of the mind, not, like Damascus, an actual location:

> When I went to Tabriz, I spoke with Shamsoddin
> Of the oneness of God, without needing any words

At least once, Rumi heard news of Shams in Tabriz that was believable enough for him to write a poem excitedly about the possibility of his being alive, more visceral than his whimsical payments given to strangers claiming a sighting here or there. Rumi compared the reception of this news to the Quranic story of Joseph's father, Jacob, catching the scent of his vanished son, who was said to have been murdered and cast down into a well by his brothers—suspiciously similar to the murder rumors about Shams:

> Joseph's shirt, and the scent of him have come!
> Following these two signs, surely he too comes!

The finale of the *ghazal* fixes the living Shams's whereabouts confidently within Tabriz:

> You asked for a banquet from heaven
> Rise up, and prepare. The table descends.
> Good news, O Love! From Shamsoddin,
> In Tabriz, a new sign has come!

Finally, though, most likely in Damascus, around 1250, Rumi heard some confirmation of the death of Shams that caused him to decisively face his worst fears, which he had been avoiding as much as pursuing during the past two years, and to adopt instead an attitude of mourning, and to no longer hold out hope. The tenor of his writing, speaking, and feeling about Shams shifted. He moved toward acceptance rather than denial. From him poured a classical elegy, a container for his grief, filled with tears that were hot but not hysterical, each line of the threnody ending with the sad *radif,* "weep":

> *If my eyes could bear to cry fully for this great grief*
> > *Days and nights, until dawn, I would only weep . . . .*
> *Death is deaf to mourning, and hears no wailing*
> > *Otherwise, with a burning heart, he would weep.*
> *Death is an executioner, without a heart,*
> > *Even if he had a heart of stone, he would weep.*

The noble ode ends in a sorrowful mode unusual for Rumi's writings on his personal sun:

> *Shams of Tabriz is gone, and who*
> > *For this greatest man among men, will weep?*
> *In the world of essences, he is enjoying his wedding,*
> > *But in our world of mere forms, without him, we weep.*

Rumi might never have known the exact cause of Shams's death, or his final resting place, and he appears to have strongly dismissed all murder rumors to the end of his life. Whether inklings or doubts rose and fell over the years is not known. No one will ever know the truth about the hazy circumstances of Shams's death and burial, which were just as mysterious and obscure at the time—not entirely surprising for a lone figure, no longer young, possibly traveling incognito, and without an entourage. Tombs for Shams exist in Konya, Tabriz, and Multan,

Pakistan—the most ancient in Khoy, a town near Tabriz on the main road from Konya, its grave site, with encrusted minaret, dating back at least to 1400.

Rumi's acceptance of Sham's death, though, set him free and also set Shams free to live again in Rumi's poetry as a state of being as much as a mere mortal. During the rest of Rumi's time in Damascus, he reconciled himself to this finality while allowing himself to be remade from within to become the man he wished to be in the wake of Shams's departure. When Shams left for Aleppo, four years earlier, Rumi discovered how much he relied on the volatile teacher for his new way of life. Now he needed to accept that Shams's absence was permanent. He had the option of returning to Konya, defeated, to take on the turban and robes again to live out his life respected, if perhaps a bit pitied, or of seizing responsibility for embodying the freedom and love Shams sought to impart. To do so meant undergoing the kind of life change common in young people in transition from adolescence to adulthood, but more rare in a man in his forties.

Sultan Valad wrote of the transformation of his father in Damascus in the technical terms of medieval theology—his father went from being a "pious man" to a "mystic." A "pious man," explained Sultan Valad, obediently follows the religious laws, believing "If I do good deeds, I won't be drawn to evil." Yet the mystic, he wrote, "Out of love, says 'What will come to pass?' In a state of amazement, he waits to see what God will do." Sultan Valad probably learned of this distinction from his father, who composed another elegy for Shams at that time revealing a similar understanding of his change:

> *Each dawn, like an autumn cloud, I rain tears at your door*
> *Then wipe the tears from your house with my sleeve*
> *Whether I travel to the east or the west, or up into the sky*
> *I won't see any sign of life, until I see you again.*

I was a pious man of the land. I held a pulpit.
Then fate made my heart fall in love and dance after you.

Rumi's final days in Damascus were quieter and more formal. The madness of Konya for him had subsided. Aflaki later reported of time spent by Rumi studying in the company of a local leader of the Damascene Sufi community whom he "loved dearly." He had clearly avoided Konya, the scene of so much pain and breakdown, and was now ready to return. In another set of Sufi terms, he had graduated from "lover" to "beloved," finding the source of the power and wisdom he admired and missed in Shams within himself. The integration he experienced in his poetry occurred in his life as well. In Sultan Valad's version, Rumi discovered Shams, "in himself, radiant as the moon." As he directly repeated his father's words, either from verses Rumi recited, or from a near rendition:

> *He said, "Since I am he, who am I seeking?*
> *I am the same as he. His essence speaks!*
> *While I was praising his goodness and beauty*
> *I myself was that beauty and that goodness.*
> *Surely I was looking for myself."*

❖

At about the age of forty-three, Rumi returned to Konya, rarely to leave again. Much had transpired in the capital since he had looked on as a young man while his father was given a royal welcome when his family first arrived two decades earlier. His own reentry was now quite different, as those gilded and hopeful days were long faded. The great protector of both his father and the Seljuk Empire, Kayqobad I, had been dead for over a dozen years. Likewise Kayqobad I's profligate and inept son, Kaykhosrow II, had died four years earlier—after having temporarily placated the Mongols with a weak financial deal. He left behind an uneasy triumvirate of three young princes, all younger than twelve—Ezzoddin, Roknoddin, and Alaoddin, the son of the sultan's favorite wife, Gorji Khatun.

These royal personages and their machinations were more than distant chess pieces to Rumi. He returned to Konya a far more outspoken figure than he left—less "pious," to use the word of both his son and himself. These key personalities of the Seljuk court would turn out to be far more forgiving and protective than some of the more upright members of the religious establishment in town, and his relations with them were often quite close. Either mother or stepmother to all three sultans, Gorji Khatun became the center of a circle of noblewomen devoted to Rumi, and was mentioned warmly in a poem of praise written by Sultan Valad. At least nine letters exist from Rumi to the Sultan Ezzoddin, in which he referred to Ezzoddin as his "son" and himself as his "father." Mutual fondness also tied him to Karatay—a freed Greek slave, now regent, the true power behind all three thrones between 1249 and 1254—whose "angelic qualities" Rumi once extolled.

Karatay especially was helping preserve Konya from the sort of destruction and stripping of all beauty and subtlety that Rumi had just witnessed in Damascus. Indeed the capital was experiencing a mellifluous and florid spike in its art and architecture that lent a warm context to Rumi's wish for a spiritual life of music and poetry. The symbol of this late phase of the Seljuk Empire in Konya was the *madrase* built by Karatay as his own legacy, a theological school across from the Citadel, midway to the Madrase Khodavandgar, which was finished in 1251, just as Rumi was returning from Damascus. Its architecture was a clear departure from the sobriety of the Alaoddin

Mosque toward a more refined Seljuk classical style—covered in turquoise blue glazed tiles, encircled by bands of Kufic inscriptions, with carved interlocking triangles leading toward an open dome. The white, bluish, black, and turquoise tiles of the dome formed complex patterns of stars. At night, actual stars visible in the circle of the dome reflected in a pool below, the sort of effect never lost on Rumi, for whom reflections expressed his metaphoric way of seeing:

Just as water reflects the stars and the moon,
The body reflects the mind and the soul.

If Rumi's life had been disrupted by Shams, so had the family to which he returned, though in ways set up early on by their first responses to the stranger from Tabriz. Kerra went along rather easily with her husband's transformation following Damascus. She had always exhibited a bent toward a magical spirituality of dreams and visions as well as hovering *jinn* and lurking water monsters. Many of the more incredible tales of Rumi after his death—like being transported to Mecca during prayer and returning with dust on his feet—were traced back to her. Of his two sons, both in their midtwenties, Sultan Valad had solidified his role as his father's dutiful favorite. His white sheep image, though, was sullied by some, like Kerra, who complained of his violent behavior, out of his father's view, toward other family members in the harem. The more tortured Alaoddin left Konya for a time after the disappearance of Shams, shamed by his father's blaming him for his role in the events—the estrangement between the two never entirely healed during Alaoddin's lifetime. Rumi's third son, Mozaffaroddin, a young boy, was still in the harem, with his sister Maleke; within a decade both children would need to decide whether to lead mercantile lives or to become Sufis.

When Rumi returned from Damascus, he moved between court and family and school as he always had, yet he was somehow changed. And that change became the next mystery for those around him to notice and try to understand. Unlike Shams, truly an outsider with no stake in any place or institution, Rumi had always been an entitled member of the religious and ruling class of Konya, and his comments and actions were topics of note, especially given the ongoing drama of his very public adoration of Shams. He knew when he returned to Konya that he was walking onto a stage again. He went about his business with that air of being solitary while being among people that Shams had counseled. Yet he was now not a frightening or aloof figure to most. He had evolved into a far more accessible and concerned religious leader, without pretense, good-humored, humble and simple in approach, living life in a new way in his old town.

Many stories of Rumi following his return from Damascus report quiet acts of kindness around town. Typical was the friend who told of Rumi having asked him to purchase two trays of tasty delicacies at market. When he gave them to Rumi, he wrapped them in a cloth and departed. Curious, the friend trailed him and discovered Rumi inside a ruined building, feeding the treats to a dog that had given birth to puppies. When confronted, he explained, "This unfortunate dog has not eaten anything for seven days and nights, and because of her puppies she is unable to go off." Such mercy from Rumi, described as having walked with his head down, spoke to all the people of Konya, his humility and kindness understood as virtuous by Christians, Jews, and Muslims alike.

He appeared everywhere, mixing with everyone, in all kinds of settings. Many of those around him wished to protect him by keeping him apart and dignified. But he repeatedly showed by his demeanor that he was a changed person. Once he attended a *sama* session where a young man brushed against him during the dance, and Rumi's disciples said harsh words to the overly excited whirling Sufi about his decorum. Rumi quickly cut them off, refusing to be kept insulated or to hurt anyone's feelings in the name of piety:

> My kindness is such that I don't want anyone's heart to be hurt because of me. When someone in a crowd in *sama* brushes up against me, some of my friends try to prevent them, but I am not pleased by that. I have said a hundred times don't presume to speak for me. Only then am I content.

He was also bold and energetic in organizing his own *sama* sessions in public, drawing a clear line to show where he stood on this issue of music, dance, and song in religious meditation and prayer. While exceedingly kind, he was also galvanized and immoveable in his resolve. As Sultan Valad remembered, stressing his remarkable reinvigoration: "He went to Damascus like a partridge, and returned to Rum like a falcon. A drop of his soul became as expansive as the sea. The degree of his love became even greater. Because he became like this, don't ever say, 'He didn't find him.' Whatever he was seeking, he truly found. He again called together all the musicians, on the roof and in the yard. Not knowing his head from his feet, he shouted with all his strength, his voice boisterous. His love was filled with waves like a stormy sea. Everyone was astonished."

In trying to make sense of the meaning of his time with Shams, and its lessons for his life going forward, Rumi's thoughts often returned to a favorite Sufi guiding notion of the need for a living spiritual world axis, either known or anonymous, who was the center of love and understanding in his time, and on whom the welfare of all human beings depended. Rumi later explained this subtle, elusive concept in Book II of his *Masnavi*:

In every age a saint appears
As testing continues to the end of time
When those with good souls will be liberated . . .
He is the lamp that gives light to other saints
Lesser saints are like lamp niches, reflecting his light.

Rumi never directly said that he considered Shams as the saint of saints of his epoch. He did not attempt to place him technically within the complex hierarchy of Sufi spirituality, remaining as guarded, or ambiguous, on this as on many theological matters. Yet he implied in all his turns of phrase that he did believe Shams was such an exalted figure. He went about Konya looking for the reflection of such light in the people he met every day.

With the passing of the decades, especially the tumultuous decade of the 1240s, Sultan Valad came to present the life of his father schematically, following the basic contours, but tidying them into defined squares and boxes. As his son described his father's life, the crazed search by Rumi for Shams was resolved by 1250, when he returned to Konya having attained a station of empowerment. Yet Rumi actually remained fitfully pained by his aching memories of the loss of Shams throughout his life, while revealing or concealing that secret in different ways. Likewise his "Collected Shams of Tabriz," or at least the thousand or so poems explicitly naming Shamsoddin, were implied to have all been written during their time together, especially during the searching in Syria. Logically, if Rumi understood the need for a living spiritual saint, he would not have kept summoning the spirit of Shams in poetry. He did, though, continue writing poems of love that pointed to just such composition, as in one wrenching late *ghazal*:

I grew old mourning him, but say the word "Tabriz"
And all of my youth comes back to me

Rumi kept honoring the memory of Shams and marked his continuing presence, his enduring spirit. He often visited Shams's cell near the *madrase* portico. Evoking his own nicknaming of Shams, Rumi, according to Aflaki, "one day lowered his head before the door of Mowlana Shamsoddin's room and, with red ink, inscribed in his own blessed handwriting, 'The place of the beloved of Khezr.'" The cell was kept untouched as a timeless shrine to Shams. Years later, when Rumi heard someone doing repairs, and hammering a nail into the wall of the cell, he cried out, "They feel no fear in hammering a nail in this place? Don't let them do it again. I imagine that they are driving that nail into my heart!" No one could spend time in the Madrase Khodavand-gar without sensing the resonance of Shams's lasting impact upon Rumi. Folded into his aura of solitude, and his faraway look, was the absence of the one man who would have understood him.

Even Rumi's way of dressing was a constant reminder for him of Shams. As a sign of respect, when he accepted Shams's death, Rumi put aside the white turban that had been his headgear until that time, the standard designation of the scholar and mature religious leader, and wrapped a smoke-colored turban about his head instead. He also dispensed with his wide-sleeve jurist's robe, like the *atabi* robes worn by academics in Baghdad, made of shimmering silk. He fashioned an inexpensive *faraji* cloak woven from thick linen cloth, made in India or Yemen, and dyed dark blue. Such was the garb associated with traveling Sufis, their dark hues masking the clotted dirt of the road, while Rumi associated them as well with the rich violet hues of the early morning skies:

> *Morning rises, and draws his polished blade,*
> *In the heavens, a light as white as camphor bursts forth*
> *The Sufi of the skies slices his blue robe and shawl*
> *Downwards, deliberately, until he touches his navel.*

Dark blues and violets were also the colors of sorrow and distress in medieval Persian society, and family members wore blue clothing as often as black during their formal forty days of grief. As Aflaki reported, "This was his clothing until the end of his life."

PART III

CHAPTER 10

"Last year in a red cloak . . . this year in blue"

ONE day Rumi, in an energetic state, was walking down a street in the goldsmiths' quarter within the commercial market district of Konya. When he happened to pass by the familiar, small shop of Salah, the sound of the steady hammering of the goldsmith struck his ear in a musical way. He responded to the percussive rhythms and, according to the story told by Sepahsalar, began to whirl spontaneously in the street: "When Salahoddin saw his *sama* and his movement to the rhythm of his beat, he did not stop his hammering, not caring about the damage to the gold. After a while Salahoddin stepped out of his shop to converse quietly with Mowlana." As Sepahsalar recounted their portentous reunion: "Salahoddin polished his inner mirror by speaking with Mowlana."

The two had known each other for twenty years, most memorably during the early days when Rumi and Shams first met and Salah opened his home to the two men, giving them a safe haven, while many of Rumi's family and school, outside those walls, were growing irate and agitated. For his trust and sharing in a special time kept secret from most others, Rumi cherished Salah. On the afternoon he began whirling in front of his shop, he and Salah shared a magical moment of recognition rekindling the memory of Rumi's first glimpse of Shams outside the inn at least six years earlier. Following this encounter, Salah became the second of the three beloveds central in Rumi's life.

Salah was also a living link to Rumi's original tutor, Borhan, and so to the spiritual legacy of the lost world of Khorasan and Rumi's father. Both Salah and Rumi had been helped by Borhan, who recognized promise in Salah because of his close following of Borhan's austere regimen in fasting and meditation. Salah's daughter Fateme recalled an occasion in their home when Borhan pointed out the different temperaments of Rumi and her father. If the traditional teacher of the time passed on his very style and behavior to his students, Borhan spoke of splitting that legacy: "I passed on my eloquent speech to Jalaloddin, since he already had abundant spiritual power. I bestowed my beautiful spiritual state on Salahoddin, as he has no capacity for any form of eloquence." No trait of Salah's was more commented upon than his inarticulate manner of public speaking.

Rumi was a member of the Persian cultural elite, by dint of not only his family but especially his immersion in the rarefied university atmospheres of Baghdad, Damascus, and Aleppo. Salah, if he read at all, had never even attended a *maktab*, the elementary school emphasizing reading, writing, and Quranic recitation so important in Rumi's life as a boy in Central Asia. Salah's Persian and Arabic were broken. When he had returned to the fishing village of Kamele, following Borhan's departure for Kayseri, Salah fit easily into the simple rustic life of his father, Faridun, and mother, Latife. He married and had several children of his own. Returning to Konya, according to Aflaki, he and Rumi then followed the separate paths laid out by Borhan: "As Mowlana was engaged in the study of the religious sciences, disputation, teaching and giving sermons, Salahoddin was striving in his goldsmith shop to earn a living while gaining power in his spiritual state."

Closer in age to Shams than Rumi, Salah cut a fabulist figure of a wizened mystic in his shop. He was especially given to seeing colored lights and visions from a world made visible only with the inner eye, perhaps enhanced by the extremes of his fasting. "I see so many wondrous lights," he told Rumi. At other times, he would say, "I have seen an ocean of white light," or "I see an ocean of dark blue light," or "I see a green light and I see a yellow light. I see a smoke-colored light and behold, the ocean of black light has become agitated with waves." When Sultan Valad asked his father if their renewed companionship was based on these hallucinatory visions, Rumi replied, "No, rather I love him because of his character and our special affinity." In most of the poems that he began writing evoking Salah, Rumi stressed his otherworldly demeanor and his faraway gaze:

> *That lion-hunting deer, clearly from his eyes,*
> *Roams another desert, beyond heaven and earth*

Rumi was not shy about casting Salah as a substitute for Shams. The logic of the medieval Sufi notions of love and sainthood led to his understanding that the love in human hearts was universal and, therefore, similar. The life of the spirit required two hearts beating as one to work its alchemy. Rumi wrote transparently of his substitution of Salah for Shams, following their afternoon of dance and conversation outside his shop:

> *Last year in a red cloak, he rose, like the moon,*
> > *Only to return this year, in blue*
> *The Turk you saw last year in Turkestan*
> > *Returned this year as an Arab*
> *The same beloved, but in different clothes*
> > *He changed his clothes, and then he reappeared*
> *The wine is the same, but in a different glass.*

Signifying the growing claim of Salah on his heart, Rumi began dropping his name into poems. He introduced him tentatively at first in lines referring to a "goldsmith," or a "crucible," much as he first camouflaged Shams's name in the Arabic word for "sun." He finally mentioned Salah directly in a poem that still carried the name of Shams as its *takhallos,* soon enough advancing to advertising his name as a new *takhallos* in many of the over seventy love poems inspired by him over the next decade:

> *The grace of Salahoddin shone in the midst of my heart*
> *He is the candle at the heart of the world*
> *I am nothing but the basin where his wax drips*

Some of these poems came to express an intimacy and beauty equal with those to Shams:

> *At the end of time, no one will help you*
> *Only Salahoddin, only Salahoddin,*
> *If you've learned the secret of his secret*
> *Don't breathe a word. Let no one know.*
> *A lover's chest is a fresh, flowing stream*
> *Souls float on its waters, like sticks and straw*
> *When you see his face, don't breathe a word*
> *Breathing will only fog the mirror.*
> *A sun rises from within the lover's heart*
> *Filling the entire world with light.*

Because these were quite different men, if Salah replaced Shams as Rumi's spiritual axis, then the resultant poems to Salah registered a change of mood from the Shams years. Gone was the fiery sun, threatening to singe or burn if too closely approached. Salah was a mirror in which Rumi saw a reflection of his own face, or a candle softly lighting a room, a deer, a gold mine, a lily, or a rose. The tenor of these poems was tender and warm. Salah was not Rumi's intellectual equal, and did not provide him with sharp challenges and debates, yet neither did he lay traps of disturbance, constantly raising the punishing, if salutary, threat of separation. In his simplicity, his ability to mirror rather than enflame, Salah had a soothing effect, allowing Rumi to regain some semblance of balance and sanguinity. Aflaki writes of them engaging lightly in *"eshq-bazi,"* a sort of "amorous playfulness."

Compared with Shams, a respectful formality also persisted between them. Everything was not always *eshq-bazi*. Rumi later shared a memory of Salah with students, making a point about etiquette while revealing their almost comic propriety:

> It happened to me that once in the bathhouse, I was acting with excessive politeness toward Sheikh Salahoddin, and he was being excessively polite toward me. As I complained of his politeness, the thought occurred to me that I was overdoing my own humility and that it would be better to reveal my humble nature gradually. First you rub someone's hands and then his feet until little by little he becomes so accustomed to it that he no longer notices. You should not make him feel awkward, but rather match courtesy with courtesy. Whether showing friendship, or anger, you need to proceed by gradual steps.

Unlike Rumi and Shams, the pair never vanished for long periods into a timeless cocoon. Rumi was often in seclusion, but usually in solitary prayer and reverie. From the time of Shams's final disappearance, he kept about him a nimbus of distinct separateness, a mysterious otherness, and a touching aloneness, which was never completely dispelled.

The shock for Konya and the Madrase Khodavandgar in

this newfound focus on Salah was Rumi's decision to raise the humble goldsmith to the exalted rank of his successor. Sultan Valad labeled him the *nayeb,* or deputy and successor of Rumi—in the law schools of the time, a precise rank and position. As professors would hold more than one academic position—Rumi held four different posts when Shams appeared on the scene—their *nayeb* would teach some of their classes, and deliver sermons in their stead, for a small fee, paid from the professor's salary, with the promise of future promotion to a full position. Salah did begin such preaching, as Aflaki reports that Rumi had given up delivering sermons ever again, except for one final occasion, when Salah coaxed him to elaborate on his own instruction. This appointment of a nearly illiterate local merchant to a position intended for the nuanced articulation of refined theological points was a forced variation on the usual expectations, if not an outright mockery of the entire system.

Rumi's bonding with Salah was a response to his need for a kindred soul. As Sultan Valad recalled him saying, echoing his own *ghazal:* "He said, 'That Shamsoddin I was talking about has returned again! Why am I sleeping? He just changed his clothes and returned.'" But he was also being artful and strategic. Rumi no longer wanted to be in a position of daily authority. He preferred to be left alone. Salah was the figure he put in place as a buffer between him and his ever-needy group of students. As Sultan Valad recorded the blunt—even harsh—words of his father, passing on his official leadership role: "Dedicate yourselves to Salahoddin. I am not in the mood for being a sheikh, for no bird can match flight with my wings. I am happy with myself. I need no one. Having others around me, like flies, bothers me. From now on just follow Salahoddin—seek him with all your heart and your soul, and like him, walk along the straight and narrow path."

Either intentionally or by chance, by appointing Salah, Rumi was beginning to tamper with the fundamental nature of the former *madrase*, and to attract a new and potentially much larger and inclusive group of followers. Salah was able to appeal directly to the local working-class Greeks and Turks, rather than only to the more select religious class of Persian and Arabic émigrés. His mispronunciation of words, which so horrified many of the educated class, would have been reassuringly familiar to his fellow laborers. Salah even had trouble with the word "*al-hamd*," or "praise," in the "al-Fatiha," the opening sura of the Quran recited at the beginning of all five daily prayers, as well as a number of other Arabic and Persian words. To cover for him, as well as make a point, Rumi began mispronouncing these words in the same manner as Salah. "Words have been changed by people in every age since the beginning of creation," he argued. His raising up of Salah solidified his reputation as a lover of all people, opening spirituality to everyone, not only to those who had special religious training and education.

If Salah was Shams reborn for Rumi, he reinvigorated some of the old conflicts around Shams for those traditional members of the *madrase*, especially the remnant of the disciples of Rumi's father. They began their lamenting again, even wishing for the return of Shams as the lesser of two evils, the devil they knew: "Again envy spread among the distrustful. Again, the hypocrites gathered together. Again, jealousy was boiling up, because they were drowning in their delusions. They said to each other, 'We were freed of the other one, but now we fear that we are entrapped again. This one is worse than the first one. . . . At least he was articulate in his speech, and well-spoken, with knowledge, intellect, language and writing. . . . This one does not know writing, or science, or rhetoric. He does not have any worth or value for us. He is an ordinary person, and foolish. He does not know good from evil. He was constantly day and night in his shop hammering, so much so the neighbors closed their doors and windows from the noise." Much of their resistance was based on issues of class. Salah had actually received deep spiritual training from Borhan and was perceived by Rumi as a true successor to Shams, yet they were blinded to these virtues because he was less articulate and had not read widely.

Rumi had no patience with criticism of Salah, especially given the history of complaints against Shams. He had learned a lesson in conviction and was now indifferent to pressure from others, whether princes or students, family or strangers. For all his starry distractedness, he had an inner rudder by which he was now navigating, its course known to him alone. Ebn Chavosh, a friend of the goldsmith, went behind his back to inform Rumi of grumblings around town claiming Salah amounted to "nothing," and that his counsel was corrupted by mixed motives. Rumi was swift in his dismissal of both messenger and message, in a disquisition on the wise compassion of Salah, delivered mostly in Arabic:

As a matter of principle Ebn Chavosh should guard against backbiting with regard to Sheikh Salahoddin— both for his own good and so that this dark covering might be lifted from him. Why does Ebn Chavosh think that so many people have abandoned their homes, fathers and mothers, families, relatives, and tribes, and worn out the iron in their boots traveling from "India to the River Sind" in hopes of meeting a man who has the aroma of the other world? How many people have died from regret because they were unsuccessful in meeting his equal? In your own house you have encountered such a man in the flesh and yet you turned your back on him. This is both unfortunate and unwise.

Rumi trusted his heartfelt instincts. He also understood himself to be living in a spiritual world of mirrors, as much Sufi thought conceived of the sort of affinity he was experiencing with Salah through the imagery of light and reflection, candles and mirrors. The heart of the beloved was a mirror in which the lover saw himself, and saw his reflection dignified by a shared light. True enlightenment only took place in a relationship:

> *Without a mirror, you can't see your face*
> *Look at your beloved. He is your mirror.*

This bouncing light created "flashes" (as Ahmad al-Ghazali described) of divinity in humans, in a physics of love, and in the natural world, mirroring divinity, when properly seen. Engaged in this optics rather than logic, the saint merely reflected. As Rumi wrote:

> *I'm a mirror, I'm a mirror, I'm not a debater—*
> *You only see me if you turn your ears into eyes.*

The ultimate beloved reflected in this purified heart was understood to be God: "Take a polished heart to God so that He may see Himself." For Rumi, he and Salah were two such mirrors, gazing into each other, their affinity inexplicable in words or thought. The polishing took place together and involved maturing through union and separation. Rumi's passion around Salah was driven in part by his embrace of these concepts, and this vision of a world of ricocheting light and love compelled him for the rest of his life.

❖

Rumi's deputizing of Salah not only reverberated in his community but also in his family. The decision had the greatest impact on Sultan Valad, especially in the absence of Alaoddin. Sultan Valad wrote in detail of this phase of his father's life, the memories vivid because he was by then a grown man in his midtwenties and a close observer of the dynamics described—rather than the teenager who tried to make sense of the disruptions caused by the even more inexplicable Shams of Tabriz. He was also alertly engaged, since he had been viewed universally as the inevitable successor to Rumi.

One day Rumi summoned his son and said, "Look at the face of Salahoddin. That king of truth carries such insight!" Sultan Valad agreed, though a bit unenthusiastically, pointing out to his father, "Yes, but only in your eyes. Not in the eyes of ordinary people." Rumi pushed his argument that Salah was the embodiment of Shams, insofar as he carried for him the essence of love: "This is Shamsoddin the King, just without a horse and saddle." While Sultan Valad hinted delicately at his disappointment, his entire life had been predicated on obeying and pleasing his father, and so he capitulated to his wishes. "I see him the way you do," he reassured Rumi. And his father gave his clear command, "From now on follow Salahoddin. Follow that true kin." "Whatever he commands me, I will do," Sultan Valad vowed. "I am at his service with all my soul."

Salah felt the need to assert his position more strongly with Sultan Valad. Either coached by Rumi, or on his own volition, he pressed for an oath of loyalty, saying to Rumi's son, "If you become my disciple, commit to me with all your heart and soul." Sultan Valad responded, hedging slightly to allow a higher status to the previous favorite, Shams: "Oh king, no one can match you in *this* age." Another sign of loyalty Salah shrewdly demanded was that Sultan Valad stop delivering sermons, which reminded Rumi's followers of his articulateness and fueled resentments: "My friend, stop preaching. From now on, only speak of my goodness. . . . I want to be sure that you are all mine." Sultan Valad swore, in the highly florid medieval Persian manner: "Day and night, I will turn my face towards you. You are the king and I am the servant. Whatever you want me to say, I will say. Wherever you wish to send me, I will follow your orders."

Salah spoke with Sultan Valad about the agitation he knew was growing in the community, familiar to them from the time of Shams. He explained his promotion in rank using the metaphor of the mirror, which dominated Rumi's understanding of their relationship: "They are upset because Mowlana made me special, above everyone else. But they know not that I am but a mirror. The mirror does not reflect itself. In me, he sees his own face. So how could he do otherwise but choose me?" Salah was more adept than Shams at dealing with the rough-and-tumble of violent threats. Sultan Valad never wrote of any murder plots against Shams, but he did discuss a conspiracy directed at Salah, who was brusque in his response: "When this news reached the king Salahoddin . . . he laughed loudly, and said, 'Those blind men, they are lost unbelievers. They are not aware of the power of the truth that nothing moves without God's command, not even a straw.'"

Rumi not only commanded his son to submit to Salah, but he also soon arranged for him to marry Fateme, Salah's eldest daughter. In his time living at the home of Salah with Shams, during their first intense seclusion of three months, Rumi had grown close with Salah's family, including his wife, Latife; his mother, also named Latife, who lived in the house after her husband's death; Fateme, about ten years old at the time; and her younger sister, Hediye. Latife and her daughters were allowed before Rumi "with their faces fully unveiled," as he was considered *mahram,* or part of the family. He once exclaimed, of his bonds with them, "Fateme is my right eye, and her sister Hediye is my left eye."

Of all the women in the family, Fateme was definitely Rumi's favorite. When she was still a little girl "because of the extreme affection he felt for her," he began teaching her writing and reading the Quran—quite unusual for a girl of the period. So the choice of Fateme as a bride for Sultan Valad, now that she had come of age, was natural for Rumi. He was also accomplishing a spiritual version of a state wedding, merging their two families, with great hopes for a resulting baby, combining the strains of Rumi and Salahoddin. For Sultan Valad, the marriage was less ideal, and some hard days would lie ahead for the newlyweds because of his attitude. Never as visionary as his father, a marriage to the daughter of a goldsmith remained a social demotion for Sultan Valad.

Balancing any misgivings of his son, Rumi expressed nothing but ecstatic joy and happiness. He wrote at least two poems, either on the occasion of the wedding contract or the wedding celebration, or both, replete with mentions of "the Sheikh," the father of the bride, and raining down upon them blessings from all the religious holidays at one time:

> *May the blessings that flow in all weddings*
> *Increase with even more blessings, for this wedding,*
> *The blessings of the Night of Power, and fasting, and the feast*
> *The blessings of the meeting of Adam and Eve*
> *The blessings of the meeting of Joseph and Jacob*
> *The blessings of the vision of the heavens above*
> *The blessings that cannot be put into words*
> *For the daughter of the Sheikh and my eldest son.*

In another of these nuptial poems, Rumi gives a glimpse of the celebrating that took place, full of the percussive drumming now central to daily life in his community:

Dance you saints! Whirl you righteous ones!
  In the kingdom of the king of the world, lift our spirits!
With drums hanging from your necks, in the rosy nuptial bower
    Tonight, full of tambourines and drums, the best of the best . . .
  At this moment Sufis are gathering together out of joy
    Glimpsing an invisible world, through my shouts of praise
  A throng of clapping guests, clapping like the waves of the sea,
    A throng of upright guests, like sharp arrows, bundled in a quiver.

By the time of the wedding of Fateme and Sultan Valad, Rumi
was adrift in a continuous outpouring of music and poetry. He
performed the five daily prayers, as no one was more assiduous
at adhering to the religious regimen than his self-designated
Sheikh Salahoddin. (Once when he left his robe outdoors in
winter, Salah was said to have put on the frozen garment and
rushed to morning prayers rather than risk any infringement
of the letter of the religious law.) Yet Rumi was mostly living
in an atmosphere of musical instruments and altered states
brought on by whirling, fasting, and meditation, while sleep-
ing only a few hours a night. The result was the accumulating
creation of the rest of his nearly 3,500 lyric *ghazals,* written in
fifty-five different meters, including obsolete classical meters.
The creativity that had begun under the dramatic influence of
Shams continued apace and expanded in its breadth through-
out the 1250s.

An apparent source of this virtuosity was Rumi's natural
talent and knack for music. His favorite instrument to play was
the *rabab,* which he customized for his purposes with a hexag-
onal box rather than the traditional square shape. His favorite
musician, Abu Bakr Rababi, named for his mastery of the *rabab,*
was remembered clearly enough to make his way into the histo-
ries. "His knowledge of music, which, in reality is the source of

rhythm, provided Rumi with the necessary wherewithal and artistic skill to write poetry that has greater metrical variety than any other Persian poet," concluded the Iranian scholar Badi al-Zaman Foruzanfar of Rumi's technical skill, "and that is why a number of meters can be found in Rumi's lyrics which are absent in the poetry of other Persian poets."

His method of composition was often collaborative. Not only Rumi's expertise explained his experimenting in different meters, but also the knowledge of the musicians around him, trying out different musical modes as Rumi took up the challenge to fit his words and messages to their rhythms and beats. If Shams had been the designated representative of *sama* and its evils during their time together, Rumi was left standing alone as its defender. "One day they asked my father, 'Why is the sound of the *rabab* so strange?'" recalled Sultan Valad. "He replied, 'It's the creaking sound of the door of paradise that we hear.'" When a local religious eminence heard the remark, he quipped, "But we also hear the same sound. How is it that we don't become as passionate as Mowlana does?" Rumi wittily responded, "God forbid! In no way! What we hear is the sound of the door opening, while what he hears is the sound of that same door closing."

Amid all this provoked and controlled ecstasy—in a society where personal *gravitas* was expected—while cultivating the delicate cult of friendship between men of God, Rumi still managed to be alert to the competing practical needs of his circle, especially his family. His most pressing concern, following the wedding of Sultan Valad and Fateme, was their married life together, which turned difficult quickly and continued to present challenges when Fateme did not bear her husband any children during their first few years. Quite possibly the aggressive behavior that Rumi's wife reported witnessing from Sultan Valad toward family members in the harem was toward his wife, as Rumi was moved to write a supportive letter to Fateme, promising his advocacy:

> If my dear son Bahaoddin is being mean to you, truly and with all my heart, I will withdraw my affections from him, and I won't respond to his greetings, and he won't be allowed to come to my funeral. Don't be sorrowful, and don't be unhappy, because God is by your side and He will help you. Whoever brings harm to you, if they swear a hundred thousand oaths that they are innocent, I will still find them guilty, because they are not kind to you and don't appreciate you. . . . Do not hide anything from this father, but tell me in detail about whatever happens to you so that with God's help I will be able to provide you the utmost possible assistance.

He likewise wrote a letter to his son, with whom he was more politic, almost gingerly in his approach, revealing his expertise at persuasion and tact. He made a case for his son to modify his behavior around his wife, while presenting an astute argument for respect toward women, an approach not always required of husbands at the time:

> Because of the white hair of her father, and because of our family, I want you to treat her dearly, and every day and every night, treat her as if it were the first day, and every night as if it were the night of the bridal chamber. Don't think that you have caught her and you don't need to pursue her anymore, because that is the manner of superficial people. She is not the sort of woman who will ever lose her freshness. I swear to God that she has not complained, and is not sending any messages to me, either by

hinting or by gesture. . . . I'm not going to tell anyone of this advice. This letter is a matter between us.

Rumi was similarly engaged in bringing about the marriage of the second daughter of Salah, Hediye, to the young calligrapher Nezamoddin, a scribe of the sultan and teacher of the young princes. The obstacle was the poverty of Salah, who had given up his livelihood as an artisan to take over full-time as the spiritual leader of Rumi's community, as well as being his closest companion and deflecting as much business and workaday concern from him as possible. Yet the father of a bride was responsible for providing a dowry, an expense out of reach for Salah. Though living within the tight constraints of poverty, which sometimes weighed on his own wife and family, Rumi expended much energy in letter writing to procure jobs and loans for his dependents. And so he approached a female tutor of the royal princesses, and a "child" of Rumi's, to take a request to the powerful and wealthy queen mother, Gorji Khatun.

The request met with a charmed response, as was often the case when the women followers of Rumi were involved. Gorji Khatun ordered her treasurer to conjure two or three clothespresses and prepare five outfits, as well as veils, hats, and jewels as accessories. According to Aflaki, "They collected rugs and curtains and delightful carpets from Georgia, Shiraz and Aksaray, as well as a tray, a pan, a cauldron, copper and porcelain bowls, a mortar, candlesticks and a complete set of kitchen utensils." The value of the goods, transported to Rumi's school on mules, was high, and he divided the value of the trousseau between the two sisters to prevent any hurt feelings. Rumi next began writing helpful letters on behalf of Nezam, whom he praised as "my dear child and an accomplished artist," as well as "my eloquent, literary, competent, and honest son."

As expected, Rumi created a nuptial poem for the wedding

of Hediye and Nezam. These occasional poems are not among his most inventive. They are formulaic and—even if Rumi was not a patronized courtly poet—tailored to the expectations of his audience and their degrees of understanding. But these standard poems stood in clear contrast to the tortured odes that had poured out of him publicly and privately over so many years not even a decade earlier. Rumi truly did seem to have found some balance of mystic solitariness with the patriarchal pleasures of seeing his family grow and flourish into the next generation. The palm dates, cups of red wine, and streams of milk and honey in these happy matrimonial poems of the 1250s exude felt life. As Rumi sang that day:

> *May this wedding still be smiling like the angels*
> > *Today, tomorrow, and for all eternity . . .*
> *May this wedding be fortuitous, beautiful, and acclaimed*
> > *Like the moon, and like the blue wheel of the sky.*
> *I grow silent, unable to find the words to say*
> > *How radiantly my soul glows on this wedding day.*

CHAPTER II

The Fall of Baghdad

DURING the autumn of 1257, Hulagu, a grandson of Genghis Khan, began a march on Baghdad, sweeping with his Mongol forces across the Great Khorasan Road, the route traveled by Rumi's family four decades earlier. Since the death of Genghis Khan, in 1227, the Mongols had limited themselves to incremental conquests of the south of China, Russian territories, or parts of modern-day Iran, but nothing on the scale of their earlier leveling of an entire civilization in the Central Asian capitals of Samarkand, Bukhara, Balkh, and Merv. Hulagu had renewed global ambitions and was now focused on the ultimate prize of Baghdad, the financial, political, and cultural capital of the Muslim world, where much wealth had been conspicuously displayed for five centuries.

Following the standard practice employed by his grandfather with Khwarazmshah, Hulagu sent Caliph al-Mustasim an ultimatum urgiung him to atone for a contrived list of grievances, including not providing the Mongols with military aid in various conflicts, as the caliph had sworn allegiance to Genghis Khan. The Abbasid Caliph, the thirty-seventh successor in a direct line from the Prophet Mohammad, as well as ruler of a metropolis legendary at least since the creation of its most famous fictional resident, Scheherazade, in *The Thousand and One Nights*, was dismayed by these blunt demands. A hybrid of pope and emperor, al-Mustasim replied that the entire Muslim world, from as far as North Africa, would wage a holy war to defend the capital and its caliph.

The holy war never materialized. By January 1258 the forces of Hulagu had surrounded the city walls of Baghdad and occupied its suburbs, stretching beyond the confines of the old "round city," which was quickly filling to capacity with refugees. The Mongols bombarded the city with innovative ammunition, including missiles fashioned from the trunks of local date palms and gunpowder treated with oxygen to create more powerful explosions, as well as rudimentary grenades, smoke bombs, and fire rockets.

The destruction of Baghdad was catastrophic and matched the brutal razing of Termez or Nishapur, decades before, by the unsurpassed creator of terror, Genghis Khan. Destroying dams and diverting the Tigris to create a barrier of water around the city, on February 5, 1258, Hulagu and his forces broke through the walls, burning its great libraries to the ground, massacring scholars and soldiers alike, and piling up their skulls. Hulagu then summoned the captured caliph to his camp outside the city, where the leader of the Islamic faith and his male children would be executed. According to different reports, they were wrapped in carpets or sacks, and either kicked to death by booted warriors or trampled by fierce horses. The Islamic caliphate that had existed for more than six centuries was destroyed within a week, along with its rarefied culture of meticulous Arabic scholarship and research, while the control of the central lands of the realm of Islam passed to an utterly foreign power.

This news could have taken a couple weeks to reach Konya. Eventually Rumi did speak to his circle of the nearly apocalyptic event for orthodox Muslims. As with other historical incidents, he was quite accurate in his basic account, down to the exact dating:

> When in the year six hundred and fifty-five Hulagu Khan arrived in the region of Baghdad . . . the Khan ordered the vizier of his kingdom and the pivot of his affairs: "Write a letter on my behalf to the caliph telling him to be obedient and to submit and not to act insolently." . . . The caliph refused, acted with insolence, and uttered much abuse. That same day Baghdad was conquered and the caliph was taken away as a prisoner.

In his rendition of the imprisonment, Rumi tells of the caliph begging for food and being given instead bowls of jewels, pearls, and coins from his treasury as a lesson for his profligacy in spending monies on luxury rather than armies. Marco Polo chronicled a parallel tale of the caliph imprisoned in the treasury tower where he stored gold. Rumi then detailed his ignominious execution, "in a sack . . . kicked to death."

The Arabic poets of the time were traumatized by the fall of Baghdad and the caliphate and mourned its passing in rhyme and meter. As one poet sorrowfully wrote of the incomprehensible event, "Oh seekers of news about Baghdad, the tears will tell you." He saw no benefit remaining as "the beloved has departed." For yet another poet, the unthinkable disaster signaled a "loss for the kingdom, for true religion," which could turn a child's hair white. For some, the waters of the Tigris ran red from the bloodshed, for others, black from the ink of the books. Regarded as marking the apex of an Islamic golden age, Baghdad would remain much depopulated and mostly in ruins for centuries.

Rumi never joined in the wailing chorus. Rather than focusing on damage done to the religion of Islam or the insult to the caliphate, he mostly dwelled on the benefits of fasting, using the Mongols as examples, as they fasted for three days before the battle:

> Now if not eating and fasting had such an effect on the affairs of unbelievers and doubters of the faith so that they could attain their goal and become victorious, imagine what would be achieved and bestowed upon supporters of religion and upon all good and pious people if they were to do the same.

As Aflaki summed up Rumi's treatment of this crucial historical event of the Muslim era: "Mowlana brought forth this story on behalf of the excellence of hunger and not eating."

The crisis was even less seismic in Rumi's poetry, dedicated to a spiritual world that had become even more powerfully attractive as the events on the ground in the Middle East and Anatolia grew more dire by the year. Rumi did pay his respects to the power of the caliphate in his *Masnavi* but in lines likely written years after its demise:

> *The deputy of the Merciful God, the Caliph of the Creator*
> *Because of him, the city of Baghdad is like springtime*

These words of praise, though, were put in the mouth of the Bedouin wife, perhaps purposely dated as a character from times past. He never revealed any orthodox reverence for the figure of the caliph or for any of the symbolic trappings of religious power in Baghdad.

Mongol armies had been appearing intermittently at the gates of Konya, too, ever since their victory over the Seljuks in 1243. In one *ghazal,* Rumi included a personal nightmare of the Mongols threatening Konya. He atypically dated the dream within the lines of the poem as having occurred on November 25, 1256, perhaps inspired by an actual threat by Baiju, the commander of the occupying Mongol forces in Anatolia:

> *The Tatar armies, with bows and arrows, swelled the sky*
> > *Ordered to rip apart the pregnant sky, to give birth to a baby . . .*
> *On Saturday night, on the fifth of the month of Qa'de*
> > *In the year of six hundred and fifty-four*
> *Turbulence shook the town. An earthquake seized the town.*

While the poem was phantasmagoric, Konya never suffered the horrific fate of Baghdad. At its conclusion, Rumi was unharmed, calming his own spirit, "Help yourself to sleep."

Rather than the dramatic reversal of fortune suffered by Baghdad, Konya endured an interregnum of decades of appeasement and subjugation, with some benefits as well as much anxiety and uncertainty. In his letters, Rumi gave glimpses of his own worries as a citizen of the Il Khanate—the vassal empire that was now formidably ruled by Hulagu and his extended family, and stretched from Central Asia to Anatolia, or the entire arc of the world Rumi had traversed. He complained of the greed of the Mongols for demanding endless "taxes and camels." In one letter to a Seljuk official, away from Konya on military business, he reported horrid disruptions of daily life by rough bands of Mongols:

> During your absence, troubles began to occur in this town. Every night they captured a house, and killed women and children, and stole their belongings. . . . Anyone concerned with education during that time had no choice but to close their schools and end their classes. When the mind is filled with frightening thoughts, when every day there is bad news, then there is no time for education. . . . I hope that the prince will protect them, as they are dis-

tracted and unemployed. Those used to drinking sweet water, and sitting with scholars, cannot live with such constant distress.

In the same letter, Rumi imaginatively expressed the nature of the power of the Mongols, always menacing, while still allowing the Seljuks a semblance of normal life:

Since this group has gained power over us, fear has prevailed. If it has stopped for an hour, it is as if a viper, sated with its prey, was asleep for a while in the corner. But it is the same viper. It will awake again eventually. Konya today is clearly one of the great centers of knowledge in the world and, God willing, will be allowed to remain so for longer into the future.

One of the ironies of this twilight epoch was the greater freedom granted figures such as Rumi. Islamic culture was allowed to flourish under Mongol rule in Anatolia, and the indifference and tolerance of these rulers toward Sufis, and religious matters generally, overlapped with the fine velleities of Persian and Seljuk culture to create a zone where exploratory mysticism was given leeway—though heatedly disputed—rather than leading inexorably to the brutal executions endured by al-Hallaj and others under the rule of the caliphs in earlier Baghdad.

❖

The shadow sultan of Konya and the Seljuk Empire during all the remaining years of Rumi's life—and the main foil for his ambivalent relations with the power politics of the era—was Moinoddin Solayman Parvane, the de facto ruler of the Seljuk

state in Anatolia during most of the period of the Mongol Pro-
tectorate, as well as a somewhat mercurial disciple of Rumi.
His father, born in northern Iran, had gained prominence as a
trusted vizier of Khaykhosrow II, and negotiated the peace with
the Mongols that spared weakened Konya after the Seljuk defeat
in the battle of Kose Dag. The son then became a regional com-
mander in Tokat until summoned, in 1256, by the Mongol chief
Baiju, who awarded him the more princely and powerful titles
of *emir hajib* and *parvane.*

The title that stuck to him, and by which he was known in
his time, and down through history, was simply "Parvane"—a
Persian word with the whimsical-sounding meaning of "butter-
fly." He was officially lord chancellor and president of the *Divan,*
or council, and, so, the representative of the sultan in all inter-
nal affairs. "Butterfly" referred to his dual function as the chief
of the twenty-four secretaries in a sort of department of state,
concerned with foreign affairs, especially the constant rustle of
communications with foreign powers. Written on finely textured
white Chinese paper, these memos were generally in Persian,
though the Mongols had begun to introduce Turkish into the
chancelleries. In the pantomime of Seljuk power on display at
state ceremonies, the Parvane wore an inkpot hung about his
neck—the emblem of his office.

Early on during his time in Konya, the Parvane made a point
of meeting and cultivating Rumi. A son-in-law of the Parvane
was a disciple of Rumi in attendance at many of his talks and
was sometimes their go-between. On one introductory occa-
sion, the Parvane sent him to invite Rumi to a gathering of re-
ligious scholars at his palace. "How would it be if Mowlana also
deigned to honor us with his light-filled presence?" the Parvane
asked. "Indeed, that would be the honor of a lifetime." Rumi
came along but created an edifying distraction by seating him-
self in the courtyard rather than on the high platform reserved

for honored guests. The Parvane occasionally sent Rumi gifts, which were invariably refused, eluded, or redirected. When he suggested building a cupola over the simple grave of his father, Rumi replied that the azure arch of the sky would suffice.

Rumi was not at all hesitant about speaking truth to power. When the Parvane appeared one day to ask him to give counsel and advice, Rumi, raising his head after several moments of silence, replied, "I hear that the commander Moinoddin has learned the Quran." He answered, "Yes, I have." "I also hear that you have listened to the important works written on the study and classification of the sayings of the Prophet Mohammad." He replied, "Yes, I have." Rumi said, "Since you have read the word of God and the Prophet, and you know how to discuss as is required, and yet you do not take counsel from these words and you are not acting in accordance with any Quranic verse or saying of the Prophet—why ever do you wish to hear something from me and then follow that?"

Rumi was known to reassure the Parvane when he worried aloud to him that he was devoting all his time to the brutal machinations of power and politics rather than to his spiritual life. He once sent a message apologizing for not attending one of Rumi's talks: "Day and night my heart and soul have been at your service, but I have not been able to attend because of my preoccupation with Mongol affairs." To which Rumi responded:

These are also the works of God, since they have to do with the safety and security of the faithful. You have sacrificed your all, both materially and physically, to give tranquility to the hearts of a few Muslims so that they may occupy themselves with acts of devotion. This is good work, too.

On other occasions, when the Parvane arrived unannounced to solicit wise advice from the spiritual teacher, Rumi hid from him and his retinue. He guarded his privacy and was careful not to show any special favor to the rich and powerful. After keeping the Parvane waiting at length—uncustomary treatment for him—Rumi emerged to find that his guest had learned an important lesson. "For my part, because Khodavandgar was late in coming, I imagined as follows," said Parvane. "'This lateness is a lesson for you, Parvane! How bitter and what a hardship it is for people in need to have to be kept waiting to speak to you.' Your being late has caused this benefit for me." His newfound humility freed Rumi to indulge in a soaring example of excessive Persian etiquette:

> This way of thinking is very good. But the truth is that if a supplicant comes to someone's door and has a request but his voice and his face are not attractive, he will be quickly sent away. However, if someone arriving with a request has a beautiful voice and is good-looking and pleasant, he would not so quickly be given a piece of bread, to keep him there longer. I came late because your supplications, your love, and your longing are so pleasing to all the men of God that I wished for the benefits to linger.

The Parvane was so happy with this elaborate compliment that he ordered six thousand sultani coins to be delivered to the *madrase*, which Rumi then distributed among his companions.

Rumi was increasingly displaying otherworldly behavior during this decade—praying until dawn on his rooftop or preaching to a pack of wild dogs. Yet he never abdicated his role as a civic diplomat. He turned out to be skilled at managing the expectations of Seljuk sultans and their emissaries, providing them a connection to a spiritual practice that was sincere but also constituted good public relations requisite with their position. Rumi could create metrically precise poetry while whirling, or deliver legal opinions from the midst of extreme fasts and meditation, due to his scholarly training. Likewise his years of learning the manners of court and academy were never lost. In that sense, he fit a description by the scholar of Sufism Omid Safi of "premodern Muslim saints" as "men and women of power. Their power derived from their sanctity."

Many were the reports of haughty behavior on Rumi's part toward the Parvane. In dozens of surviving letters to the statesman, though—more than to any other correspondent—he was quite formal and respectful, which suggests perhaps exaggeration in the reporting of his public rebuffs or a kind of elaborate role-play acceptable to both. In these letters, Rumi employed all the titles of office of the Parvane, including his title among the Mongols, while soliciting favors for children or disciples, such as jobs, tax exemptions, or pardons. Almost all contained the bartering promise of "praying for your prosperity."

Sometime after the death of the sultan Kaykhosrow II, the Parvane had consolidated his authority within the palace by marrying the wife of the deceased sultan—and mother of the young sultan Alaoddin—Gorji Khatun, the "Georgian lady," otherwise known as the "Queen of Queens." While she was the most powerful woman in the Seljuk state, and had become a committed devotee of Rumi, no clear evidence exists that she ever officially gave up her Christian faith, as she never took on a traditional Muslim name. Arriving on the Citadel hill, as a young bride, the Georgian princess had been accompanied by senior Christian ecclesiastics. Later in life after Rumi's death, she acted as patron of a church in Cappadocia and was depicted in one of the sanctuary murals.

The fervent devotion of Gorji Khatun to Rumi as her personal saint and spiritual guide, though, was never in doubt. When she needed to travel to the royal palace in Kayseri, she commissioned a Greek portrait painter to draw Rumi to console her during her absence. Of the proposal, Rumi said to the painter, "It's fine, if you are able." As Aflaki reported, "He drew a very delicate face, but when he looked a second time, the expression was different from the first time." The painter wound up with twenty sketches, since his subject's likeness was proving resistant to capture. Unfazed, Gorji Khatun packed all twenty sheets of paper into her trunk and gazed at them whenever she needed to be comforted. Her relationship with Rumi was apparently more satisfying than with her husband, as the Parvane once had to approach Rumi as a marriage counselor when Gorji Khatun demanded a divorce. She said, "I want you to divorce me." Rumi advised the husband to keep promising "I will do it," but not follow through, until her mood passed.

The wife of a treasury official and later viceroy, Aminoddin Mikail, was likewise one of the women in Rumi's circle, and was dubbed by him "Sheikh of the Ladies," as she hosted weekly Friday evening women's *sama* sessions. These sessions, which Rumi often attended, were far more potentially scandalous and incendiary than his public gatherings in the *madrase*. When he was present, the husbands would stand guard outside. After evening prayers, bending all rules of religious propriety, Rumi visited the women "all alone without any followers." As Aflaki reported:

> He would sit down among them and they would form a circle and gather before him. They would scatter so many rose petals over him . . . Mowlana, in the midst of roses and rose water, would be immersed in sweat, and until midnight he engaged in uttering higher meanings and secrets, and giving advice. Finally, slave-girl singers and rare tambourine players, as well as female flutists would start to play. Mowlana would begin performing the *sama* and

all the women became so ecstatic that they could not tell their heads from their feet, or even whether they were still wearing any covering on their heads. They would cast all their jewels and gold into the shoes of this sultan in hopes that he might accept some small thing or pay them some regard. He did not glance at anything at all. Having performed the dawn prayers with them, he would then depart.

As Aflaki clarified, at that time and in their traditional society, "No Friend of God or prophet . . . behaved in such a manner or style."

The spirit of tolerance and creativity allowing such expressions of spiritual ecstasy continued to influence, as well, the public building still taking place all over Konya, especially the *madrases* funded by ministers in the extended circle about Rumi. Rising to power as vizier after the death of the sympathetic regent Karatay was a younger politician, Fakhroddin Saheb Ata, praised by Rumi in letters to him as "my brother" and "lofty and pious." Perhaps competing with the Karatay *madrase*, about a hundred yards away, the vizier had built his own Ince Minareli, graced with an innovative slender minaret. Completed during the same year as the fall of Baghdad, the Ince Minareli marked a final baroque phase in Seljuk architecture, its gateway decorated with sinuously twisted Quranic lines in cursive Kufic script, one of the first uses of this more fluid style in architectural inscription, similar to the tumbling and kinetic intricacies of Rumi's own fluid poetics.

Rumi also maintained relations with the three young sultans, though with differing intensities of feeling and commitment. He knew Alaoddin Kaykobad III particularly, as he was the son of his devotee, the queen mother Gorji Khatun, and had been the designated successor of Kaykhosrow II—even though he was the youngest—since she was his favorite wife. Yet Alaoddin, who was part Muslim and part Georgian Christian, was unlucky in his final destiny. When Mongke, the descendent of Ghengis Khan, summoned the leaders of the Seljuks to his capital in Mongolia, Alaoddin accepted, as the representative of the royal triumvirate but was mysteriously murdered en route.

Rumi was also close with Ezzoddin Kaykaus II, the oldest brother, who was ruling in Konya during much of the latter third of the decade of the 1250s, though he spent most of his time in the pleasant Mediterranean town of Antalya, where he invited Rumi to visit. Rumi declined, telling his circle that while Antalya was warm, "the people there are mostly Greeks, who don't understand our language, although a few Greeks do." In one letter, Rumi compared their separation, when Ezzoddin was away from Konya, to that of the patriarch Jacob missing his son Joseph. As his brother Roknoddin Qelij Arslan IV was the favorite of the Parvane, Ezzoddin suffered many setbacks. Rumi's letters, whenever Ezzoddin found himself again in exile, were always supportive and consoling:

> Your kingdom is a shelter for the poor and weak, and a shrine for the innocent and for those who are victims. I am hoping that soon happy news arrives that will tell us of your blessed return, bringing us joy.

Eventually Ezzoddin fled into a final exile in Constantinople, where he wore the purple slippers of Byzantine royalty and practiced Christianity. Roknoddin was then propped up by the Mongols as sole sultan with the Parvane as his designated political intelligence.

❖

Far more troubling to Rumi than the effects of the conquest of Baghdad or internal Seljuk politics during the fall and winter of 1258 was the deteriorating health of Salah, who had grown older and frailer and was bedridden. The decade that Rumi spent with Salah had been nurturing and marked a peak period of his playing musical instruments and whirling in *sama* sessions. With such different characters, they had often been alone, even when together. Attuned to his friend with the multicolored visions, while creating his own far more delineated and fabulous images of an invisible realm in poetry, Rumi felt freer to explore his contemplative inner world of silence with Salah reliably nearby. He honored this closeness during his friend's illness by visiting him daily for long periods and neglecting most of his other obligations. Writing to one of the princes, Rumi apologized profusely:

> I wanted to come and be at your service and visit your blessed face but I have not had the opportunity because of the weakness and illness of our great Sheikh Salahoddin, because I am busy only with him.

He went on to say that he was praying steadily by the bedside of Salah, but to little avail.

The only friction in an otherwise smooth friendship between these two companions—in contrast to the tumult of his time with Shams—had been caused by jealous tendencies in Salah. Rumi inspired an unusual pitch of rivalry around him, made more pronounced by his air of detachment. Knowing of Salah's acute sensitivity, Rumi advised his son Sultan Valad not to even mention Shams or the younger Hosam, who Rumi had put in charge during his time in Damascus, in the presence of Salah. "Even though there is no difference between them, one should not mention them," he said. Sultan Valad reported that his father decided against inviting to Konya, his dear Sufi friend from his time in Damascus, to avoid exacerbating these tensions with Salah.

Mostly, though, Rumi and Salah harmoniously shared in the daily events of each other's lives. Salah was one of the few with Rumi regularly at intimate family moments or in mundane domestic situations. At the burial of Salah's mother, Latife, dear to both of them, Rumi stayed behind at the grave with him. "Come let us go," Rumi encouraged, but Salah wished to linger to pray for her delivery into the hands of angels. When Rumi next saw Salah, he was smiling, his graveside mission complete. On another day Salah hired Turkish laborers to do some work in his garden. Echoing comments common in the polyglot culture, Rumi advised, "For demolition, hire Turks, for building, Greeks." When Rumi needed a fireplace built, he hired a Greek. Such were the ordinary tales told of their calm and stable companionship.

The final illness of Salah was protracted over weeks and then months. Rumi visited constantly, but such attentiveness, Salah came to realize, was keeping him alive. He finally asked Rumi to release him from his affliction. As Sultan Valad recorded, "He accepted his request and said, 'So be it.' He rose from his bedside, and left quickly, setting off down the road towards his own house, and he became engaged with consoling his own pain. He didn't visit him again for two or three days. . . . Salahoddin, our king, grew lucid, and said to himself, 'My soul is departing my body. Now I am certain that I am leaving the world of the living. I am heading towards the world of eternity. His not visiting me is the sign that I should leave. This is the sign for me to bid farewell.'"

In one of their quiet conversations before his death, Salah laid out his wishes for an unconventional burial, a blueprint for a style of funeral that advertised the meaning of the kind of life to which he and Rumi were committed. As Sultan Valad remembered these deathbed wishes, "The Sheikh said, 'Around my dead body, bring the drums and the tambourine. Process towards my grave, while dancing, happy and joyful, ecstatic and clapping, so that all may know the friends of God go towards eternity joyful and smiling. Mine is a death that will be made joyful by the *sama*." He envisioned a tuneful procession of dancing accompanied by drums, tambourines, flutes, and snares.

Salah died on December 29, 1258. Baring his head in grief, Rumi then carried out the wishes for Salah's funeral carefully and explicitly. He ordered that the wind instruments and kettledrum players be gathered, and all processed through the streets of Konya to the family burial site in the sultan's rose garden. Before the funeral bier, carried on the shoulders of disciples, walked eight troops of singers and reciters, while Rumi spun in *sama* all along the way. Salah was buried to the left of the sepulcher of Rumi's father. At the emotional funerary banquet that evening, Rumi recited a sorrowful elegy, echoing in some of its lines and in its *radif,* or repeated refrain, "weep," his earlier ode to Shams:

> *Gabriel and the wings of all the angels turn blue*
> *For your sake, the saints and all the prophets weep.*
> *Stunned by my grief, I am too weak to even speak*
> *Unable to create any comparisons, I simply weep.*

The joyous and frenzied funeral of Salah was yet another shock to the orthodox Muslim population of Konya. Muslim funerals were traditionally marked by gravity and restraint, the only remotely musical expression being the somber chanting of the Quran by reciters trained to modulate their tones of grief with an austere solemnity. Called to account for this raucous spectacle—anticipating in its music and song his own funeral—Rumi was sharply questioned. "Ever since time immemorial the bier of the dead has always been preceded by

Quranic readers and muezzins," he was reprimanded. "Now, in your time, what is the meaning of these singers?" Rumi calmly answered their concerns:

> The muezzins and Quranic readers and Quran memoriz-
> ers in front of the bier testify that the dead person was
> a believer who died in the Muslim religion. Our singers
> testify that the deceased was a lover as well as a believer
> and a Muslim.

CHAPTER 12

"Sing, flute!"

DURING the years following the death of Salah, Rumi, in his mid-fifties, did not immediately fill the leadership post left vacant. More accessible than in years past, he was taking an expanded role in running the *madrase,* now operating closer in style to a Sufi lodge, though without much formal hierarchy, or reliable income or wealth. The bulk of his surviving talks, collected in the volume titled *Fihe ma fih*—as well as much official correspondence—date to this middle period. In these talks, he often stressed that no progress was possible without guidance from a wiser soul. He had entered a phase of embracing his teaching again and often looked for metaphors for his vision of his work such as an astrolabe, an instrument used in the period to determine the positions of planets:

> A human being is an astrolabe of God, but you need an astronomer to know how to use the astrolabe. If a seller of leeks or a greengrocer possessed an astrolabe, what would be the use? How could he fathom the conditions of the celestial spheres, or the turning of the houses of the zodiac, or their influences? Only in the hands of an astronomer is the astrolabe beneficial, for whoever knows himself knows his Lord.

Rumi felt a kind of spiritual expertise, like the scientific knowledge of an astronomer, which he wished to share, while knowing such learning required the passion of a lover. He was confident now in who he was as a daring religious leader, and where he fit in.

While committed again to his school, he was hardly confined to its walls. Probably no figure was more singular, and recognizable, on the streets, or walking in the gardens or cemeteries beyond the city gates of Konya, during the decade of the 1260s. Of medium height, with gray hair, a sallow complexion, and an intense stare, and dressed always in his tightly wound turban, rough linen cloak, and orange shoes or boots, he kept his head shaved, and beard trimmed, unlike the pious religious. Often remarked on was his thinness—"as thin as the rim of a cup"—a natural trait, as his steady diet was a bowl of yogurt with cloves of raw garlic and a crust of bread. His identifiable silhouette sometimes made him a target for derision. As a rival Sufi complained, snidely, "Look at Mowlana! What a dark figure he is, and what a silly path he follows, with his smoky turban and his dark-blue *faraji*. Who has bestowed that cloak upon him?"

Teaching the circle of Khorasani emigrants remaining from the days of his father, and the widening number of working-class Turks, Kurds, or Greeks recently brought in by Salah, he was just as compelling in giving lessons while walking about. He did not pay much attention to markers of class, race, or religion. At every random turn he was met by new opportunities to confound expectations. One day a Jewish rabbi ran into him on the street and asked, "Is our religion better or your religion?" "Your religion," Rumi surprisingly answered. In many of these accounts, the result of Rumi's responses was instant conversion to the Muslim faith, which may or may not have occurred, though certainly Sufis were attractive representatives of the faith, as the Seljuks had calculated.

Rumi had more than passing relations with the Christians, not just the indigenous Greek population, but also with the many Tuscans, Genoese, and Venetians who were resident in Konya. He often visited the nearby Monastery of Plato the Philosopher, and—according to a learned old monk who would later tell Rumi's grandson stories of his grandfather—would take retreats there, where monks from the Byzantine Empire, Europe, Armenia, and Trabzon on the Black Sea would be staying. When he once saw a young Christian, Theryanus, about to be executed for murder near the Gate of the Horse Bazaar, Rumi, as a friend of the local Greek community, intervened with the prefect of police to save his life by covering him symbolically with his cloak. The young man became a devoted convert and changed his given Greek name to Alaoddin Theryanus.

A visiting Christian monk from Constantinople, having heard of Rumi's reputation for such gestures of kindness, encountered him on the streets of Konya and bowed three times. As he raised his head, he found that Rumi was bowing back but had continued well beyond three bows. "Mowlana lowered his head thirty-three times before the monk," reported Aflaki, suggesting immoderation. When the monk asked why he was showing such extreme humility before him, Rumi answered, "How could I not act with humility towards one of God's servants? If I were not to behave this way, why would I have any worth, and who could I truly help, and what work would I be fit for?"

Following the example of Shams, Rumi continued to frequent the Armenian tavern district, considered definitely off-limits for Muslims. After one *sama* session at the residence of a nobleman, Rumi was wearing luxurious gifts he had been given of a red cloak with a lynx fur collar and golden knot buttons as well as an Egyptian woolen turban. Walking past a rowdy wine tavern, he heard the irresistible tune of a *rabab* being played inside and, filled with joy, wound up whirling in the street and giving away his cloak and hat. Regarded as scandalous was his ongoing friendship with a beautiful dancing girl, from a nearby caravanserai, who freed the slave girls working for her after meeting him. When one cleric complained, "It is not proper for so great a person to spend time with a prostitute of the tavern," Rumi responded, "At least she is honest about who she is."

If Rumi was misunderstood, or felt to be a threat, by a number of the religious leaders of Konya, both orthodox and Sufi, he found an entirely receptive audience in children. Even when his own children were older, he often used games and stories to teach them lessons. One day, noticing that Sultan Valad, now a grown man, was sad and depressed, Rumi put on a wolf skin, covering his head and face, and crawled up to him and said, "Boo!" When his son laughed, he said, "If a beloved friend were always joking and cheerful and then said, 'Boo,' would that frighten you?" His point was that life experiences might be scary or threatening, but never the loving essence. When his daughter Maleke complained of the stinginess of her husband, Rumi told her a story of a rich man so miserly he wouldn't open his door for fear the hinges would wear out. According to Aflaki, "Maleke became happier. She laughed and was free from her cares."

He could teach his children difficult lessons, as well. Rumi's temper flared when he once came across Maleke beating her female slave. Pushing through the door, he shouted at her, "Why did you hit her? And why are you harming her? If she was a lady and you were a slave girl what would you wish from her? Do you want me to issue a *fatwa* that there should be no male or female slaves in the whole world, except those belonging to God? In reality, we are all brothers and sisters." Shocked by her father's reaction—a *fatwa* against slavery would have been remarkable in the Middle Ages—Maleke freed the slave, dressing her in her own clothes, and, as long as she lived, behaved with the utmost kindness and consideration to both male and female slaves.

One day he left his neighborhood and came across some children playing. When they spotted Rumi they ran over, bowed to him, and he bowed back. A little boy shouted from the distance, "Lord, wait for me to finish my work and I'll come, too." Rumi waited for him to finish his "work" and then embraced him. He often interceded to prevent cruelty to animals. While riding beside him, a Quranic reciter began beating the head of his donkey for braying. Rumi asked, "Why are you beating that poor animal? He is either hungry or excited. But all beings share these responses. Why don't you hit everyone on the head?" He could bring sweets to a litter of puppies but was also a clear-eyed observer. When a friend noted the "happy union" of dogs asleep in the sun, he corrected:

If you really want to see their friendship and unity, throw a piece of meat or some tripe into their midst. Then you will discover their true situation. This is the condition of people attached to the world and worshiping wealth. As long as there are no worldly goods or self-interest involved, they are friendly and loyal. But throw in a trifle of worldly goods and they forget their friendship and unity.

Rumi remained keen about the dangers of high position or any kind of wealth. He reserved his strongest and most stinging criticism for the rich and powerful, and could be as censorious about them as he was welcoming to the poor and marginal. When a wealthy townsman was brought to visit to pay his respects, Rumi bolted from his place and went into the toilet. After much time had passed, one of his students went looking and found him hunched down in a dark corner. Rumi heatedly explained to him:

The stench of this clogged-up toilet is a hundred times better to me than the company of the anxiety-laden rich.

For the company of worldly people and the wealthy turns enlightened hearts dark and only causes confusion.

He put the matter a bit more elegantly when speaking in public to a circle of his students:

> The danger in associating with kings is that anyone who converses with them, claims their friendship, or accepts wealth from them, must in the end tell them what they wish to hear, and hide their own opinions about their evil behavior to preserve themselves. They are unable to speak in opposition to them. Therein lies the danger, for their religion suffers. The further you go in the direction of kings, the more the other direction, which is essential to you, becomes strange to you. The further you go in that direction, this direction, which should be beloved by you, turns its face away from you. The more you accommodate yourself to worldly people, the more the true object of your love grows estranged from you.

Equally challenging to Rumi was fame, creating another sort of status, which was based on a more subtle currency, intimately and increasingly familiar to him. Aflaki reported that one day Rumi turned to his companions and unexpectedly confided:

> As my fame increased and people came to visit me and desired to be with me, from that day, I have had no peace or rest from this affliction. The Prophet was correct when he said that "Fame is an affliction, and repose lies in obscurity."

He often lashed out at fame, claiming that each degree of removal from obscurity and anonymity increased the deep pain of separation from God. As he wrote in the *Masnavi*:

Make yourself thin and wretched
To be let out of the cage of fame
Fame is a strong and powerful chain
Heavier along this way than iron.

He felt similarly about the sort of false praise or flattery bestowed on the rich or famous:

Words of praise taste delicious,
But be careful, they are filled with fire

So Rumi avoided any privilege of rank or status both for himself or anyone around him. He quickly exited a bathhouse minutes after entering when he discovered that an attendant had removed someone from the edge of the pool to make room for him. "I began to sweat in shame and I quickly came outside," he said. He would always wait for his disciples to enter the house of noblemen first for fear they would be stopped at the door after he entered. When he saw Sultan Valad bumptiously riding on a horse while others walked, he ordered him to dismount, warning of the "affliction of high position . . . You are looking at everyone from above, and so you see them as beneath you."

To keep his own appetite for food, money, or fame in check, Rumi exercised extreme austerities, rarely slept, and was continuously close to prayer. He distrusted comfort, and while embroidering a beautifully inviting theology of love, music, and poetry, relied for its practice on a forbiddingly hard regimen. Instead of candles, he would insist on linseed-oil lamps, which the poor used. When his wife complained of their extremes of penury, he replied, "I am not keeping you from having the things of the world, I am keeping the world from having you." After a female servant in the women's quarters complained of being allotted such a small amount of money to spend for food, he reminded her that she still had her eyes, nose, and limbs, which were extremely valuable.

In a public bathhouse, Rumi was shocked to catch sight of a reflection of the result of his abstemiousness—his weak and emaciated body. "I have never in my whole life felt ashamed before anyone but today I am extremely embarrassed before my thin body," he said. "How my body laments, 'You don't leave me be in peace for even a single day so that I might gain some strength back to bear your load!'" His startled recognition, however, did little to change his behavior. In the middle of that difficult winter, while even young men were huddled in front of ovens and stoves in furs, Rumi was on the roof nightly, praying—all done in the interest of achieving further visionary glimpses of the loss of self, of becoming freer:

> One morning, a moon appeared in the dawn sky
> Descending even closer to get a look at me
> Like a hawk, seizing a little bird, while hunting,
> That moon seized me, and as we climbed the sky
> I looked within myself, only to find no self there
> Within that tender moon, my body had become a soul . . .
> The entire ship of my existence had vanished in the sea.

❖

On one of those evenings, around 1261 or 1262, Hosam chanced upon Rumi in his private quarters. Rumi's loyal follower was now in his midthirties, and had been serving, at his request, as the treasurer of the unofficial order so that Rumi never needed to touch money or pay much attention to its allotment. Hosam had recently been mulling over a suggestion and was looking for an opportune moment to approach. He had noticed that many of the younger students were eagerly reading aloud from Attar's *Conference of the Birds* as well as Sanai's *Garden of Truth*— both *masnavis* or long poems in rhymed couplets on spiritual themes. They preferred such poems to the drier prose manuals on Sufi theory. So he decided that Rumi should write his own extended poem, full of moral pith and wisdom. "Collections of your *ghazals* have become numerous," he proposed. "Yet a new book in the manner of Sanai, written in the meter of Attar, as a memento for the souls of lovers, would be a kindness."

In response, Rumi supposedly plucked from the folds of his turban a page on which he had already written eighteen couplets, the beginning of a poem in rhyming lines of eleven syllables that followed just the meter requested—the flowing *ramal mahzuf*, stressed in drumming feet of four syllables each, with the last foot of each line losing a syllable. He handed the page to Hosam, who read the prologue of a poem-in-the-making that eventually grew so famous as to simply be referred to by its form—as the *Masnavi*—eclipsing all other verses composed in the same rhyming pattern:

> Listen to the reed flute and the tale that it tells
> How it sings of separation:
> Ever since I was cut from my bed of reeds
> Men and women have joined in my lament
> I keep seeking other hearts, torn by separation,
> To share my tale of painful longing
> Everyone cut at the same root
> Longing for the time when they were joined.

In the guise of this mournful flute—perhaps a flute cut from the reed beds of Khorasan—Rumi found a voice that allowed him to sing of separation, which had been Shams's last and greatest lesson to him before his departure over a decade earlier, as well as of secrets, which could only be expressed in the allusive language of lyric poetry:

> *Out of curiosity, they drew close to me,*
> *But none discovered my secret*
> *My secret is woven into my lament*
> *Yet no eyes or ears can find its light*
> *Soul is woven into body, and body into soul*
> *Yet no eyes have the power to see the soul*
> *Fire, not wind, makes this flute sing*
> *If you don't have fire, don't play.*

The poetic flute of the eighteen-line prologue was a symbol at once mystical and familiar for its intended audience, as an instrument carrying tunes from Central Asia, but also akin to the Anatolian Phrygian flute, its plangent tones, like a human voice, commented on already in ancient writings. In one such local tale, King Midas of Gordion—not far from Konya—had been cursed by Apollo with a pair of donkey ears that he hid beneath his Phrygian cap. Unable to keep the secret, a courtier whispered the truth to a lake, where he thought it was safe. Yet a reed growing on the banks heard, and when a shepherd cut the reed to make his own flute, the flute began singing of the king's secret.

The result of the meeting of minds of Rumi and Hosam at this time was dramatic and significant. For Rumi to make any major shift in his life at this stage, he needed to align his roles as sheikh, preacher, father, teacher, mystic, and poet. In the confluence of Hosam with his emerging *Masnavi,* he had discovered a diligent secretary, a respected deputy, and a beloved companion for his later years, as well as a medium of poetry that allowed him to be both ecstatic and didactic, both a mystic seer and a moral preacher.

Hosam was hardly a newcomer. His involvement in Rumi's life dated to the arrival of Shams, who took an interest in the young man, a teenager with the maturity of an older man because of having lost his father at an early age, while inheriting power and respect among Kurds and followers of the *akhavan* youth movement. Much noted had been the handsome appearance of Hosam. As Aflaki recorded, "When Hosamoddin reached the age of puberty, he was extremely beautiful and the Joseph of his day." (The reference was to the young Joseph, so irresistible to women, as described in the Quran.)

By the evening of his proposal of the *Masnavi*, Hosam had begun making his transit into the much more intimate poetic cosmology of Rumi, and was soon to be affixed in his shining firmament as the third of Rumi's beloveds, both muse and companion. In this personal universe, Shams was the sun, and Salah either moon or mirror. Like Salah, Hosam was only gradually introduced in the poems—sometimes in puns on the Arabic word for sword, "*husam*." Sultan Valad wrote that his father came to think of Hosam as a star, or a constellation of stars. Yet in his poems, he usually identified him with sunlight—not *shams*, the source, but rather *ziya*, which is a sunbeam or "ray of sun." Rumi codified this private image in the prelude, introducing Book IV of the *Masnavi*:

> *You are a ray of the sunlight of Truth, Hosamoddin*
> *With your light the* Masnavi *glows brighter than the moon*

Though Hosam was busy as a community leader, and devoted to his wife, he and Rumi set to work almost instantly on their project, which was taxing, time-consuming, and intensive. The poem was collaborative, as nothing was written unless Hosam was there to record it, and then to read it back and help revise it. For months and eventually years, he accompanied Rumi every-

where, writing down verses as Rumi spoke them, whether walk-
ing along the street or in a bathhouse, at home, or turning about
a pole during *sama*—his informal version of the whirling dance
that sometimes accompanied the meditation. Hosam recited the
lines back, and Rumi would correct them, before they would be
read to the disciples, as sermons or stories in serial form. Rumi
preferred nighttime for poetic composition—as for prayer—and
included apologies to Hosam for keeping late hours:

> *It's dawn. You who support and shelter the dawn,*
> *Please grant me pardon from Hosamoddin*
> *You who grant the release of intellect and soul*
> *You, the soul of souls, and the radiance of coral,*
> *From whom the light of dawn now begins to shine.*

Rumi would occasionally confuse his scribe, playing tricks on
him, teaching him personal lessons beyond those expressed in
his verses. As Hosam told of one incident: "One day Mowlana
came to our house. Choosing the winter room for seclusion, he
went inside and did not eat anything at all. . . . He asked that
the doors be closed and the windows covered. He ordered me
to bring several packets of Baghdadi paper. He then began ut-
tering divinely inspired knowledge, and I wrote down whatever
he dictated in Arabic and Persian. I would read aloud whatever
I had recorded, page by page, and set them aside when I was
finished. He then ordered me to light the oven. He took hold of
around one hundred sheets of paper, one page after the other,
and threw them into the oven. . . . When the fire sent up flames
and kindled the pages, he smiled, and said, 'They came from
the invisible world and shall return to the invisible world.' . . . I
wanted to hide a few pages, but he shouted, 'No! No! That's not
correct!'"

The poem survived such treatment, though, and thrived, and

their work of the early 1260s was finally fashioned into a co-
herent first volume of about four thousand lines, with a begin-
ning, middle, and end. Introducing the poem was a traditional
enough Arabic prose preface, replete with Quranic references,
identifying the poet, as Rumi used his first name; giving his
family pedigree, "Mohammad the son of Mohammad the son of
Hosayn from Balkh;" and crediting the inspiration for "this long
work of rhyming couplets" to Hosam, the "Sword," or "*husam*,"
of truth and religion. Less traditional was Rumi's appearing to
make the long poem analogous to the Quran, or at least, as he
wrote, "the unveiler of the Quran," as well as not including the
usual invocation to the Prophet.

After the plangent opening aria of the flute, bemoaning
"love's path, full of pain," a few lines into the first tale concern-
ing the love of the slave girl for the goldsmith of Samarkand,
Rumi halts to share an aside on the creation of the *Masnavi*.
Among the key verses of the *Masnavi* is this dramatized vignette
in which Hosam understandably enough requests that Rumi
speak to him more about his beloved Shams of Tabriz. Like the
royal physician in the tale, Hosam is seeking love's pulse. Rumi,
the "I," in the segment, tells Hosam, the "he," that the truth of
love can only be expressed by metaphor:

> *"It's better the secret of the loved one be disguised," I said,*
>   *"Even if you're telling the story, be sure to cover your ears,*
> *It's better that the lover's secret*
>   *Be told through the tales of other lovers."*
> *He said, "No, tell it openly, and unveiled,*
>   *It's better to reveal than to hide your devotion*
> *Lift the veil and speak nakedly.*
>   *I don't wear clothes when I sleep with my beloved."*
> *I said, "If you were allowed to see the beloved naked,*
>   *You would no longer exist, neither your chest, nor waist.*

Please don't request what you can't endure
   A blade of straw can't endure the weight of a mountain,
If the sun, illuminating our world, came any nearer
   Then everything would be burned and go up in flame
Don't seek to make such trouble, or turmoil, or strife,
   From now on, never ask again about the Sun of Tabriz!"

In the twenty-five thousand verses of the *Masnavi* that follow, the name of Shams is rarely again mentioned, though his presence shimmers throughout. Only when Rumi neared its final sections would he again press harder at revealing in code the true begetter of his poem.

The key term in these verses of rhymed conversation between Rumi and Hosam was "*serr*," or secret, which for Rumi conveniently elided with "*sher*," or poetry. (Which elided further with "*shir*," sweetness, reminding him of the beautiful *Shirin* of Persian love poetry, and so on.) He never bothered to title his poem, known already in his lifetime as the *Masnavi*, or, sometimes, *Masnavi-ye manavi,* or *Spiritual Couplets*. In the heat of composition, he once called the poem *Hosamname* or *The Book of Hosam*. Had the title not already been claimed by Attar, *Asrarmame*, or *The Book of Secrets*, would have fit. For Rumi circled in its accumulating lines around his most cherished secrets—the nature and identity of the beloved, and the borderline between the human and the divine.

Rumi exhaustively played in his *ghazals* on the ambiguity of the Persian pronoun "*u*," which could refer to either "he," "she," "it," or "God." The gender of the beloved was a game built into the language that was occasionally played by Persian poets, but Rumi especially exploited its metaphysical confusions: Were his poems truly to Shams? Or God? Was he praising the natural sun, the human Sun, or the eternal Sun? In the *Masnavi*, which was more of a teaching poem, he engaged in theological issues, but with the same coy gamesmanship. In the *Masnavi*, edgily dubbed "the Quran in the Persian tongue," probably by the Sufi poet Jami two centuries later, Rumi explored the nearness of the human to the prophetic or the divine. Such intimacy seemed especially granted to the lover, or to the poet of love, as Rumi cast himself as the thin reed flute played by Love:

> *You blow into me. I am in love with your breath.*
> *I am your flute! I am your flute! I am your flute!*

The *Masnavi* expanded into a grand book of tales, like much of the literature Rumi had grown up with as a boy in Khorasan. A number of the stories in its first book are set in the locations—either geographical or imaginative—of his childhood. The slave girl has been carried away from her goldsmith of Samarkand, perhaps during the siege of Khwarazmshah. The lion and hare of *Kalile and Demne* appear early on, as the hare tricks a marauding lion into lunging after his own reflection into a deep well. From Attar, Rumi retooled a number of stories, such as the parrot of India who escapes her cage in a greengrocer's shop by playing dead. Unlike the originals, though, these tales are not framed or continuous, but are linked or interrupted by Rumi's musings in a manner closer to the rambling style of a Sufi master adlibbing a mixture of stories and morals.

Other stories came from Rumi's memories of tales told by Shams, not only the secret pulse of the poem but also a source of much of its raw material. If Rumi maintained his closeness with Shams by whirling in *sama*, he did so, as well, by retelling his stories. During his time in Konya, Shams especially liked to tell of a vain gentleman who fussily instructed his barber to pick out all the white hairs from his beard. The barber espied so many white hairs that he snipped off his entire beard and laid out the hairs before his customer, saying, according to Shams, "You pick them out. I have work to do." (In Rumi's version in the *Masnavi*, the moral is the unimportance of theological hairsplitting for lovers of God.) Or his tale about the mouse that took the reins of a camel and started walking, fancying he pulled the beast by his own strength. Rumi used many of these lines and stories, like bits of colored glass or tile, in his complex epic arranged in mosaic form.

After a year or two, Rumi concluded the first volume of the *Masnavi* by reciting to Hosam an incident told of Ali, the nephew and son-in-law of the Prophet Mohammad, who was on the battle-field and about to deliver a death blow to an infidel knight. As Ali lifted his sword, the knight spat in his face. Suddenly Ali, instead of stabbing downward, let his sword drop. Not spun as a parable of nonviolence by Rumi, the incident is a showcase of the mysterious ways of God. Held by Sufis as a model of the mystic saint, like Arjuna on the battlefield in the Bhagavad Gita, Ali sees beyond mere winning or losing to a larger divine pattern:

> *I am a mountain. He is my solid base.*
> *Like straw blown about by the thought of Him.*
> *My desire is stirred only by His wind,*
> *I am ridden by the love of Him alone,*
> *Anger is the ruler of kings, but my slave;*
> *I have tied anger beneath my horse's bit,*
> *I have beheaded anger with the sword of patience*
> *God's anger has been turned within me into kindness*
> *I am plunged in light, though my roof lies in ruin*
> *I am turned into a garden, though I am filled with dust.*

Rumi concludes his first book, perhaps still conceived as the entire work, with the true lover, the lover of God, and emphasizes his essential theme as religious and spiritual. He would eventually quotes or alludes to 528 Quranic verses in thousands of the lines of the epic.

As Rumi was absorbed in the composition of his *Masnavi*, he became clearly aware of the tremendous changes he had undergone in the two decades since his first poems encouraged by Shams of Tabriz. If the beloved were a mirror in which the lover could see his soul, poetry was a mirror, too, in which the poet could glimpse personal reflections. Rumi had matured, and like many poets still creating into their later years, he had advanced from lyrical abandon to a more classical and meditative mode. A measured clarity replaced the earlier divine madness. Rumi recognized, and shared with the audience for the new *Masnavi*, his sense of the loss of his more torturous rapture, his late work framed as the calmer product of his sunset rather than his sunrise years:

When I first began to compose poetry, there was a strong inspiration that caused me to compose. At that time it was very effective. And now, even though this inspiration has weakened and is setting, it still is effective. It is God's way to nurture things while they are rising, and create great effects and much wisdom. Yet even during the setting time that nurture still stands. The noble title *Lord of the East and the West* means that God nourishes both the rising and the setting inspiration.

CHAPTER 13

"A nightingale flew away, then returned"

SOON after Rumi completed the first book of the *Masnavi*, around 1262, revealing his expanded powers as a poet of richly animated spirituality, production came to a sudden halt. Hosam's wife had died, and the young man's response was severe. Like Rumi, Hosam had a single wife, rather than the conventional harem of wives kept by Rumi's father, Baha Valad. Hosam was also a notably devoted husband. From the earliest days of their marriage he would not look at other women, whom he could have married according to Islamic law. And he took care to avoid the bathhouse during the day when he might catch sight of women entering and leaving, instead going at night when only the men bathed.

The death of his wife caused Hosam to plunge into a severe depression, and he exhibited a lack of energy for completing daily tasks. He experienced an inner darkness that led him to withdraw. As Aflaki described his condition, "In his emotions and in his body, he became sluggish and slow. Within himself, every moment he experienced a new mood and a new perplexity so that he could not be engaged with anything else." Rumi later described this hidden phase in his life as leading to Hosam's "spiritual ascension." During the long interruption, the two men neither visited nor spoke with each other.

Equally disruptive, the death occurred in mid-September of the same year as that of Alaoddin, who had been estranged from his father since the disappearance of Shams, nearly fifteen years earlier. Dying young at about the age of thirty-five, Alaoddin had children who were living separately from the *madrase*. He had continued to follow the orthodox path of teacher and preacher, questioning the musical and mystical practices of his father, and embarrassed by the changes wrought upon the family legacy bequeathed by his grandfather. Rumi, in turn, had never forgiven his son for his part in the disappearance of Shams and for joining the insurrection against him. He did not even attend his funeral. As Aflaki recapped the family history, "Having waged war against Mowlana Shams of Tabriz, he hastened to ally himself with the rebellious disciples. It is said that they led him astray and put him up to this. Afterwards, being angry with him, Mowlana cast out of his blessed heart the love he had for him. . . . And during those days after Alaoddin had died, he was not present at his funeral and did not pray over him."

The reported hard feeling for his son, even at the time of his funeral, was harsh and not always accepted as accurate. Some explained Rumi's absence at his son's funeral as extreme grief. Others took the report as propaganda against Alaoddin in a conflict between his descendants and those of Sultan Valad over the family heritage. Indeed many signs pointed to Alaoddin's continued engagement with his family. Sultan Valad wrote two elegies for his brother—if not especially moving quatrains—and he was buried in the family plot, near Baha Valad and Salah. Rumi had written at least three letters to Alaoddin in recent years, addressing him as "my dear son," "light of my eyes," and "pride of professors," pleading in one for him to return home, where he belonged, and to ignore accusations leveled against him. Filial relations were strained but not broken:

Dear pride of professors, and beloved of the pious, accept
greetings from this father, and pray for him. I wish for you
to look into your generous spirit and shut the window of
anger. . . . If someone does not fulfill his duties as a son,
he will never feel peace and his heart will never grow light,
even if he prays and fulfills all his religious duties.

Though their relationship remained tense at the time of his
death, his father eventually came to forgive Alaoddin for his part
in the traumatic events of the decade of the forties. A school-
teacher told of having accompanied Rumi one day to visit the
tomb of Baha Valad: "After he prayed for his father and recited
litanies for him and meditated for quite some time, he asked me
for an inkwell and a pen. When I brought them, he stood up and
went to the tomb of his son Alaoddin, and wrote a couplet on
the whitewashed tomb. . . . Mowlana immediately forgave him
and said, 'I had a vision that my Lord Mowlana Shamsoddin
Tabrizi had made peace with my son and forgave him and inter-
ceded on his behalf so that he became accepted as one of those
pardoned by God.'"

While the conflicts with Alaoddin were resolved for Rumi
after his son's death, the theological issues that had separated
them continued to divide Rumi from other prominent members
of the local community of learned Muslims. Rumi often found
himself at odds with both the pious clerics and other Sufis. Aflaki
described the ceaseless criticism of his practices among the cler-
ics: "At this time people expressed so many complaints and so
much resistance, issued *fatwas* and read out so many chapters
forbidding *sama* and the *rabab* that it would be impossible to
describe in an entire book. He tolerated all of this because of
his extreme kindness, compassion, and generous spirit, and he
said nothing."

In spite of Aflaki's stress on his magnanimous serenity, Rumi was not always impassive about internecine conflicts, especially those involving other Sufis. By the 1260s the religious figures known as "Babas," who often accompanied Turkmen emigrating from Central Asia, had been spending more time in Anatolian cities, attracting large followings and princely patronage. When the Sultan Roknoddin chose one of these popular Babas as his personal spiritual leader, Rumi responded peevishly. He had been invited to a ceremony at the palace in honor of this Baba, but entered with a mere "Salam" and sat alone in a corner. When the sultan announced his oath of fealty, Rumi, in extreme jealousy, shouted, "If the sultan has made him his father, I will take another son." He departed barefoot, without bothering to collect his shoes.

Adding to Rumi's outsider status, even among his protectors, was the rough working-class background of some of his followers. As many often took their job description as part of their title, the names of those relating firsthand stories about Rumi in later accounts was a catalog of the varieties of labor—hat maker, tanner, carpenter, physician, astrologer, butcher, harpist, as well as such religious jobs as Quran reciter and schoolteacher. At a gathering at his home, the Parvane complained to one of his guests, "Khodavandgar is a king without equal . . . but his disciples are an extremely bad and gossiping lot." A supporter of Rumi overheard the remark and reported back to him. Seeing hurt in the faces of some followers, Rumi dispatched a response to the Parvane:

If my disciples were good people, I would myself have become their disciple. It is because they were bad people that I accepted them as disciples, so that they might change into good people and enter the company of those who are good and do good works.

Even Sultan Valad felt moved to comment on the unruly nature of Rumi's growing corps of followers and their difference in demeanor and style from the softer, more restrained, and otherworldly Sufis seen everywhere in those days on the Konya streets. "These Sufis seem very content with each other, and talk without ever arguing," he observed to his father. "But our companions fight with one another, for no reason, and they do not get along together." Rumi answered, "Yes, indeed, Baha-oddin. If a thousand hens are in one house, they will get along together. But two roosters in the same place do not get along. Our companions are like roosters and that is why they raise a ruckus." The decidedly virile virtues Rumi was praising were attributes of the *akhavan* movement, as close in manner to the chivalric knights of Europe as to the Muslim Sufis.

Exhibiting the sublime sensibilities of Sufism more pleasingly, and with fewer rough edges, was the godson of Ibn Arabi, Sadroddin Qonavi, reputed to be so devoted to learning that he rigged a contraption suspending a bag of stones held by a rope above his bed; if he fell asleep studying and lost grip on the rope the stones would fall on him. He was known in Konya by the honorific title of Sheikh al-Islam, making him a sort of archbishop among Sufis, with his well-appointed Sufi lodge more like a grand governor's palace, replete with doormen, eunuchs, and porters. His residence was quite different from the modest, drafty Madrase Khodavandgar, with barely enough food to keep its residents nourished and identifiable by the makeshift cell on its roof where Rumi passed his solitary nights.

Qonavi was drawn to systematic mystical thought and gave much-appreciated lessons to the Parvane as they spun abstruse webs of theory together, while Rumi followed the practical path of love, dispensing with the Damascene knowledge of his youth. Tensions could exist between them. Qonavi did not like Rumi at first, and one of Rumi's admirers voiced offense at Qonavi's aristocratic airs, saying he felt as if he were visiting the house of a ruler rather than a man of poverty. Yet Rumi advised the Parvane to give a stipend to Qonavi, as he had so many more students to feed in his kitchen. Eventually a quiet respect grew between them, and on at least one occasion Rumi and Qonavi were seen quietly meditating together, their prayer rugs facing, knees touching. When a student approached during this session to ask Rumi "What is poverty?" he would not answer—his point being that silence itself was a kind of poverty.

Rumi's sincerity, coupled with the entrancing spell of his evolving poetry and the infectiousness of his message of love, granted him freedom from the rules that another might not so easily have been given. At one point the Parvane was considering appointing the son of the vizier Tajoddin as *qadi,* or chief judge of Konya. The young man was learned in religious law but impervious to the charms of Sufism, especially those of the least manageable of Sufis, Rumi. He agreed to accept the post on three conditions: the outlawing of the *rabab*; removal of corrupt bailiffs from the court; and paying bailiffs a stipend so they would not accept bribes. The Parvane accepted the last two conditions, but not the first, knowing its repercussions for Rumi. When word reached Rumi, he said, "Such a blessing, *rabab*! And praise God that the *rabab* also saved the son of Tajoddin from the trap of being a judge!"

The presiding *qadi* during most of Rumi's mature years, and so the most influential in his legal fate, which was always somewhat in jeopardy, was Serajoddin Ormovi, imported to Konya by the Seljuks in 1257, and lasting through all the shifts in imperial administration, mostly because of the support of the Parvane. A Persian speaker, born in Azerbaijan, Serajoddin was already sixty years old when he settled in Konya, after having lived in Mosul, Damascus, and Egypt as part of the civilian elite. A philosopher-theologian of the rationalist school, equally at home in the court or the *madrase,* he was particularly suited to the Seljuk post, as he spoke Arabic, Persian, and Turkish, and was familiar with Jewish and Christian scriptures as well as Islamic legal tomes and studies.

As a meticulously trained logician versed in analysis, Serajoddin was not by nature sympathetic with *sama* and some of the more illogical practices of the visionary mystics. He and Rumi held predictably opposite positions on many issues. Given the seat of honor at most public ceremonies, he embodied for Rumi the hypocrisy of rank and position, and Rumi judged him handicapped by his reliance on the finer points of logic. When Hosam asked Rumi his opinion of Serajoddin, he answered, "He is a good man. But he circles about the watering hole. He just needs one kick to reach it." As with Qonavi, though, Rumi gradually developed a respectful friendship with Serajoddin.

As chief judge, Serajoddin often needed to rule on issues involving Rumi. In one instance, Rumi wrote to him to intervene to insure that the children of Alaoddin not be deprived of their rightful inheritance. Another time, Theryanus, the Greek convert saved by Rumi from execution, was brought before the judge and charged with going about town proclaiming that Rumi was God—which was obviously not encouraged in Islam. Questioned by the *qadi,* he answered, "No, I said he is a God-builder. Don't you see how he has remade me into a knower of God?" Case dismissed, he reported the proceedings to Rumi, who smiled and replied, "You should have said, 'Shame on you, if *you* don't become God!'"

The crucial rulings of Serajoddin concerned *sama,* an issue of spiritual life and death for Rumi, who had by then given up on traditional instruction in favor of teaching with insights gained with the help of such tavern pastimes as music, song, and poetry. At least once, formal charges were brought against Rumi by a group of the religious scholars in Konya, their pressing for a legal ruling reminding the *qadi* of the radical nature of Rumi's liberated life and teachings. "Why must this kind of innovation advance and this practice be promoted?" they demanded. The answer of the *qadi* focused on the person of Rumi, not on any theological principle: "This heroic man is strengthened by God and is without peer in learning. You should not quarrel with him. He is the one who knows, as does his God."

❖

After two years, in June of 1264, Hosam finally recovered from his protracted mourning and depression. He had been feeling the predictable wish to marry again, and was searching for a wife. He awoke one summer morning, though, pining again for the spiritual life, and also for the poem-in-couplets that he had abandoned in his sorrow. As suddenly as he had been overcome by lassitude, Hosam felt its release and went straightway to the *madrase* to propose starting up again just where he and Rumi had left off, "requesting the remainder of the *Masnavi* from the luminous heart of the Sheikh."

Rumi assessed Hosam as having matured and was thrilled by his return. Wasting no time, he dictated a new prologue for him to write down, on the spot, starting again at the beginning— this time of Book II—with a date and gloss explaining the interruption:

> *The light of God, Hosamoddin,*
> > *Pulled back the reins at the summit of heaven*
> *During his ascension, while seeking for the truth,*
> > *Without his springtime, buds would not bloom*
> *When he returned from the ocean to the shore*
> > *The harp strings of the* Masnavi *were retuned*

This Masnavi *has burnished every soul*
    His return was a day of beginning again
    The date of the renewal of this great gift
    In the year six hundred sixty-two
A nightingale flew away, then returned
    As a falcon, hunting for mystical truths.

Mystic and scribe fell quickly back into their old way of working, with Hosam revising and adding vowel signs. As Aflaki confirmed, "There was no further delay up to the end of the book. Mowlana continually recited in unbroken succession and Hosamoddin wrote it down and repeatedly read out loud what he had written until the work was completed."

His harp strings retuned, Rumi also realized a wish he had been harboring for some time—making Hosam the sheikh of his unofficial order. For the third time, Rumi elevated a chosen companion into a position of esteem, a position he himself might more naturally have held. The maneuver was loving and passionate, a reflection of the feelings in his heart, but also savvy, as he again put a barrier between himself and his followers, allowing more space for mystical abstraction and his own rapt devotion to prayer and dance. The difference between Hosam and the others was that he was accepted by most of Rumi's students without as much conflict. Hosam was now forty years old—a respectable age for a religious leader—and had been espousing Rumi to his band of young men for years, attracting resources and a more diverse group of followers.

Passed over again, of course, was Sultan Valad, who described the transition without any evident slighted feelings, telescoping six years into a single poetic frame: "When Salahoddin left this world, Sheikh said, Hosam, the Way of Truth, you are the successor and caliph. The Sheikh seated him in place of Salahoddin and scattered light above his head. He asked all the followers to bow to him, and be humble before him, and obey all his commands with all their heart, and plant his love within their souls." The exception in this smooth transfer of power was Sultan Valad's wife, Fateme. She kept alive the jealousy and suspicion of her father, Salah, toward Hosam, resenting that her husband had not ascended to the position of leadership she felt belonged to him.

Rumi's worship of his appointed beloved was always a challenge for the community. Shams had presented special difficulties because of his irascible temper and eccentricity. Salah, as a practically illiterate teacher, confounded every expectation of a school or Sufi lodge. Hosam was well liked and a natural leader since adolescence, but the social reversal was of an older man humbling himself before a younger man. Yet humble himself Rumi flagrantly did. Once when a group was setting out for a ceremony at a Sufi lodge, Rumi took Hosam's prayer rug from the shoulder of a follower and carried it on his own shoulder, walking the entire way through the center of town. Shopkeepers and passersby recognized the gesture as proper for a well-behaved servant.

As with Shams and Salah, Rumi pushed his devotion to friendship to extravagant lengths. On one occasion, the Parvane held a gathering of ministers and prominent men at his home and invited Rumi, hoping for him to entertain in a spiritual key with choice words and perhaps bursts of lyric poetry and ecstatic dance. Noticing that Rumi was sullen and silent, the Parvane realized that he had not invited Hosam and sent for him. As soon as he arrived, being led in with a torch, Rumi jumped down from his rug on the dais to join him in the palace courtyard, exuberantly greeting him, "Welcome my soul, my faith, my light!" Aware of the Parvane, who was suspicious of the exaggerated compliments, Hosam explained, "Even if not true, once Mowlana says so, it is like this and a hundred times more!"

Hosam understood—as had Salah, in his sense of mirroring—
that the intensity of Rumi's adoration could inspire the recipient
to rise to the challenge.

Most of the more relaxing periods of visiting between Rumi
and Hosam, especially during the warmer months, were passed
in Meram, where Hosam owned a garden. Every year during the
later decades of his life, Rumi spent forty days each summer at
the hot springs of Ilgin, reached by wagon, about sixty miles
northwest of Konya. He would teach his students at twilight next
to a frog pond. Otherwise he often stayed with Hosam in Meram,
a settlement where gardens and orchards were cultivated, just a
carriage or mule's ride from Konya. Here he would picnic with
friends and enjoy listening to the splashing of its many water-
wheels. Running water was believed to calm the spirit, and was
used to treat the mentally ill in an Anatolian hospital built in
Rumi's lifetime in Divrigi, outfitted with watercourses empty-
ing into basins. Yet watermills throughout the Middle East also
made loud creaking noises. In their endless turning, and plain-
tive screaks, Rumi imagined lovers pining for each other, and
for reunion with God:

> Lovers are like waterwheels turning day and night
> Restlessly revolving, endlessly moaning,
> The turning of the wheel teaches those who seek the river.
> No one may say to them this river is ever still.

Many fond memories by followers of Rumi date from these re-
treats in Meram, as he was otherwise mostly secluded in Konya.
One told of the time a group of travelers from Bukhara sought
Rumi in Hosam's garden, and a close woman friend, who often
stayed up late into the night talking with him, brought out a tray
of homemade desserts. "If you asked for the banquet table of
Jesus it would have descended for you in this house," said Rumi,

referring to a story of Jesus feeding the hungry with food from heaven. (This woman "kept constant company" with another follower of Rumi's, who also held *sama* sessions locally in her home.) Especially coveted by Rumi's extended family of wife and children from two marriages, as well as Salah's widow and children, was the white honey from Hosam's garden, which was used in medical potions. Rumi felt comfortable in Meram, and whenever he went missing, which happened frequently, he could most reliably be discovered praying alone in the Meram mosque.

During all the seasons of the year, though, whether in Konya or Meram, Rumi and Hosam kept up their unflagging work on the poem, which Rumi was imagining might grow so lengthy as to need to be carried by forty mules. Rumi paused every so often in the poem to exult in Hosam. Midway through Book II, he stopped to duly credit him:

> *Come light of God, Hosamoddin,*
> *Without you no plants grow in this dry soil*

Hosam could be just as extravagant in his praise of the importance of the poet and his poem to which they were both committed. More than once, he reported having a dream in which the Prophet Mohammad was reading the *Masnavi* with great interest and approval.

The writing of the *Masnavi* was not solely a production undertaken by Rumi and Hosam in privacy—though it was often so. Rumi also composed with listeners gathered, as oral performance was an important quality of its rhythmic power. Unlike *sama* gatherings, these sessions required absolute silence, as the teasing out of meanings from fables, and their weaving, was a delicate procedure. Implied in the poem were hints of occasions when witnesses fell asleep, while the creation evolved within the deep silence of the insulating stone pillars and heavy roof of the main hall. Rumi was anxious to make sure that these recitations were not seen as mere entertainment. He discounted himself as a poet to his followers—a bit disingenuously, given his skill and lifetime love of poetry:

> When friends come to visit me, I am worried that they will be bored, so I recite poetry. Otherwise why would I have anything to do with poetry? I am vexed by poetry. There is nothing worse for me. I do poetry the way someone puts his hand into tripe to wash for guests because they have an appetite for it. That is why I must do so. A man has to look at the town where he is living to see what goods the people need and what kind of goods they wish to buy. People will then buy such goods even if they happen to be of the lowest quality.

Casting himself as a humble merchant, peddling second-rate wares, Rumi also spoke of the disparagement of the art of poetry by religious long beards in his native Khorasan, which may have been true in orthodox circles, but certainly not in the highly poetic culture generally, or by his father, who often quoted Sanai and other poets:

> What am I to do? In our country and among our people there was nothing more disgraceful than being a poet. If I had remained in our native land, and wished to live in harmony with their tastes, I would have done only what was desired of me, such as teaching, writing books, preaching, fasting and performing pious deeds.

Even if a reluctant poet—and a self-deprecating one—Rumi either took exacting pains with the structure of the *Masnavi*, or a lifetime of rigorous intellectual activity manifested itself spontaneously. The second book matched the structure of the first book, and both set the template for the books to come. At about 3,800 lines, the second volume is almost the same length as the first. Both contain about a dozen core stories, which are broken up by digressions and expostulations, and are fed into by less complex anecdotes. The sections are also introduced by rubrics, *Kalile and Demne*–style, probably inserted by Rumi or other scribes later, such as "How a king tested two slaves he had just purchased."

While neither book settled into a single succinct theme, Book I conformed loosely to the Sufi genre of a pilgrim's progress, where a soul progresses from the pain of separation from God, like the mournful reed flute, longing for reunion, to the divine illumination experienced by Ali. The stories of the second book center more on the split between appearance and reality, with the spiritually undiscerning always mistaking surface for essence, and so succumbing to painful or deadly moral errors: a Sufi leaves his cherished donkey with a servant who swears he needs no instruction in caring for the animal, which nearly dies of neglect; a king entrusts his falcon with an old woman who clips its claws to try to domesticate the royal bird. Most darkly comic, was the tale of the man who befriends a bear that winds up swatting a fly on his friend's face with a giant boulder:

> *A fool believes the love of the bear is true*
> *Yet his love is anger, and anger is his love*

The lesson of the tale of the bear was care in choosing a friend whose spiritual insight was compatible, an important lesson for Sufis selecting their companions along the way.

Following through on his promise in the first book, Rumi included private memories of Shams, all of them camouflaged, and known to him alone, or to a few intimate disciples such as Hosam, who had been present for the original talks of the stranger from Tabriz. Only once does he make any kind of direct reference to Shams:

> *From love of Shams, I have grown weak*
> > *Or else I would give sight to the blind*
> *Light of the Truth, Hosamoddin*
> > *Quickly heal them, and make the envious blind.*

Yet the penultimate set piece of Book II, "The story about the ducklings raised by a hen," is stocked with memories of Shams. During his time in Konya, Shams often spoke about his adolescence as a misunderstood mystic with this analogy: he felt he was a duckling raised by a hen. As he said, "Now father, I see that the ocean is my homeland. If you are of me, or I am of you, come into the ocean. If not, go back to your hens." Rumi universalized Shams's experience, as shared by all landlocked mystics:

> *You are the child of a duck, even if a hen*
> > *Held you beneath her wing, and raised you*
> *Your real mother belongs to the ocean . . .*
> > *We are all seabirds. Only the ocean knows our language.*

As a seabird himself, Rumi's instinct was to soar, and his reflex in these books was to conclude with a lyric crescendo. In the first book, the epic hero was revealed to be Ali on the battlefield. In the second, following a catalog of ascending birds—falcons, nightingales, parrots, and peacocks—Rumi introduces his hero, an ascetic in the desert. Rumi classified the *Masnavi* as a "Shop of Unity," and his ascetic, or mystic, lives beyond the differences that confused seekers in earlier stories, as he prays in a terrain without variation. Rumi had envisioned his solitary desert mystic in a separate *robai*:

> *Beyond belief and doubt is a vast desert*
> *In the middle of this desert, we find ecstasy*
> *When a mystic arrives here, he bows to the ground.*

At the climax of the spiritual tale, a group of pilgrims, doubtless on the way to Mecca, pass by the mystic. Though the land is parched and dry, the mysterious, lone figure turns to them from his prayers, dripping with water from hands and face, his clothes damp. A perplexed pilgrim asks for an explanation, so the saint prays to Him who "opened the door to me from above" to reveal the nature of the place. Rumi at his most visionary then describes a shower of bountiful rain, the rain of love he felt was assured and was to become an even more effusive and unorthodox theme as the poem went on:

> *As he was praying, a beautiful cloud appeared*
> > *Like an elephant, spraying water from its trunk.*
> *Suddenly a shower began pouring down*
> > *And settled in the ditches and the caves.*
> *While the cloud kept pouring rain, like tears,*
> > *The pilgrims turned their faces to the sky.*

CHAPTER 14

The Religion of Love

RUMI was living in a society of conventions, where the decades of life were assigned set significances—maturity was believed to arrive at age forty, which he respected when he waited to appoint Hosam to a leadership role, while sixty marked a graduation to the age of sagacity, the proper time for the consideration of last things. Almost immediately on completion of Book II, around 1266, Rumi and Hosam began work on Book III, which was finished in 1268, as Rumi was moving into his sixties, his own final decade. He was seizing on this ripe moment to express his increasingly radical and personal wisdom in as liberated, joyful, confident, and even reckless a manner as ever.

Rumi described his *Masnavi* as a "box of secrets." With each installment of the expanding poem-in-progress, he was allowing the box to become further ajar, its contents more clearly and unapologetically exposed. By the late 1260s the *Masnavi* had become a public attraction and, like much about Rumi in Konya, a generator of debate. The orthodox were shocked by some of its theology, while even more sniping for its storytelling came from the intellectual Sufis in the lodge of Qonavi. Rumi described one such slur:

Suddenly a fool, from out the stable,
  Poked his head, like a sarcastic old woman,
Saying, "This Masnavi *is cheap and low*
  Just stories of the Prophet, on how to follow,
No mention of the loftier secrets of divinity,
  Which cause the steeds of saints to gallop,
Or of the many stations of renunciation
  Stage by stage up to union with God."

The poet's brash defense was to compare his inspired verses to the holy Quran:

When the Quran came down
  Disbelievers were just as sarcastic and mean,
Saying, "These are just legends and myths,
  Without any depth or lofty speculation
Something little children can understand
  Nothing but lessons about right and wrong.
The story of Joseph and his long, curly hair
  The story of Jacob, the passion of Zolaykha
It is simple and plain, and everyone understands
  Where is the exposition in which intellect gets lost?"
God answered, "If this seems so simple to you,
  Try composing a single chapter in the same style.
Let the spirits of heaven and the men of earth
  Try writing a single verse in this 'plain' style."

Many were protective of Rumi, and tried their best to keep him from straying too far into dangerous territory and to shield him from the most serious charges of innovation in religious matters. Rumi did little to bolster their helpful cause. Once a companion informed Rumi that when interrogated by a suspicious religious scholar, "Why do they call the *Masnavi* the Quran?" he had corrected him. "It is a commentary on the Quran." Sultan Valad recalled, "My father remained quiet for a moment and then exclaimed:

> "You dog! Why is it not the Quran? You ass! Why is it not the Quran? You brother of a whore! Why is it not the Quran? Truly contained in the words of the Prophets and the Friends of God are nothing but lights of divine secrets. The speech of God has sprung up from their pure hearts and has flowed forth upon the stream of their tongues. Whether it is Syriac or the Fateha prayer of the Quran, whether in Hebrew or in Arabic."

He grew convinced that all divinely inspired speech, including the poetry of the *Masnavi*, in whatever language or format, was equal, whether from the living or the dead.

At the outpost of such skirmishes with tradition was Mansur al-Hallaj, executed in Baghdad for his heretical pronouncements, the most famous being "I am Truth." In these later years, Rumi adopted Hallaj as a personal saint and his infamous self-blessing as a favorite inspiration for teaching. Defending the Sufi's possibly apocryphal statement, Rumi grappled with his own experience. He explained Hallaj's paradox to students:

> People think that to say "I am Truth" is a claim of greatness, but it is actually extreme humility. Anyone who says, "I am God's servant" is really claiming two existences, his own and God's, while the one who says, "I am Truth" erases himself and gives up his own existence as nothing. When he says "I am Truth," he means, "I do not exist. Everything is He. God alone exists. I am utter, pure oblivion. I am nothing." There is more humility in this than any claim to greatness.

He spoke approvingly of the remark, on another occasion, inviting its embrace by others:

> Everyone who exhibits some form of perfection and beauty, whether through actions or words, and has pride and grace, may actually claim, according to their own state and condition, "I am Truth"!

The figure of Hallaj and his pronouncement "I am Truth" haunt the last few books of the *Masnavi*, like a faint clue to a mystery, or a motto for any knowing mystic:

> *When Hallaj said, "I am Truth," and kept on*
> *He throttled the necks of the blind*
> *When the "I" vanishes from our existence*
> *What remains? Consider this thought.*

Nothing was more rousing to Rumi both as mystic and poet than the contemplation of annihilation and the erasure of self and all the mundane details of life, including the need for speech and language. He wished to whirl them away. This ecstatic freedom was embodied in Hallaj, and many of Rumi's more exquisite *robai* quatrains, which he was writing late in life, evoke him:

> *He dove into the sea of his own oblivion*
> *Then pierced the pearl of "I am Truth"*

As an early Arabic Sufi poet—Rumi often retold Hallaj's parable of the moth drawn by a passionate love for a flame—Hallaj could be found subtly mixed with imagery of books:

> *I am the servant of those who know themselves*
> *Who free their hearts from error at each moment*

Composing a book from their own essence and traits
And making the title of that book, "I am Truth."

Like Hallaj's fluttering moth, Rumi circled the flame of truths that were inexpressible, or only expressed at great cost or danger of being misunderstood. Yet by the time he arrived at writing the third book of the *Masnavi,* and in talks written down by scribes, he was more baldly and directly stating his challenging secrets. He clearly felt that divine inspiration was universal and reflected in the mirror of the hearts of living saints, and he implied that he had experienced just such immolation in the divine spirit of love. Modeled on the story of the composition of the Quran by Mohammad, Rumi recited his *Masnavi* in an inspired state and imagined he was a mere instrument like a reed flute:

Be empty! Sing like a flute, full of passion.
Be empty! Tell secrets with your pen.

Rumi and Shams first discussed such matters while they were in seclusion, and the force of these revelations had changed his life remarkably. Yet Shams was even more adamant about "following" the Prophet Mohammad, and he strongly rejected Hallaj and his involuntary shout "I am Truth!" In his embrace of Hallaj, Rumi appeared to have gone beyond even Shams in the radicalism of his ideas about God and man. He no longer stood in anyone's shadow, having fully realized his own voice. Although he stayed faithful to Sunni practice, and the *Masnavi* is filled with Muslim piety, the logic of a religion of the heart led him beyond denominations and religions to a universal vision:

The mosque inside the hearts of holy men
Is a place of worship for everyone. God is there.

He sang of a "religion of love," and a "religion for lovers," and its daring implications:

The religion of love is beyond all faiths,
The only religion for lovers is God

In Book III of the *Masnavi* he put this creed as simply and unambiguously as possible:

Since we worship the one God,
Then all religions must be one

❖

While celebrating love and his religion of lovers with such exuberance and freedom, Rumi, though, was beginning to show signs of physical aging, and to share hints of his sense of the divergence of his stiffening body from his timeless heart, mind, and soul. As he wrote in Book III of the *Masnavi*, "My heart is a field of tulips that can't be touched by age." Other parts were more susceptible. Rumi had put his body through punitive trials of fasting and deprivation, and pushed himself with damaging nightly sessions of spontaneous composition and prayer. Of all the memories so carefully collected of his life from his disciples, none ever recalled seeing him asleep in his bed at night during these decades of his life. For the era, he was reaching life expectancy.

In a surprising aside in Book II of the *Masnavi*, Rumi had even departed from his usual invective against worldly pleasures and the lures of the senses. He mused on the strengths of bygone youth, when springtime was flourishing, and life was a rose garden in full bloom:

Youth is a garden, fresh and green
Easily yielding leaves and fresh fruit
Fountains of strength and passion flow
Making green the soil of the body
A well-built house with a high ceiling
Its columns straight and tall and standing free.

The ensuing caricature of old age as the head of a horse being forced into a halter was harrowing by contrast, as he listed the loss of moral strength as one of its infirmities:

The eyebrows droop and are almost white
The eyes dim, and wet with tears
The face wrinkled, like a lizard's back
Speech is gone, as are teeth and taste
The day late, the path long, the mule limping
The shop in ruins, the business failing
The roots of bad habits having taken firm hold
And now the strength to dig them up lost.

Rumi was hardly as bowed by age as the decrepit figure of his meditation on the stages of man, yet he was marked with the lines and strains of a life lived forcefully at a steady pitch of intensity even if its main activities were composition, prayer, and meditation. He might well have thought of his teacher Borhan, who grew more carefree and joyful in his daily life at about the same time his body began to lose its former powers of endurance. Unlike Borhan, Rumi never relaxed his regimen of fasting and daily prayer, though he did relax the constraints of conventionally pious thinking and dogma to the extreme. With his gait of an elder combined with almost juvenile unchecked energy, no one in Konya was remotely like peripatetic Rumi.

The final decade of his life also marked the final decade of

Konya maintaining even a pretense of independence as the capital of a Seljuk Empire. Its most compelling spiritual figure, Rumi, felt unfettered enough to trust in a steady light at the heart of events as civilizations collapsed and maps were redrawn, while his counterpart in the political world—the Parvane—lived with increasingly complex problems and acted with greater desperation. A respite from the Mongol threat was promised by their first defeat—by the Egpytians at the battle of Ayn Jalut in Syria in 1260—shifting the Muslim power base from Baghdad to Cairo. Yet for the Parvane, machinations became more elaborate, as he engaged in a perilous game of playing the Egyptian Mamluks against the Mongols.

Internal politics in Konya were just as brutal. With power came paranoia for the Parvane. He grew convinced that the Sultan Roknoddin, who had been given of late to childishly imprudent language and stormy behavior, was plotting against him. So the Parvane took the proactive measure of having Roknoddin murdered at a banquet, in 1265, and in his place put Roknoddin's son Kaykhosrow III, less than seven years old and obviously not a threat. Taking no chances, the Parvane then set himself up as the boy's tutor and regent. Among those the Parvane termed Rumi's "gossiping" followers was talk of Roknoddin's fall as divine retribution for his having spurned Rumi in favor of the more rural Turkish Babas.

As distracted as Rumi might appear, he was still engaged with his family, and still shrewdly maintained an air of studied indifference toward political intrigues at court and in the Sufi lodges. In his family life, a rare incidence of Rumi becoming angry with his wife was provoked around this time by her interest in a group of flamboyant silk-clad traveling Sufi dervishes attracting great attention in Konya for walking on hot coals, swallowing snakes, sweating blood, bathing in boiling oil, whipping themselves, and making animal noises. They were members of the Refaiyya

Order, known as far as Europe as "the howling dervishes" for
their wild and loud *sama* performances. While Rumi was away
in Meram on a day trip, a group of noble ladies came to Kerra
to convince her to go with them to Karatay Madrase, where the
dervishes were performing their circus magic. When Rumi re-
turned that evening he was livid with her for attending a session
of this troupe, though even Afalki reported that his upset arose
"out of jealous anger."

At most times, though, Rumi's manner with his wife was
tender and bemused, the testing of the Shams years replaced
with mellow companionship. Kerra remained superstitious.
When he traveled to Ilgin in the summer, she worried that he
might fall prey to the water monster believed to live under a
bridge near a meadow he enjoyed. "How wonderful," Rumi
joked. "I have wanted to meet the lord of this river for years." As
her husband grew more impractical, Kerra became increasingly
protective. When Rumi went to the bathhouse, she told his com-
panions, "Take care of Mowlana because he pays no attention
to himself at all." They toted a rug and towel to spread for him
in the cooling chamber. Whatever light eating and sleeping he
managed was due to her insistence.

All of Rumi's children were now grown and pursuing adult
lives. Sultan Valad was closest, as he remained at Rumi's side.
His great disappointment was his wife's lack of children, while
Rumi also remained hopeful for grandchildren from the line
of Salah. Maleke, the daughter of Rumi and Kerra, was still
married to the miserly Konya businessman who had been en-
during a losing streak in his petty trading deals in Sivas. Rumi
tried to help his son-in-law by writing to the Parvane to request
his exemption from the high road tolls and taxes along the
way. Their son Mozaffar worked in the sultan's treasury and
government service until—to Rumi's great joy—he decided to
don the cloak of the Sufis.

Rumi's main focus remained Hosam, who was not only leading the community and transcribing Rumi's poetry and correspondence but also staying active in the spiritual politics of the wider Sufi community in Konya, one of the most vibrant at the time in the Muslim world. When the sheikh of another Sufi lodge died, Hosam took over leadership of that community after a letter-writing campaign on his behalf by Rumi, overriding objections by rivals. At an inauguration, after the issuing of a royal decree, violence broke out because of continued opposition, and knives were drawn. "Why do these men with donkey tails show such ingratitude for God's blessings?" asked Rumi on his way out. Hosam eventually went on to be in charge of yet a third such lodge in Konya.

A technicality more important to Hosam than to Rumi was his affiliation, like Shams of Tabriz, with the Shafii School of jurisprudence, as opposed to the Hanafi tradition. In Sufi practice, a master and his disciple were always of the same school. Hosam lowered his head and said, "I wish from this day to belong to the Hanafi School, as Khodavandgar is a follower of the Hanafi School." Rumi was absorbed by then in his religion of love and the mosque of the heart and had little interest in such divisive legal issues. "No, no!" he answered. "What is proper is that you remain in your school, and follow it, but that you travel our mystic path, and guide people on our road of love."

The gatherings for Rumi's talks, transcribed under the supervision of Hosam, were continuing, though they often evolved into discussion groups or question-and-answer sessions regarding the burgeoning *Masnavi* as the poem was being circulated. On one occasion, a student asked for an explanation of a few of its more perplexing lines:

> *Oh brother, you are nothing but your thoughts*
> *The rest of you is merely skin and bones*

If your thought is a rose, you are a rose garden
If your thought is a thorn, you are fuel for the fire.

Rumi explained that what is seen or heard is secondary to the more essential force of thought, which is the invisible creator of words and actions, like the sun in the sky:

Although the sun in the sky is constantly shining, it is not visible unless its rays strike a wall. Similarly, if there is no medium of words and sound, the rays of the sun of speech cannot be seen.

In these talks, Rumi explored the practical relevance for the lives of those who were drawn to him and his increasingly unorthodox *madrase* of the "religion of lovers":

People work variously at all sorts of jobs, crafts, and professions, and they study astrology and medicine, and so forth, but they are not at peace because they have not found what they are seeking. The beloved is called *delaram,* or "he who gives the heart repose," because the heart finds peace through the beloved. How then can it find peace through anything else? All these other joys and goals are like a ladder. The rungs on the ladder are not places to rest but for passing along.

In a surprising departure from the enlightened and ethereal tone of many of his remarks, Rumi announced one evening that he had been weighing in on current political difficulties with the Parvane, lecturing him on his appeasement of the Mongols rather than allying himself with the Muslim Mamluks of Egypt. He had obviously not lost his alertness to politics nor to the side of himself capable of being engaged and partisan:

All this I said to the Parvane, I told him, "You have united yourself with the Tatar, whom you aid to annihilate the Syrians and Egyptians and so to lay waste the realm of Islam. What was supposed to be a cause for the expansion of Islam has become the cause for its diminishment. In this state, which is a fearful one, turn to God. Give alms to the poor so that He may deliver you from this evil condition, which is simply fear."

He reserved special anger for students he felt were too prone to falling under the spell of the Parvane and his sumptuous lifestyle. Especially irritating was a group sent on a mission to Kayseri, who returned talking about the delicacies and tasty dishes they sampled at the imperial table. Cuttingly, Rumi said, "Shame on the companions for their exaggerated praise of the stuff of the table, and for being proud and saying, 'We ate such and such.' You who beheld fine fat foods, get up to look at what is leftover in the toilet."

The aging sage appeared most often in a delighted state and was refreshingly otherworldly in sightings around town. One day as he was walking in the bazaar, a Turk was offering a fox skin for sale to the highest bidder, calling out, in Turkish, "*Delku, delku,*" meaning "fox." Rumi held his heart, and whirled, repeating, in Persian, "*Del ku? Del ku?*" meaning, "Where is the heart?" When a Turkish jurist presented him with a list of abstruse legal questions while he was sitting alongside a moat next to the Sultan Gate, reading a book, he called for a pen and inkwell and dashed off exemplary answers without consulting any authorities. He also liked leaving messages on public spaces. As he had once written on his son's tomb and Shams's door, he ordered verses that he first composed in ink on paper to be inscribed on the gate of the little garden of the *madrase.*

Kindness continued to stand out as a virtue for him, as was

borne out by many testimonials. When a Christian, drunk on wine, wandered into a *sama* session, accidentally bumping into Rumi, some of his followers shoved the man. "He is the one who drank wine," Rumi berated them, "but you are the ones behaving like drunken brawlers." Preventing his companions from clearing a bathhouse pool of lepers and the sick, Rumi quickly took off his clothes, entered the water, and pourd the water they were using over his head. When a thief stole his prayer rug, he sent someone to buy it back from him at the bazaar to spare him embarrassment. Animals continued to be beneficiaries of his kindness, such as the ox some butchers bought intending to slaughter that he convinced them to set free, or a wild dog he saved from a beating on Hosam's street.

While not overly careful in guarding his own health—other than relying on a favorite drink, julep of sorrel—Rumi had begun to add to his reputation, too, an instinct for natural healing. When a favorite disciple had a high fever, which the doctors could not treat, Rumi pounded garlic cloves into a mortar and mixed the paste with the man's food, causing him to break into a sweat and recover. For a pupil complaining of falling asleep too often, Rumi successfully advised, "Extract the milk of poppies and drink it." During one of his summer retreats in Ilgin, a disciple became grievously ill. Rumi ordered him lifted in his bedding and brought to the bathhouse, where he immersed him in the central spring water pool and dunked him repeatedly until he revived. The method worked, though, according to Aflaki, "No clever doctor ever used this strange form of treatment."

❖

Rumi and Hosam were proceeding at a steady and energetic pace through the composition of the books of the *Masnavi*, with about two or three years separating the creation of Books III, IV, and V, near the turn of the decade of the 1270s. Much of Rumi's spiritual life since Shams's departure decades earlier had circled about his beloved friend's final lessons to him on the meaning of separation, which was the mystery at the heart of their friendship, as well as, explained Shams, central to the experience of love, both human and divine. Rising and falling in these later books was a meditation on death as the ultimate separation, the root of so much pain.

In Book III of the *Masnavi*, Rumi had not only identified himself as the unabashed preacher of love—as he wrote in one ghazal, "At the Festival of Unity, the Preacher of Love arrives." He also turned to considering death as fully as love, if not as a form of love, as he moved closer to the horizon of his own life. Yet he was not composing in the violet mode of sad elegy—the somber hymns of the blue-winged angels in his weeping poems on the death of Shams or Salah. Instead his message was the joy and release of death. Fear of death was nothing but a reflection in the mirror of passing thoughts:

> *You flee from death because you are afraid*
> *But truly you fear yourself. Consider this!*
> *Your own face is frightening, not the face of death*
> *Death is a leaf, but your soul is the tree*
> *Every leaf grows from you, both good and bad*
> *Every hidden thought, both pleasant and ugly.*

The tenor of much of Rumi's poetry in the *Masnavi* is cheerful and transcendent. The conviction behind this sensibility depended on his belief in the shifting qualities of the world, so that thoughts were not taken as fixed or unchanging. Soul or spirit or even attitude could recast or illuminate the perception of all experiences. As far as the psychology of approaching

death, Rumi almost reflexively counseled its embrace rather
than its fear—advice, given the timing, for himself as much as
anyone. He chose to see the "limping" physical demands of his
own aging as the fermentation of eternal love:

> God created me from the wine of love,
>   I'm still that love, even as death wears me down

As a mystic, Rumi had a more powerful and compelling in-
centive for dwelling on death in the final books of the *Masnavi*.
He lived according to the belief that not only was the invisible
world more real than the visible, but also that life after death
was a release into a cosmic experience of infinitely greater light
and love than experienced in the body. In the third book of the
Masnavi, Rumi sings of death as a release, in one homespun
simile after another. Life was like a steam bath you needed to
exit for the sake of your heart, or like wearing tight shoes in the
desert, or a confining womb after nine months had passed:

> Squeezed in the womb like a baby
>   I am eager to move on, after nine months,
> If my mother were feeling no labor pains
>   I might be left in this burning jail
> But the pains of death are telling her
>   The time has come for the lamb to be born
> So that he may graze in lush, green fields
>   Open wide the womb, the lamb is ready!

In a weirdly hypnagogic tale of a mosque where anyone
who spent the night would die and of the lover who insisted
on spending the night there, Rumi identified with the death-
radiant lover, bragging of his recklessness in facing his own
certain extinction:

He said, "My friends, with no regrets,
I have grown weary of life in this world
I'm a wanderer, seeking only pain and wounds,
Don't expect sense from this wanderer on the road
I'm not a wanderer seeking my next meal
I'm a reckless wanderer, seeking death
I'm not a wanderer seeking to make money
But a nimble wanderer seeking to cross the bridge
Not to be found hanging around in shops and markets
But rather running away from my own existence."

The tale of the lover in the mosque of death in Book III was interrupted—or illustrated—by a companion tale of a caged bird in a rose garden, visited by a flock of birds singing of their freedom on the wing, a message that causes the bird to lose its satisfaction with its gilded prison and to desire escape. Yet the bird stops itself from squeezing through its bars by the sudden appearance of a cat identified as "Death, its claws disease." Fear of the cat of death turns the hopeful bird into a spiritual gray mouse:

The bird turned into a mouse, seeking a hole
After he heard the cat's cry, "Stop!"
Just like a mouse, his soul was calmed
By finding a home in this world's hole
He started building and acquiring knowledge
That fit into just the space of this small hole
He only learned trades that would work well
Within the confines of his small hole.

Braving—even loving—death was revealed to be the secret for living a fulfilled life. For Rumi, love and death were entwined in an embrace, while love and fear were opposites.

The crescendo to Rumi's growing excitement about death as an expression of love and nonattachment was reached in a glorious hymn to death in Book V, which Rumi composed at the beginning of the decade of the 1270s, when he was sixty-three years old. He was now quickened with anticipation at the prospect of death and resurrection. The theme of transcending his mortal body had become inseparable from his religion of love:

> *When you hear them say, "That poor man is dead,"*
> *You may answer, "I am alive, you just cannot see!*
> *When my body was laid to rest, all by itself,*
> *Eight paradises blossomed inside my heart!"*
> *When the soul sleeps among roses and jasmine*
> *What matter if the body is buried in dirt?*
> *What does the sleeping soul know of the body?*
> *Or care whether its grave is a rose garden or ash pit?*
> *The soul has emerged into the sky-blue of the heavens*
> *Crying out, to those below, "If only everyone knew!"*

CHAPTER 15

Wedding Night

As Rumi was walking one day, in bright daylight, his mind elsewhere, his shoe became stuck in the mud. He simply discarded it and proceeded barefoot. At other times, and other places, Rumi's behavior was becoming similarly marked by absentmindedness, ecstatic absorption, or the freedom that came with advanced age and station. He once grew excited enough during *sama* that the knot of his drawers came undone, though he kept twirling only in a loose shirt until Hosam jumped up, clasped him in a tight embrace, and covered him with a cloak. Aflaki reported, "If a group of poor people begged from him, he would give them the cloak from his back, the turban from his head, the shirt from his body, and the shoes from his feet—and off he would go."

Provoking an even more exhilarated response was the birth of his grandson, anticipated ever since the marriage of his son to Salah's daughter at least fifteen years earlier. Born on June 7, 1272, Ulu Aref Chelebi arrived as a kind of miracle into Rumi's life. Fateme had suffered many stillborn births, or children dying in infancy, and was taking drugs and making violent movements to eliminate the fetus, not wishing to undergo the ordeal of labor again. She was convinced her pregnancy was doomed. Hearing of these practices, Rumi sent a strong message to Fateme: "Do not do such things but keep to your pregnancy. Can it be that you feel so ashamed of our lineage?"

As soon as he received news of the birth of his grandson, even before the completion of the ritual rubbing of salt on the newborn, Rumi rushed to Fateme's bedside. He gleefully scattered gold coins over the head of the mother, a blessing of good fortune, and asked whether he might take the baby. Receiving the baby from the midwife, he then wrapped him in the sleeve of his cloak and whisked him away. After spending some afternoon and evening hours alone with him, Rumi returned the baby that night to Latife, the mother of Fateme, with more gold coins tied in a loop wrapped in his sheet. Weeks later, when the baby was in his crib, Rumi lightly raised the covering veil and whispered, "Allah, Allah," teaching him the mantra for prayer first taught to him by Baha Valad.

Rumi also took responsibility for naming the child. He instructed Sultan Valad that his name should be "Faridun," the first name of the boy's grandfather Salah. But he added, "You should address him as Amir Aref, the way Baha Valad called me Khodavandgar, and never said my actual name. Let my spiritual gift to him be my title, meaning that you may write his name as Jalaloddin Amir Aref." He also marked the occasion with a poem that harked back to his formulaic wedding poems for Faridun's parents:

> *The day he was born from his mother was Tuesday*
> *In the year six hundred and seventy—Faridun!*
> *On the eighth day of the month of Zel-Qa'de,*
> *Two hours after noonday prayers—Faridun!*
> *From the family and race of the Khosrows,*
> *He was loved like Shirin—Faridun!*
> *Descended from nobility in both his father and mother,*
> *He came from Paradise, a beautiful angel—Faridun!*

Rumi imbued him not only with a spiritual pedigree, but a Persian one, saturated in the epic love for Shirin of King Khosrow, "beautiful as the moon," as he once wrote of him.

A *Masnavi* reciter—now an occupation, like Quran reciter—told of visiting Rumi and Hosam, when the grandchild was not more than a year old. "Suddenly I saw the door of the small garden open," he recalled. "Amir Aref was seated on a little wagon and his tutor was pulling him. Mowlana stood up and placed the rope of the wagon over his own blessed shoulder and pulled it along and said, 'I can be Aref's little ox.' Similarly, Hosamoddin stood next to Khodavandgar and grabbed the other side of the rope, and both of them pulled the wagon one or two times around the courtyard of the *madrase*. Aref laughed sweetly and screamed with joy. Khodavandgar announced, 'Being kind to little children is a legacy for Muslims.'" Rumi then repeated a teaching from the Prophet Mohammad in the Arabic, "'Whoever has a child, let him behave like a child himself.'"

When Aref was a bit older, Sultan Valad was often startled when the boy entered a room, as he recognized mannerisms of Rumi in his son. Aref's Quran teacher recalled that Sultan Valad told him, when the child was only six years old, "The moment Aref enters the door of the *madrase*, I imagine that my father has entered. His graceful gait, his delicate manner of walking, and his balanced movements are exactly the way my father walked. In my youth, I continually saw my father with these same characteristics and appearance, and Aref's movements during *sama* are exactly like his." *Sama*, within Rumi's *madrase* at least, had become a regular family activity practiced by all ages.

Rumi's stretches of skyward distraction, alternating with silly patches of playfulness during the infancy of his grandson, did not keep him from starting back to work on Book VI of the *Masnavi*, which he identified in its Prologue as the final book. He chose the number six as representing in Islamic medieval thought the six directions—the four cardinal points, plus zenith and nadir, which were a sort of moral height and depth:

> *Oh, Life of the Heart, Hosamoddin,*
>   *Desire for a Sixth Part is now boiling*
> *Because of your magnetic wisdom*
>   *A Book of Hosam circulates in the world*
> *Oh, Spiritual One, I dedicate to you*
>   *A Sixth Part, the ending of the* Masnavi.

The sixth book revisits in its philosophical disquisitions the concerns of the earlier books with teaching questions, especially the debate that most absorbed Rumi, between a determinist submission to the will of Allah expressed in thoughts, feelings, events, and actions and the commonsense exercise of personal free will. As in the other five books, he reached back to his childhood for animal fables—from *Kalile and Demne* came the tale of the friendship of a mouse with a frog. More novel was his growing reliance in the last two books on raw material drawn from *hazl* poems, which featured bawdy, even obscene or profane language, and lewd scenarios. (When R. A. Nicholson later translated the *Masnavi* into English he rendered these sections in Latin to spare the general public material he considered pornographic.) In one such tale, a maiden uses a donkey's equipment for her sexual satisfaction, which Rumi presents as a lesson on being in thrall to our animal nature. In another, a young man in a Sufi lodge builds a wall behind him each night to prevent being raped—an example of abuse of power in the religious life. Rumi was illustrating, to the dismay of some, that no material was too vulgar to be embraced within the rich universe of his book and of God's wisdom and understanding.

Knowing that he was drawing closer to the finale of the poem, Rumi's thoughts turned more often to its secret muse,

Shams of Tabriz, the human sun now visible only in shadows cast on a wall. In death, Shams had merged with eternity, which was the presence of God's love expressed in this world and in the world beyond death. Rumi took on this paradoxical mystery—of the sun and the Sun—in the tale of "The Poor Dervish and the Police Inspector of Tabriz"—its setting a clue. Spread over five hundred lines, the story concerned a Sufi dervish whose debts had always been paid by a kindly police chief in Tabriz, until the policeman died, leaving his treasure hidden. The dervish travels to "glorious" Tabriz only to discover that his true benefactor was God, the treasure, divine:

> *He gave me a cap, but You the head filled with intelligence*
> *He gave me a coat, but You the tall figure to clothe*
> *He gave me gold, but You the hand for counting*
> *He gave me a horse, but You the mind for riding*
> *He gave me a candle, but You the eyes for seeing . . .*
> *He gave me a house, but You the sky and the earth.*

The limits the debtor discovered in the police inspector of Tabriz were those Rumi had come to find were the human limits of Shams of Tabriz—he lit the candle of love for him, yet God imbued Rumi with the mirror reflecting the flame from Shams and other lights.

Within a few hundred lines of the completion of the *Masnavi*, and immediately preceding its ultimate "Story of the Three Princes," Rumi breaks into a moving litany, a catalog poem of all of lovesick Zolaykha's coded language, disguising her feelings for Joseph, the paragon of beauty in Rumi's poetry—the story of the Egyptian lady's love for the Hebrew slave is described in the Quran itself as "the fairest of stories." Zolaykha's dexterous ploy happened to match Rumi's in expressing his feelings for Shams of Tabriz—often compared by him to handsome Joseph—and was a parable for his poetic task of coming closer to the truth by going in circles. In talking about such ineffable love, Rumi believed, the longer the detour the more sure the arrival:

> And when she said, "The wax is melting softly!"
>   That was to say, "My friend was kind to me."
> And when she said, "Look, the moon is rising"
>   And when she said, "The willow is now green!"
> And when she said, "The leaves are trembling"
>   And when she said, "How nicely burns the rue!"
> And when she said, "The nightingale sang for the roses" . . .
>   And when she said, "Beat firmly all the rugs!" . . .
> And when she said, "The bread is all unsalted!"
>   And when she said, "The spheres are turning backwards" . . .
> When she praised something—that meant "His sweet embrace."
>   When she blamed something—that meant "He's far away!"
> And when she piled up a hundred thousand names
>   Her desire and intention was always Joseph's name.

Rumi had circled back to his dialogue with Hosam in Book I. He was confessing that all the while he was writing the *Masnavi* he had never stopped thinking of Shams. Just as Zolaykha meant Joseph with every word of hers, so Rumi meant Shams with every word, verse, and tale of the *Masnavi*. Since Shams had first awakened his heart to the transformative fire of love, the name of that sun also evoked the hidden name of God.

The *Masnavi* ends on an inconclusive note, almost midstory. Its final tale is fitting. The story of the three princes who fall in love with a portrait of a Chinese princess and travel to the royal court of a king in faraway Asia shares elements with the first tale of the *Masnavi* of the king and the slave girl of Samarkand. The story was yet another told to him—and finished—by Shams. Given their months of seclusion, most if not all the stories in

the *Masnavi* might have originally been just such teaching sto-
ries Rumi first heard from Shams and wished to keep alive in
his poem. Book VI ends on a quiet parable of a "window be-
tween hearts," without any crescendo, so the epic seems to be a
mosaic with a few pieces missing. For a poet with so little inter-
est in titles or frames, dying off into silence was an appropriate
enough statement. Some said, though, that Rumi had simply lost
interest in dictating, in spite of requests from Hosam and Sultan
Valad, as if he had descended or ascended into the distant calm
that increasingly possessed him.

❖

In the autumn of 1273 Rumi fell seriously ill. Among the closest
of his companions had always been a prominent local physician,
well regarded as a commentator on a five-volume Persian en-
cyclopedia of medical knowledge, based mainly on the ancient
Greeks Galen and Aristotle. Rumi had satirized Galen and the
reliance on medicine in general in Book III of the *Masnavi*, his
skepticism prescient, as this doctor was unable to diagnose the
cause of his weakness, other than detecting excess water in his
side. Nevertheless he remained next to Rumi to monitor his con-
dition.

The unspecified malaise lingered for weeks and months, as
Rumi's bedside became the center of heightened concern and
anxiety for his family, school, and all of Konya. Most frenzied
and upset was his wife, Kerra. "You should have a precious life
of three hundred years, no four hundred years, to fill the world
with higher truth and meaning," she pleaded with him. "Why,
Why?" Rumi answered. "Am I Pharoah? What do I have to do
with this world of dust? How can I find rest and peace in this
world?" For three full days and nights he asked that no one

speak to him, and he did not speak to anyone. When his wife
finally came to him, and lowered her head, and asked about
his health concerns and his pain, he answered, "I am thinking
about my death, which will be occurring soon." At that remark,
she shrieked and was hysterical for several more hours.

During the onset of his illness, Rumi was not entirely bedrid-
den and sometimes walked about the *madrase* in a frail manner.
Unchanging was his certainty that he was going to die, and his
preparing those close to him for the eventuality, as well as set-
ting its tenor with good humor if not outright eagerness. When
he sighed from pain while hobbling in the courtyard, his favor-
ite cat mewed and howled. "Do you know what this poor cat is
saying?" Rumi asked. "It says, 'During these days you will be set-
ting out towards heaven and returning to your original home-
land. Poor me! What am I to do?'" (When this cat died a week
after Rumi, his daughter, Maleke, buried it near him.)

Earthquakes were common enough in Anatolia, but during
that fall a particularly powerful quake occurred, interpreted
by Rumi's followers as connected to his condition. In a joking
way, Rumi agreed, saying the earth was hungering for a juicy
morsel and would soon be satisfied by his corpse, yet no harm
would come to the town. He informed his friends that most of
the prophets and mystics departed from the world in autumn
or the dead of winter, "when the earth is like iron." Weighed
down by worry about a lingering debt of fifty dirham, he tried
to repay with gold filings. When the creditor forgave his debt,
Rumi said, "Thank God I am delivered from this horrible ob-
stacle!"

Soon he was confined to his room, a pan full of water set
by his bed for him to dip his feet into and sprinkle his chest
and forehead, as he had begun to be racked with intense fevers.
Hosam and Sultan Valad were usually nearby. Visions and
dreams abounded among those gathered, at least in later retell-

ings of the events of those days by those present. Hosam told of being seated at the top of the bed with Rumi's head resting on his chest as they saw a handsome young man materialize in front of their eyes. When Hosam asked his name, he identified himself as Azrael, the Angel of Death. "What excellent, perceptive sight to be able to see a face such as that!" Rumi weakly exclaimed.

One by one the notables of the town visited to pay their respects. Leading them was Qonavi, whose earlier haughtiness toward Rumi had long since dissolved and been replaced by an admiring respect. The godson of Ibn Arabi appeared quite disturbed and began to pray for Rumi's healing: "It is hoped that recovery will take place. Mowlana is the soul of mankind. He deserves a full recovery." Rumi quickly snapped back, "Let those words be for your sake! When there is no more than a thin shirt between lover and beloved, do you not wish the shirt to be removed so that light may be joined with light?"

On another occasion the Chief Judge Qadi Serajoddin visited Rumi, his judgments in favor Rumi's *sama* practice crucial in his having been able to safely complete the *Masnavi* and teach, dance, and play music for the glory of his religion of love. Hosam was holding a cup filled with a medicinal potion in his hand, in the hopes that Rumi would drink some. Rumi paid no attention at all. "I placed the cup in the Qadi's hand hoping Mowlana might take it from the hand of so great a person, but he refused," said Hosam. When the Qadi departed, Qonavi again entered. "He took the cup from my hand and offered it to Mowlana," recalled Hosam. "After taking a few sips, Mowlana gave it back to him." A friendship and trust had deepened between them in spite of their philosophical differences, like that between Shams and the cynic Shehab in Damascus.

Hosam was there as always to copy the poems that Rumi kept producing to the end, his lucidity intact except when the fevers became too high. Rumi was well used to reciting poems in extreme states, from ecstasy in the midst of whirling to exhaustion in the middle of the night. His theme on his deathbed was the joy of death, which became the occasion he was addressing, always with the message that love rather than fear was the single choice if you did not wish to lose the only life that mattered. As a patriarch and mystic who achieved some joy and peace he was able to sing convincingly of the happiness and release of death in a set of poems unmatched on the daunting theme:

> *When you see my coffin being carried out*
>> *Don't think I'm in pain, leaving this world . . .*
> *When you see my corpse, don't cry*
>> *I long for that time, and for that reunion*
> *When they bury me, don't cry*
>> *The grave is but a veil for eternity*
> *When you see the setting, wait for the rising.*
>> *Why worry about a sunset, or a fading moon?*
> *You think you are setting but you are rising*
>> *When the tomb encloses you, your soul will be released.*

He also recited lines that would eventually be used for the inscription on his tomb. Its *takhallos,* or signature, was Shams of Tabriz, which had been replaced by Hosam, yet such a circling back to his original muse might have been his point. Rumi was increasingly summoning the name and presence of Shams on his deathbed. His happiness and excitement at death were made more real by imagining its resolution as a joyous reunion with Shams, as well as with the light of the sun, and the source of both, God:

> *Don't be sad at God's festival*
> *My chin is shut, within the grave, asleep*

While my mouth tastes bittersweet love . . .
I will never rest, until my soul flies
To the towering soul of Shams of Tabriz.

Distraught from watching his father succumb to this illness, and spending sleepless nights nursing him, Sultan Valad also became ill. As Aflaki reported, "Sultan Valad had become extremely weak from limitless service, deep sorrow, and lack of sleep. He was constantly crying, tearing his clothes, and lamenting. And he did not sleep at all." Rumi said, "Bahaoddin, I am happy. Go, lay your head on your pillow and get some rest." He then a wrote a poem that fit the moment, this "last *ghazal* that Mowlana composed," alluding once again to Shams, the name cloaked inside of his dying poems:

Go. Lay your head on your pillow. Leave me be!
Let me wander in the night, ruined and afflicted.
I am alone in waves of passion, all night until dawn
If you wish, come, have mercy, if you wish, go, be cruel.
The only cure for my pain is dying
So how may I ask him to cure my longing?
Last night I dreamed I saw an old man in the alley of love
He waved to me with his hand, as if to say, "Come to me."

During Sultan Valad's absence, Rumi addressed the question of his successor. Fateme continued to press for her husband to take the traditionally inherited position at the head of the family *madrase* and secure the place for their son, Amir Aref, as a kind of spiritual royal family. Again Rumi decisively deflected the chance to begin a lineage or form a more standard order. Some imams of Konya came to see Rumi and asked, "Who is suitable to succeed Mowlana and who has been chosen?" Rumi named Hosam. The question and answer was repeated three times. On the fourth query, they asked, "What do you have to say to Baha-oddin Valad?" Rumi answered, "Bahaoddin is a champion. He has no need of confirmation from me. He has no need to boast or make claims." His eldest son accepted this decision as he had before, in silence, without public complaint.

No one left in the room was able to comprehend fully the length and breadth of Rumi's expansive life. The companions who traveled with his family from distant Khorasan were now mostly buried near Baha Valad in the family plot of the imperial rose garden. None of his children had ever laid eyes on the Oxus River, the great natural divide separating the Balkh region of his birth, nor was it any longer possible for them to visit the capitals of his youth, Samarkand or Bukhara, as they had been destroyed as cultural centers by the Mongols, as had Baghdad. His mother remained buried in Larande, and the grave of his first wife was not included among the rest of the family. Some closest to him had known the remarkable Shams of Tabriz, but only Rumi understood the nature and extent of their months of intimate encounter that transformed him midlife from a respected religious leader into an audacious mystic and visionary poet. These experiences kept him a figure apart even in his approach to death. As everyone around him was grieving and sorrowful, he remained witty and serene.

Rumi took leave of his circle in a coherent manner with targeted words and messages, treating death as a teaching moment. He was especially understanding with Kerra, who would outlive her husband by nineteen years and during those years become a distinctive, eccentric figure in Konya, only leaving the house in the evening to go to the bathhouse, wearing a fur coat from Turkestan in the summer with a silk veil over her head, burning candles during the daylight hours, but much sought after for her reputed psychic powers. "Will there appear anyone like our

Khodavandgar?" she asked inconsolably. "If there is, he will also be I," Rumi answered. And then he added: "I have two attachments in this world, one to you, and the other to my body. When I leave my body, and join the world of Oneness, my attachment to you will continue to exist."

Rumi consoled his companions with just such a message—the emanation of the manner of spirit he exhibited would be the same as his presence. Such a belief had animated his similar relations with the two successors of Shams, Salah and Hosam, whom he believed emanated and inspired the spirit of love and so were avatars of love: "Don't be afraid when I depart, and don't be sad, because the light of Hallaj, one hundred and fifty years after his death, revealed itself to the spirit of Attar and became his spiritual director. Whatever situation you are in, try to stay with me and to remember me so that I can show myself to you. Whatever clothes I may be wearing, I will always be with you."

He concluded with practical life advice: "I recommend to you fear of God, both silently and publicly, neither eating too much nor speaking too much, avoiding causing any trouble or sin, diligence in fasting, continuous praying, the leaving behind of all passion and lust, patience in the face of injustice from all mankind, renouncing the company of fools and common people, and associating with the virtuous and the noble. Moreover, the best person is the one who benefits other people, and the best speech is brief and gives guidance." He also taught those gathered a prayer to memorize and recite for the rest of their lives, beginning, "Oh Lord God, I draw breath only for Your sake."

Hearing the finality in his tone, some of those in the room nevertheless pressed him to rest, take his medicine, and care for his recovery. "My companions pull me in one direction," Rumi sighed, "while Mowlana Shamsoddin calls to me from the other direction . . . I am obliged to depart." Closest to his pillow in the final hours was Hosam, his "pearl-shedding sea," as he had ex-

ulted recently in the *Masnavi*. Turning to Hosam, his last words,
in character, faithful yet whimsical, Rumi instructed, "Place me
at the top of the sepulchral niche, so I may arise before everyone
else." At sunset on the evening of December 17, 1273, Rumi died
in peace, having given repeated instructions that the night be
treated as his Wedding Night, a time of joy and happy reunion
with the beloved:

> *The bats of your senses fly into the sunset*
> *While the pearl of your soul rolls towards sunrise*

❖

Rumi had planned his own funeral, reviving the basic design of
the funeral Salah laid out for himself fifteen years earlier, a bois-
terous procession worthy of a wedding celebration, with singers,
musicians, and dancers, as well as Quran reciters and imams. The
burial of Salah had been controversial, a funeral unlike any wit-
nessed in Konya until that time. Its issues had hardly disappeared,
especially the shock of mixing joyous music and dance with a tra-
ditionally somber religious observance. Soon after Rumi's death,
Hosam was brought before the court of Qadi Serajoddin to once
again defend the *rabab* from being outlawed, the chief justice
ruling in its favor, simply in memory of his friend. Yet on the day
of the funeral seemingly all Konya crowded to join in the vibrant
ceremony expressly designed for them by a man popularly felt to
be a holy figure or even a saint.

On the evening of his death, Rumi's body had been placed on
a bench and washed according to Muslim practice by an imam,
several of his companions helping with pouring the water. Early
the next morning the coffin was carried on the shoulders of a
group of friends and followers out of the *madrase* that had been

the family home in Konya since the final years of the life of
Baha Valad. At the first sight of the simple coffin, all the men of
Konya, from whatever background, bared their heads, among
crowds that included numbers of women and children. The pro-
cession was led by Quran reciters intoning verses, along with
twenty groups of singers chanting poems that Rumi composed,
and musicians beating kettledrums, and playing oboes, trum-
pets, and flutes.

Most remarkable was the spontaneous appearance of re-
ligious leaders from all the other faiths practiced in town, as
well as their faithful taking part. As Aflaki chronicled, "All the
religious communities with their men of religion and worldly
power were present, including the Christians and the Jews, the
Greeks, the Arabs and the Turks. All of them in accordance with
their own traditions walked in procession while holding up their
books. And they recited verses from the Psalms of David, the
Torah, and the Gospels, and made lamentation." Sultan Valad
remembered his father's funeral, "The people of the city, young
and old, were all lamenting, crying, sighing aloud, the villagers
as well as the Turks and Greeks. They tore their shirts from grief
for this great man. 'He was our Jesus!' the Christians said. 'He
was our Moses!' the Jews said."

The occasion was marked, though, by frenzy and violence as
much as by peace and joy. The beauty of the outpouring was inter-
rupted when some of Rumi's followers tried to push others away
from a religious ceremony they felt belonged solely to them. "The
Muslims were unable to beat them off with sticks and swords and
blows," Rumi's grandson told of the occasion, as remembered
in his family. "The crowd could not be scattered and a great dis-
pute arose." When the Parvane was informed of the disturbance
some prominent monks and priests were summoned to explain
their participation. Rumi had been spending more time in the
Greek, Armenian, and Jewish districts than was realized, teach-

ing and conversing. "Whatever we read in our sacred books about
the prophets, we beheld in him," one said. A Greek priest said,
"He was like bread. Have you ever seen a hungry person run away
from bread? You have no idea who he really was!"

Because of the long pause until the dispute among the faiths
was adjudicated by the Parvane, and then the stopping and start-
ing as mourners ripped off the coffin cover, which needed to be
replaced six times, their hysterics only partly successfully tamped
down by Seljuk soldiers and police, the procession did not arrive
at the rose garden cemetery until sunset. The harshness of the
wintry day and the fading of the light added to a feeling of sad-
ness infusing many of the Sufi leaders closest to Rumi, in spite
of the affirming music and poetry. They took part one by one
in the ritual known as the "Visiting Rite" of saying farewell to
the corpse, where a master of ceremonies would proclaim their
names, as if visiting a royal court. When the announcer called
the name of Qonavi, he added many respectful titles. Qonavi
later confided that he did not realize he was being called, as all
of the effusive titles being listed sounded more fitting for Rumi.

As a surprising revelation of the closeness that had developed
between them, Rumi in one of his final deathbed wishes asked
that Qonavi be entrusted with the leading role in the funeral
service of reading the final prayers over his body before burial.
During the recital of these prayers, Qonavi became momentarily
dazed from grief. In the confusion of the day some had arrived
late at the cemetery, and given Qonavi's emotional distress, the
Chief Judge Qadi Serajoddin repeated the burial prayer once
more, or completed the prayer, if the distress of Qonavi had
caused him to simply break off. Leaving the service in the dim
light of that early evening, the Sufi poet Eraqi made his apt ob-
servation of Rumi, "He came into the world as a stranger, and
he left as a stranger."

Rumi inspired visions, especially fitting, since he had been known as a boy who saw angels. One mourner later spoke of seeing rows of blue angels that day in the cemetery, and Kerra saw her husband transfigured into an angel with four pairs of wings. More restrained and precise, Hosam claimed he never dreamed of Rumi or even sensed his presence for seven years after his death, until he encountered him once walking in the Meram garden and Rumi asked simply, *"Chuni?"* "How are you?" "I saw nothing else," said Hosam. Even less supernatural, but most evocative of the way Rumi spoke and saw things, was a dream shortly after his death by his friend Serajoddin, a *Masnavi* reciter, who dreamed of seeing Rumi hunched in a corner of the house, lost in contemplation. When the reciter asked him about his life in heaven, Rumi wryly answered, "Serajoddin, they have not come to understand me in the afterlife any more than they understood me in this world."

Afterword

In just the six years since I retraced the steps of the young student Rumi in Aleppo, history had reminded me of its cruel and destructive powers. Arriving at the end of writing about the life of Rumi, I cast back to my early, significant meeting on a Friday morning with Sebastian in the quiet covered bazaar of Aleppo and wondered where he might be. By now the civil war that had begun nearly unnoticed that same week had created unimaginable catastrophe in Syria on the scale of the Mongol devastation in Rumi's own time. I looked for and eventually found the card Sebastian handed me.

I had no luck reaching him at the email or telephone number handwritten on the back of the crinkled card for the carpet store, though I did manage to find Omar on Facebook, through a mutual journalist friend. Omar had sold rugs in the same family business as Sebastian and was now living as a Syrian refugee in New Zealand. His uncle was the brother-in-law of Sebastian, but the uncle only knew of a last sighting, in England, of my accidental friend. "I feel sad about what happened," Omar wrote to me in a message as poignant as it was brief. "I wish I can change but as you know we can't."

All signs of Rumi might have vanished, too. He lived in just such a brutal time of destruction and tumult, hardly conducive to the preservation of delicate poetry and spiritual teaching. His death marked the end of an era, and his "setting" was simultaneous with the disappearance of the refined culture—and dominant personalities—of his time and place. Within four years, Rumi's political alter ego, the Parvane, had been executed for treason by the very Mongols who propped him up for two decades, a fall from unreliable power that would not have surprised his spiritual mentor. In those same years Rumi's counterpoint Qonavi died, his simple grave in Konya still identified by a wooden honeycomb of a tomb, open to the air, according to his wishes. Finding a pattern in the deaths of these three men, the historian of the Seljuks Claude Cahen has written: "All those who had been molded politically and intellectually during the period of Seljukid splendor had now perished together, and the former brilliance had vanished with them."

Rumi's posterity, though, was fortunate in having leaders committed to his legacy in the right place at the right time. Following Hosam's death eleven years after Rumi, his son Sultan Valad, succeeded by his grandson Aref, on whom Rumi had doted, became leaders of a more formal institutional Mevlevi Order—"Mevlevi" is Turkish for "Mowlavi"—with leadership passed down in royal fashion from fathers to sons. They sent emissaries around Asia Minor and the Levant to propogate the brotherhood. "Most of these orders peter out, after a bang with an exciting leader," Professor Ahmet T. Karamustafa, an expert on Sufism at the University of Maryland, told me in a conversation. "No one follows up, and that is that. The Mevlevis ended up being pretty successful." By the time of the Ottoman Empire the Mevlevis had become *the* establishment order, and the Mevlevi sheikh, a descendent of Rumi, delegated to gird any new sultan with a ceremonial sword.

Fortune did reverse for the Mevlevis in Turkey with the Amendment of 1925, devised by the new secular president,

Kemal Ataturk, banning all Sufi orders, as he feared their po-
litical power and disliked their musty reminiscence of the Otto-
man past. The law forbade the use of Mevlevi mystical names,
titles, or costumes, impounded assets, and provided prison sen-
tences for such practices. Yet two years later, in 1927, the Mev-
levi lodge in Konya—which grew up around Rumi's tomb, the
Green Dome, built by Hosam with funds from the Parvane and
Gorji Khatun—was allowed to reopen as a museum, which it
remains: visitors can see robed mannequins posed in a dervish's
daily round.

Equally difficult to eradicate was Rumi's sublime whirling
meditation, allowed to reemerge publicly in the guise of a folk
dance in the 1950s. Present at its first "performance" in Konya
on the anniversary of Rumi's death in December 1954 was the
scholar Annemarie Schimmel, who traveled from Ankara, where
she was teaching. "Late in the evening we were brought to a large
mansion in the center of the old town, in which armchairs had
been set out for the noble guests," she recalled. "With amaze-
ment we observed as a group of elderly gentlemen unwrapped
mysterious parcels out of which emerged flutes, *rababs*, tambou-
rines, even dervish caps and gowns. . . . For the first time in
twenty-nine years the men began to perform the mystical dance
together . . . at once they found their way back to the old rhythm
of the 'heavenly dance.'" While officially cast as performers, the
dervishes performing the whirling dance in Konya are now pop-
ularly understood to be spiritual practitioners attuned to the
resonance of the *sama,* though in the more formal and elegantly
choreographed version developed by the Mevlevis during the
Ottoman period.

When I visited Konya for the memorial *sama* ceremony in
December 2010, this public rehabilitation was well under way,
helped by the election of Prime Minister Erdogan, whose elec-
toral base was centered in the politically conservative Konya

region, known as the "Quran Belt" of Turkey. Mistakenly turn-
ing down a wrong hallway in the vast saucer-shaped venue where
the ceremonies took place, I was startled to be confronted by a
security detail with oversize automatic weapons. As the prime
minister addressed the thousands gathered for the event, I could
make out the words "Rumi" and "Turkey" repeated in close jux-
taposition. Rumors circulated that the Iranian president would
be attending, too, though he did not finally appear. (Rumi had
figured in Iranian-Turkish political relations decades earlier
when Ayatollah Khomeini, exiled to Bursa, in Turkey, before
becoming supreme leader of Iran, reportedly wished to make
a pilgrimage to Rumi's tomb but was prevented for refusing to
remove his clerical garb.)

Such geopolitical relevance for a distant poet of love might
appear improbable. Rumi had warned endlessly about the
danger of engaging with politics and position:

Animals grow fat from eating grass,
People from power and fame

Yet the momentum of his words and poetry has proved as self-
propelling—if as unlikely—as the success of his whirling dance
and Mevlevi Order, and his double legacy as earnest saint and
world-class poet has proved potent. Thousands of elegant cou-
plets by other poets, from a rich moment in Persian poetry—like
strings of pearls, as one of their own critics described them—
have faded, too. Yet by accident and devoted design, Rumi's lines
are reproduced daily both in the original and in modern trans-
lations. (I've added to the dense stream with daily tweets of my
collaborative translations of lines of his poems.)

The threads connecting us back to his original poetry are
at least as fragile as those tying us to him as a spiritual figure,
and were just as susceptible to snapping. Rumi's voice first regis-

tered in the West, faintly, only in the eighteenth century, when a young Austrian ambassador in Istanbul, Jacques de Wallenbourg, translated the *Masnavi* into French. More enduring were forty-four *ghazals* translated into German by Friedrich Rückert around 1820. One critic spryly characterized a translation of Rückert's: "This poem smells of roses." Hegel admired the verses for the pantheistic philosophy he believed he detected. Schubert and Strauss set a few to music as *lieder*. The classic English "orientalist" scholar R. A. Nicholson produced a grand and enduring translation of the six volumes of the *Masnavi*, which began appearing in print in 1925. His students at Cambridge University reported that he would weep during his *Masnavi* lectures. Nicholson's office was decorated in the oriental style, and he would toil over his lifework while draped in long Sufi robes, with a tall, round Mevlevi hat set atop his head.

Rumi's words have found receptivity in the "ear of the heart"—as he put it—through translations in dozens of languages, though not uniformly. His poems have been most popular on the Indo-Pakistan subcontinent since the early fourteenth century and in Afghanistan, where recitation is probably closest in pronunciation to Rumi's own speech, as Afghani Persian has barely changed since medieval times. While Rumi is currently popular in Israel, his poems are less so in Arabic countries, as they are associated with Persian and Iran. Equally ironically, when the Rumi scholar Foruzanfar was studying as a young man in Mashad, in eastern Iran, he had difficulty finding texts of Rumi, as this "Sunni poet" was considered superfluous reading for the many Shia seminary students.

Something of the American heartbeat has always quickened to Rumi, beginning with the transcendentalist Ralph Waldo Emerson, who retranslated lines from the German of Rückert:

Of Paradise am I the Peacock,

Who has escaped from his nest.

A decisive event in raising awareness of Rumi even more in the United States occurred in the mid-1970s, when Robert Bly handed a copy of the scholarly translations of A. J. Arberry to the poet Coleman Barks, saying, "These poems need to be released from their cages." The ensuing flutter of renditions in a free-verse American idiom has been vivifying, and often when someone says that they *love* Rumi they mean Barks's versions. Barks took some heat for not knowing Persian—he works with a native speaker or from literal English academic versions. Yet Rumi has ever been a permissive muse. While less a publishing phenomenon than Barks, the German poet Hans Meinke, who died in 1974, wrote over a hundred odes in Rumi's name, channeling his spirit, as Rumi had Shams's:

> *O Rumi, since I became you,*
> *The turmoil stopped . . .*
> *O Rumi, since I became you,*
> *North has become south and south has become north.*

❖

I suppose that my frustrated wish to speak with Sebastian at the conclusion of my journey had arisen from a need to talk with him once again of his notion of Rumi's "secret," which helped guide me on my way and fortuitously turned out to be as significant to the mystic poet as to his readers and listeners. I'd come to agree with Sebastian that mystery was an essential ingredient in Rumi's enduring power. Rumi spoke of *serr* often and in many contexts. This veil of secrecy was a virtue and an artistic style in the broader culture of the time. It was the atmosphere

Sufi mystics and Persian poets breathed, as—a favorite meta-
phor of Rumi for lovers—fish swam obliviously in the ocean.
Rumi, though, created an unmistakably personal version that
resonates in our time beyond the others.

The greatest and most guarded secret in Rumi's life con-
cerned the nature of his fiery and transformative friendship
with Shams of Tabriz, "the sunshine of the heart." Some have
explained the torrent of passionate love poems that ensued
when Shams disappeared from Rumi's life as fitting into a tradi-
tion of devotion of disciple for sheikh. Yet Rumi and Shams—as
well as other witnesses—emphasized the complexity of their re-
lationship, its failure to conform to such a neat teacher-student
model. While no evidence exists of an erotic component, Rumi
chose to speak of their spiritual love in the mode of Persian ro-
mantic love poetry, and from weaving the two came his evanes-
cent message. Most ironic in his current appeal in our age of
telling-all and exhibitionism is Rumi's conviction—especially in
the *Masnavi*—that even the name of his beloved Shams must be
steadily disguised.

His poetry, too, operated from an aesthetic of secrets. Rumi
spoke in code. Shams was the light of the sun, but so was God,
and in speaking of the beloved he was also speaking of the un-
speakable, or approaching the unspeakable, as the essence of
God is love. His stress on the pain of separation applied to both
human and divine as well. All Persian love poetry was built from
a reservoir of stock images: the young wine-bearer with black
eyelashes; the nightingale in the rose garden; cypresses and nar-
cissi, stars and moons. Yet in writing around and toward God,
Rumi was writing, too, in the tradition of mystical poetry, in-
cluding Sufis of the East, but also St. John of the Cross or John
Donne of the West. Rumi would have agreed with Emily Dick-
inson's "Tell all the truth but tell it slant." He used Shams as
his *takhallos* but also Silence, or *Khamush*. The most successful

poems for Rumi were failures. Nearing God, they collapsed into silence:

> *Explanations make many things clear*
> *But love is only clear in silence*

The most practical of secrets for Rumi concerned his faith. Rumi was born into a religious Muslim family and followed the proscribed rules of daily prayer and fasting throughout his entire life. Yet equally devout Muslim Sufis, such as his beloved Hallaj, had been executed in centuries past, and discretion and speaking in allusive poetry became more than just a stylistic preference among them. At least once, legal charges were pressed against Rumi for his use of music and dance in religious practice, as they had been against Shams for wine drinking. In the *Masnavi,* Rumi grew bolder in making claims for a "religion of love" that went beyond all organized faiths. As Jawid Mojadeddi, who is currently embarked on retranslating into English the entire *Masnavi,* said to me, "Rumi resonates today because people are thinking post-religion. He came to see mysticism as the divine origin of every religion." Rumi said as much, subtly, in verse:

> *When you discover the source of sunlight . . .*
> *Whatever direction you go will be east*

When I spoke with Coleman Barks by phone from his home in Athens, Georgia, he agreed with Mojadeddi that the sensational response to his own translations in English in our time has much to do with Rumi's emphasis on ecstasy and love over religions and creeds. "I do believe that Rumi found himself going beyond traditional religion," said Barks. "He has no use for dividing up into the different names of Christian and Jew and Muslim. It was a wild thing to say in the thirteenth century, but he said it, and he was not killed. He must have said it with such gentleness and such authority that they couldn't attack him. None of the fundamentalists attack Rumi. They just don't. They leave him alone because he is so beloved. There is a music of grace inside Rumi's poems that people can hear, not physical music, a psychic music that makes them feel ecstatic."

These exquisitely calibrated ideas and lyrics matter to many readers today then, not simply for their beauty, or even mystery, but also for truths they find helpful in their lives. One evening I had supper in a garden restaurant in lower Manhattan with Asma Sadiq, a pediatrician at Beth Israel Medical Center. Born in Pakistan, she spoke of having been brought back to her roots, as well as to a concept of mental health, by reading Rumi. "I felt befriended by Rumi," Asma said. "It was very strange but he gave me a connection to something beyond." Her father recited Rumi to her as a child, as well as Urdu poets, and at the time of his death, she found solace in Rumi. She also found her way back to her religion and the Quran, especially embracing Sufism, though a disaffected sister failed to see the connection: "She said to me, 'Rumi was a gentle, smart man, a humanist. Why are you connecting him with religion?'" Going through difficult times in her personal life, she kept Rumi's poems in her office, to read between patients: "We're a society in love with love, but Rumi takes that love deeper and acknowledges the pain beyond the high."

I recognized at the end of my travels a sensation present with equal force when I first discovered Rumi in my friend's apartment in Miami two decades earlier: the texture of a voice. No matter whether in the echoing lyrics of the *ghazal,* the sermonic tales of the *Masnavi,* or his extemporaneous talks, Rumi communicated urgency and intimacy, love and humor, as well as a need to be heard, even while circling secrets. In what I might sniff at or admire in various translations something irresistibly recognizable comes through. While reticent in sharing all the minute details of his everyday life, Rumi remained open, loving, vulnerable, candid, and even confessional. His great achievement—to articulate the sound of one soul speaking:

> *Don't speak so you can hear those voices*
> *Not yet turned into words or sounds*

Acknowledgments

A great benefit in writing about Rumi is being refreshed daily by his wise statements and life advice. Early on I was taken with one such line from a *ghazal,* which became a compass needle in the travels both geographic and literary that have engaged me for nearly eight years: "Sit close to someone with a big heart, sit in the shade of a tree with fresh leaves." Fortunately, Rumi tends to attract scholars, curators, translators, tour guides, devotees, religious leaders, librarians, artists, musicians, and close readers with big hearts. To all of them, who are finally too numerous to name, I owe a debt of gratitude for the extended experience of sitting in the shade of this tree with fresh leaves.

Rumi's was a big life, and the world of interest that has grown around him in over eight hundred years is immense. My predecessors in studying the life and work of Rumi include writers and scholars of such accomplishment that I could only hope their contributions register however faintly in my own language and thought. The contemporary American scholar who has devoted himself most exhaustively to Rumi is Franklin D. Lewis, chair of the Department of Near Eastern Languages and Civilizations at the University of Chicago. His *Rumi: Past and Present, East and West* was my authoritative source for many of the facts of Rumi's life. I am also grateful to Professor Lewis for taking time to have a conversation over lunch when he was in New York City. Of bygone Rumi scholars of similar stature, I am indebted to the great editor Badi al-Zaman Foruzanfar, of the University of Tehran, and to the vibrant books on the subject by Annemarie Schimmel, formerly Professor of Indo-Muslim Studies at Harvard.

Writing this biography has required many meetings with experts, several of whom have been extraordinarily generous, ignoring any impulse to territoriality in sharing their knowledge—a testament to them and, again, perhaps, to Rumi. Standing out among these is the Iranian-American novelist and essayist Salar Abdoh, codirector of the Creative Writing MFA program at the City College of New York. Dividing his time between Tehran and New York City, Salar was invaluable in finding books for me in the original Persian that were unavailable in the United States. For securing the remainder of such elusive texts through interlibrary loan, I am grateful to W. Gregory Gallagher, the diligent librarian of The Century Association. For other such guidance, I thank: Ahmad Ashraf, managing editor of *Encyclopedia Iranica*, Columbia University; Mohammad Batmanglij, publisher of Mage books; Dick Davis, the excellent translator of Hafez and other Persian poets; and research specialist David Smith, formerly at the New York Public Library.

As Rumi wrote and spoke in Persian and most of the contemporary accounts of his life are in Persian as well as some of the most fascinating scholarship, much still not translated, the initial phase of this project involved learning the language. For leading me through the beauties and peculiarities of Farsi my greatest debt is to the writer and native Persian speaker Maryam Mortaz, my first tutor. As the project grew, so did her role, as she was my collaborator on the translations of Rumi and other sources from the original Persian used in this biography. At the University of Texas in Austin, where I took part in the Summer

Persian Language Institute in 2011, my talented instructor was Blake Atwood, with whom I subsequently studied in an online graduate-level Persian language course. At the University of Wisconsin in Madison, where I attended the Arabic Persian Turkish Language Immersion Institute in the summer of 2012, I am similarly indebted to Seyede Pouye Khoshkhoosani, Parvaneh Hosseini Fahraji, and Mehrak Kamalisarvestani. For seven years I have also studied on-and-off in the collegial evening classes of Persian taught by Fahimeh Gooran Savadkoohi at the New York University School of Continuing and Professional Studies. For guiding me to all of these programs, and for our stimulating discussions of Persian poetry over coffee, I acknowledge the esteemed literary critic and Iranologist, Mohammad Mehdi Khorrami, clinical professor of Middle Eastern and Islamic Studies at New York University.

Traveling in the lands known to Rumi requires expert help and guidance. Among those who made my travels both possible and most rewarding: the Harvard Museum of Natural History Travel Program; Dmitry Rudich at MIR Corporation in Seattle; and my guides Muzafar Ibragimov in Tajikistan, Mahmood Daryaee in Iran, and Üzeyir Özyurt in Konya, Turkey, where I was also shown around by the highly informed Dr. Naci Bakirci, associate director of the Mevlana Museum, and Dr. Nuri Şimşekler of the Selçuk University of Konya. Of helpful friends, I wish to thank: Saadi Alkouatli for his part in arranging my trip within Syria; for her advice on traveling in Central Asia, Dr. Emily Jane O'Dell; Dr. Robert Finn, formerly the United States ambassador to Afghanistan; Frederick Eberstadt; Omer Koç, for his hospitality in Istanbul and for providing me with an introduction to Esin Celebi Bayru, Rumi's granddaughter from the twenty-second generation; and Joshua W. Walker. I am also grateful to Richard David Story, the editor in chief of *Departures* magazine, for commissioning the article "Turkey's Magical Mystical Tour."

For interviews kindly granted either in person, through email, or on Skype, I wish to thank: Coleman Barks; William Chittick, professor of Asian and Asian American Studies at Stony Brook University, to whom I was kindly introduced by his student Behrooz Karjooravary; Kabir Helminksi; Ahmet Karamustafa, professor of History at the University of Maryland; Jawid Mojaddedi, associate professor of Religion and director of Graduate Studies, Rutgers University, and translator of *The Masnavi*; Asma Sadiq, M.D., director of the Division of Developmental-Behavioral Pediatrics, Beth Israel Medical Center; Professor Dr. Kelim Erkan Türkmen; travel writer and linguist Bruce Wannell; and Professor Ehsan Yarshater, founder of The Center for Iranian Studies, and Hagop Kevorkian Professor Emeritus of Iranian Studies at Columbia University.

For invaluable ongoing advice on the writing of this book, I wish to thank my perceptive friend and longtime "first reader" Barbara Heizer for her generous and characteristically insightful responses. I relied as well on my two resourceful research assistants Mariam Rahmani and Jacob Denz, and on the cartographer Anandaroop Roy for designing the accompanying maps. For expert readings of later versions of the book, I am indebted to Imam Feisal Abdul Rauf, chairman of The Cordoba Initiative, Joel Conarroe, and Daniel Rafinejad. I cannot imagine this book existing in its present form without the influence at critical moments of my editor at Harper, William Strachan, as well as the early, bold, and continuous support of my publisher, Jonathan Burnham, and the tiger in my corner, my agent, Joy Harris, whose passion for this project has never wavered.

Rumi's name will always be synonymous with love. He is the poet of love and, as he put it, "the preacher of love." Nowhere has love been more real to me during the writing of this book than in my family, a kind of team of love. I could never decide whether my partner, Paul Raushenbush, was the Rumi in my life or the Shams, but he was certainly the loving and listening collaborator and fellow traveler in the creation of this book in more ways than I could ever spell out. The miracle of love, who happily arrived during the last year of *Rumi's Secret,* our son, Walter, has by now made everything new, including writing, and the sort of reading that takes place on cardboard pages, bringing to life for us Rumi's essential line, "Your love claps its hands, creating a hundred worlds."

Note on Transliteration

THE guiding principle in transliterating Persian and Arabic words in this biography has been to ease the difficulties of non-specialist readers. Persian words have been rendered into Latin script according to the standard Iranian pronunciation of today. Words of Arabic origin that have entered English parlance, such as hijab or Kaaba, have retained their common spellings. Proper names of Arab historical figures have been transliterated according to a simplified version of the system used by the *International Journal of Middle East Studies*. Diacritic marks have been entirely omitted, except in the bibliographical citations, where a stricter system of transliteration, which adheres more closely to the titling of articles or books in library catalogues, has been used.

Glossary of Names

Alaoddin Mohammad. One of Rumi's two sons by his first wife, named after Rumi's brother.

Bahaoddin Valad, or *Baha Valad.* Rumi's father.

Fateme Khatun, or *Fateme.* Daughter of Salahoddin; wife of Sultan Valad.

Gowhar Khatun, or *Gowhar.* First wife of Rumi.

Great Kerra, the. Mother of Rumi's first wife; a Samarkand disciple of Rumi's father.

Kerra Khatun, or *Kerra.* Second wife of Rumi.

Kimiya. In harem of Rumi; wife of Shams of Tabriz.

Kimiya Khatun, or *Kimiya.* Stepdaughter of Rumi; daughter of Kerra Khatun.

Maleke Khatun. Rumi's daughter, with Kerra Khatun.

Momene Khatun, or *Momene.* Rumi's mother, one of Bahaoddin Valad's wives.

Mozaffaroddin Amir Alem Chelebi. Rumi's third son, with Kerra Khatun.

Shamsoddin Yahya. Stepson of Rumi, son of Kerra Khatun.

Sultan Valad, or *Bahaoddin Mohammad.* One of Rumi's two sons by his first wife.

Ulu Amir Aref Chelebi, or *Jalaloddin Faridun.* Rumi's grandson, son of Sultan Valad and Fateme.

FRIENDS

Badroddin Gowhartash. Fortress commander, built *madrase* in Konya for Rumi's family.

Borhanoddin Mohaqqeq, or *Borhan.* Born in Termez, Rumi's tutor, godfather, and guide.

Gorji Khatun, "the Georgian lady," or *Tamar.* Noblewoman, devotee of Rumi.

Hosamoddin Chelebi, or *Hosam.* Rumi's final beloved companion; wrote down *Masnavi.*

Ibnal-Adim. Poet, historian, and diplomat, as well as Rumi's prime teacher in Aleppo.

Sadroddin Qonavi. Godson of Ibn Arabi; in Konya, taught a path of mystical knowledge.

Salahoddin Zarkub, or *Salah.* Goldsmith; Rumi's beloved companion after Shams.

Serajoddin Ormovi. Religious judge in Konya during Rumi's mature years.

Shamsoddin, Shams of Tabriz, or *Shams.* Rumi's beloved companion, and the "face of the sun."

POETS AND WRITERS

Attar. An herbal apothecary, in Nishapur; wrote *The Conference of the Birds.*

Jami. Fifteenth-century Naqshabandi Sufi poet of Khorasan.

Khayyam, Omar. Twelfth-century mathematician from Nishapur, famous for his *robaiyyat.*

al-Mutanabbi. Major eleventh-century Arabic poet, a lifelong favorite of Rumi.

Nezami. Court poet in Azerbaijan; wrote classic romance in couplets, *Layli and Majnun.*

Rudaki. Tenth-century innovative poet in Bukhara said to have invented the *robai* form.

Sanai. From Ghazna, Central Afghanistan; adapted courtly forms for spiritual subjects.

Yaqut. Muslim geographer and travel writer; a contemporary of Rumi.

POLITICAL FIGURES

Alaoddin Kayqobad I. Seljuk Sultan (r. 1219–37); invited Rumi's family to Konya.

Alaoddin Kayqobad II. Seljuk Sultan (r. 1246–57). Youngest son of Kaykhosrow II, his mother was the Georgian princess Gorji Khatun; died on mission to the Mongol court.

Aminoddin Mikail. A treasury official and viceroy, his wife was a disciple of Rumi.

Ezzoddin Kaykaus II. Seljuk Sultan (r. 1246, or 1248–60). Eldest of three sons of Kaykhosrow II, his mother was the daughter of a Greek priest.

Ghengis Khan (c. 1162–1227). Founder and Great Khan of the Mongol Empire.

Ghiasoddin Kaykhosrow II, Seljuk Sultan (r. 1237–46) married to Gorji Khatun.

Ghiasoddin Kaykhosrow III (r. 1264–82), Seljuk Sultan set up, when no more than seven years old, by the Parvane.

Hulagu Khan (c. 1218–1265). Grandson of Ghenghis Khan; conquered much of western Asia and led the siege and attack on Damascus.

Khwarazmshah, Alaoddin Mohammad, b. *Takesh* (r. 1200–1220). Ruler of Khwarazm, in Central Asia, during Rumi's childhood; besieged Samarkand.

Moinoddin Solayman Parvane ("The Butterfly"). Statesman, and
  de facto ruler of Seljuk Anatolia during the period of the
  Mongol protectorate; married to Gorji Khatun.

Nezam al-Molk. Eleventh-century Seljuk vizier; founded Ne-
  zamiyye University in Baghdad; patron of Omar Khayyam,
  and author of a handbook on statecraft.

Roknoddin, Qelij Arslan IV (r. 1246–64), Seljuk Sultan. Second
  son of Kaykhosrow II, his mother was a Greek slave and con-
  cubine. Apparently murdered at a banquet.

RELIGIOUS FIGURES

Bayazid Bestami. Ninth-century Sufi; promoted a "drunken"
  School of Sufism.

Fakhroddin Razi of Herat. Muslim analytic philosopher and
  preacher disliked by Rumi's father.

al-Ghazali, Abu Hamed Mohammad. Eleventh-century luminary of
  Nezamiyye College, Baghdad; rejected logical philosophy in
  his *The Revival of the Religious Sciences.*

al-Ghazali, Ahmad. Radical Sufi poet and mystic; brother of Mo-
  hammad al-Ghazali.

al-Hallaj, Mansur. Tenth-century ecstatic or "drunken" Sufi, exe-
  cuted in Baghdad.

Ibn Arabi. Spanish-born Arab mystic; wrote *Meccan Revelations,* a
  synthesis of mystical thought in Rumi's era; taught in Damas-
  cus and Aleppo.

Jonayd. Tenth-century Sufi; promoted the "sober" School of
  Baghdad.

Glossary of Terms

Abbasid. The third of the Islamic caliphates to succeed the Prophet Mohammad, the Abbasids ruled mostly from their capital in Baghdad in modern-day Iraq after assuming authority from the Umayyads in the eighth century.

akhavan. A sodality of craftsmen, laborers, and merchants, similar to early guilds, with overtones of chivalry and brotherhood.

Ayyubid. A Muslim dynasty founded by Saladin and centered in Egypt with sultans often vying for power in Syria and other parts of the Middle East.

Baba. Religious figures, often accompanying Turkmen immigrating to Anatolia from Central Asia.

caliph. A term meaning "deputy" or "successor" of the Prophet Mohammad after his death, applied to the governing religious leader of Muslims.

caravanserai. A roadside inn, also known as a *han.*

chelle. Sufi initiatory practice of an extended period of isolation from the world.

dervish. The Turkish version of a Persian word for those who renounced the world, or for the poor in God; commonly used for Sufis.

divan. A collection of poems.

fatwa. A ruling of a religious scholar on questions of Islamic jurisprudence.

fotovvat. A widespread brotherhood within Islam, which included some caliphs as members, and combined chivalric morals and a set of ethics with Sufi mysticism as well as a touch of militant power.

ghazal. Lyrical, rhymed poems, often on romantic themes, sometimes including *radif,* or repeated words or phrases at the end of each line, and not usually exceeding sixteen lines.

hadith. Recorded sayings or teachings of the Prophet Mohammad.

hajj. The annual pilgrimage to the holy city of Mecca, incumbent on able Muslims at least once in a lifetime.

harem. Separate quarters for women and young children in a traditional Muslim household.

hazl. Bawdy Persian poems featuring course satire and vulgar language.

jinn. Invisible, mischievous spirits, or genies.

Kaaba. The most sacred shrine in Islam, located in the courtyard of the Great Mosque at Mecca, and believed to have been built by the patriarch Abraham.

khaneqah. A Sufi lodge.

Khorasan. The eastern region of the former Persian Empire, including much of modern-day eastern Iran, Afghanistan, Uzbekistan, Turkmenistan, and Tajikistan.

lale. A tutor for children.

madrase. An upper-level school or college.

maktab. Elementary school.

malamatiyya. Followers of the "path of blame," who purposely disguised their piety in unorthodox clothing and behavior.

Mamluk. A military or warrior caste that rose from the ranks of slave soldiers to eventually control sultanates in Egypt and Syria in the thirteenth century.

masnavi. A long poem in rhyming couplets, often on spiritual themes; also the preferred form for narrative in classical Persian.

mihrab. A wall niche in mosques indicating the direction of the holy city of Mecca.

minbar. Pulpit in a mosque.

Mowlana. Rumi's title, meaning "Our Master," or "Our Teacher." The term in Turkish is "Mevlana," the basis of the name for the Mevlevi Order.

nay. A reed flute.

qasida. A longer ode, often of praise, but also written with elegiac, satirical, didactic, or religious content.

qadi. A local Muslim judge of religious law.

qibla. The direction of Mecca, which is the orientation for Muslim prayer.

rabab. A rebec, or small, stringed, upright instrument, sometimes bowed like a fiddle.

robai. A poem consisting of a four-line quatrain, often including short, pithy observations about life.

sama. Meditative sessions of listening to music and poetry, sometimes accompanied by a whirling dance.

Seljuks. Originally one of dozens of nomadic Turkic clans in Central Asia, the Seljuks enjoyed a two-century hold on power in the central Islamic lands—the Great Seljuks the "protector" of the Abbasid caliphate in Baghdad, and the Seljuks in Anataolia defeating the Byzantines to establish a Seljuk Sultanate.

Sharia. Religious law, differently interpreted in such Sunni schools of law as Hanafi, which was followed by Rumi's family, Shafii, and Hanbali.

sheikh. In the Sufi tradition, a spiritual leader or guide.

Shia. The minority branch of Islam believing that the leadership of Islam should reside with the descendants of the family of the Prophet Mohammad, beginning with his cousin and son-in-law Ali. "Shia" literally means "Party of Ali."

Sufism. The mystical branch of Islam, from the root word "*suf,*" or wool, perhaps for the woolen robes worn by early Sufi ascetics, rejecting wealth and worldliness.

Sunni. The majority branch of Islam, believing leadership of Islam was rightfully passed down through the Companions of the Prophet, following the "sunna" or example of the Prophet, rather than residing necessarily with the family and descendants.

takhallos. A signature, tag, or pen name, used by a poet, and usually reserved for the last line of a *ghazal*; also described as a "clasp," holding together its strung pearls of single lines into a necklace.

Umayyad. The second of the Islamic caliphates to succeed the Prophet Mohammad, the Umayyad dynasty ruled mostly from Damascus, beginning in the seventh century until overturned by the Abbasid dynasty in the eighth century.

Maps

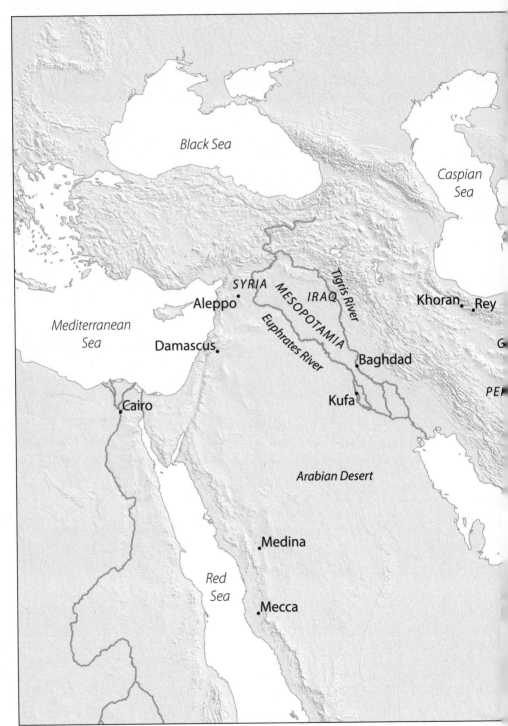

Central Asia and the Middle East in the Thirteenth Century CE

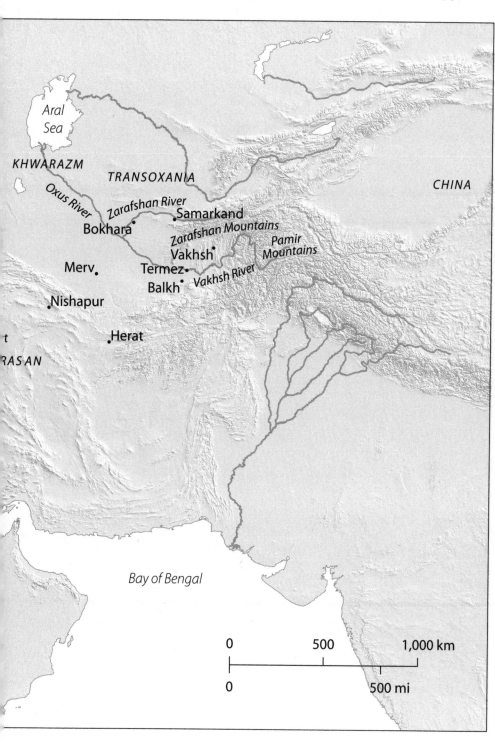

Anatolia and Neighboring Lands in the Thirteenth Century CE

References

WORKS CITED [DIRECT TRANSLATIONS]

al-Aflaki, Shams al-Din Ahmad. *Manâqeb al-'ârefin*, ed., Tahsin Yazici, 2 vols. (Ankara: Türk Tarih Kurumu Basimevi, 1959). Reference is made to the offset reprint, 4th edition (Tehran: Donyâ-ye Ketâb, 1985/2006).

Bahâ al-Din Valad. *Ma'âref: majmu'e-ye mavâ'ez va sokhanânan-e Soltân al-'olamâ Bahâ al-Din Mohammad b. Hosayn Khatibi-ye Balkhi*, ed., Badi' al-Zamân Foruzânfar, 2 vols. (Tehran: Edâre-ye Koll-e Enteba'ât-e Vezârat-e Farhang, 1955 and 1959.) A 2nd edition was published in Tehran in 1973.

Borhân al-Din Mohaqqeq. *Ma'âref: majmu'e-ye mavâ'ez va kalamât-e Seyyed Borhân al-Din Mohaqqeq-e Termezi*, ed., Badi' al-Zamân Foruzânfar. 2nd edition. (Tehran: Markaz-e Nashr-e Dâneshgâh-e Tehrân, section edition, 1998). First published 1961.

Faridun b. Ahmad Sepahsâlâr. *Resâle-ye Sepahsâlâr*, ed. by Sa'id Nafisi (Tehran: Eqbâl, 1325/1947); reprinted as *Zendeginâme-ye Mowlânâ Jalâl al-Din Mowlavi* in 1983).

Foruzânfar, Badi' al-Zamân. *Resâle dar tahqiq-e ahvâl va zendegâni-ye Mowlânâ Jalâl al-Din Mohammad mashhur be Mowlavi*, rev. 4th edition (Tehran: Zavvâr, 1978). First published 1951.

Rumi. *Divân-e Shams-e Tabrizi*. Following the edition of Badi' al-Zamân Foruzânfar, *Kolliyât-e Shams yâ Divân-e Kabir*, 10 vols. (Tehran: University of Tehran Press, 1957–67). Reference is made to the edition of the entire series reprinted by Amir Kabir in nine volumes, 2535/1977. The *Divân* gives the number for each *ghazal*, *robai*, and *tarji-band*.

_____. *Fihe mâ fih az goftâr-e Mowlânâ Jalâl al-Din Mohammad mashhur be Mowlavi*, ed. Badi' al-Zamân Foruzânfar (Tehran: Negâh, 1389/2010). First edition published by Amir Kabir, 1951.

_____. *Majâles-e sabe'e* (Tehran: Kayhân, reprint 1994). First edition published in 1986.

_____. *Maktubât-e Mowlânâ Jalâl al-Din Rumi*, ed., Towfiq Sobhâni (Tehran: Markaz-e Nashr-e Dâneshgâhi, 1992).

_____. *Masnavi-ye ma'navi*, ed., R. A. Nicholson as *The Mathnawi of Jalalu'ddin Rumi*, E. J. W. Gibb Memorial, new series (London: Luzac & Co., 1925, 1929, 1933). Reference is made in these pages to the one-volume edition subsequently printed in Iran (Tehran: Gooya Books, 1386/2007).

Shams al-Din Tabrizi. *Maqâlat-e Shams-e Tabrizi*, ed., Mohammad 'Ali Movahhed (Tehran: Sahâmi, Enteshârât-e Khwârazmi, 1990).

Sultan Valad. *Divân: Divân-e Sultan Valad*, ed., S. Nafisi (Tehran 1338/1959).

_____. *Masnavi-ye Valadi, enshâ'-e Bahâ al-Din b. Mowlânâ Jalâl al-Din Mohammad b. Hosayn-e Balkhi, mashhur be Mowlavi*, ed., Jalâl al-Din Homâ'i (Tehran: Homâ, 1389/2010. Second Printing. First edition published by Eqbâl, 1316/1937.) Known as *Valad nâme* in Iran, and as *Ebtedâ nâme* in Turkey. [My translations are in prose; the original was written in *masnavi* verse couplets.]

WORKS CITED (SECONDARY SOURCES)

Barthold, W. *Turkestan Down to the Mongol Invasion* (Exeter, Great Britain: E. J. W. Gibb Memorial Trust. First published in English in 1928, 2012 reprint).

Bennison, Amira K. *The Great Caliphs: The Golden Age of the Abbasid Empire* (New Haven and London: Yale University Press, 2009).

Bobrick, Benson. *The Caliph's Splendor: Islam and the West in the Golden Age of Baghdad* (New York: Simon & Schuster, 2012).

Browne, Edward G. *A Literary History of Persia: 1000–1290* (Cambridge, UK: Cambridge University Press, 1969; first published in 1906).

Chamberlain, Michael. *Knowledge and Social Practice in Medieval Damascus, 1190–1390* (Cambridge, UK: Cambridge University Press, 1994).

Chittick, William C. *The Sufi Path of Love* (Albany: State University of New York Press, 1983).

Hansen, Valerie. *The Silk Road: A New History* (New York: Oxford University Press, 2012).

Harvey, Andrew. *The Way of Passion: A Celebration of Rumi* (Berkeley, California: Frog, Ltd. 1994).

Hirtenstein, Stephen. *The Unlimited Mercifier: The Spiritual Life and Thought of Ibn Arabi* (Ashland, Oregon: Anqa Publishing, 1999).

Karamustafa, Ahmet T. *Sufism: The Formative Period* (Berkeley and Los Angeles: University of California Press, 2007).

Le Strange, Guy. *The Lands of the Eastern Caliphate: Mesopotamia, Persia, and Central Asia from the Moslem Conquest to the Time of Timur* (New York: Cosimo Classics, 2010; first published in 1905).

———. *Baghdad during the Abbasid Caliphate* (New York: Cosimo Classics, 2011; first published in 1901).

Lewis, Bernard, editor and translator. *Music of a Distant Drum: Classical Arabic, Persian, Turkish and Hebrew Poems* (Princeton and Oxford: Princeton University Press, 2001; first published in hardcover by Oneworld Publications, 2000.)

Lewis, Franklin D. *Rumi: Past and Present, East and West* (Oxford: A Oneworld Book, 2008, revised paperback edition). First published in hardback by Oneworld Publications, 2005.

———. "Reading, Writing, and Recitation: Sanai and the Origins of the Persian Ghazal" (Ph.D. dissertation, University of Chicago, 1995).

Morray, David. *An Ayyubid Notable and His World: Ibn al-Adim and Aleppo as Portrayed in His Biographical Dictionary of People Associated with the City* (Leiden: E. J. Brill, 1994).

Rypka, Jan. *History of Iranian Literature* (Dordrecht-Holland: D. Reidel Publishing Company, 1968).

Safi, Omid. *The Politics of Knowledge in Premodern Islam: Negotiating Ideology and Religious Inquiry* (Chapel Hill: University of North Carolina Press, 2006).

Schmimmel, Annemarie. *As Through a Veil: Mystical Poetry in Islam* (Oxford: Oneworld Publications, 2001, originally published 1982).

———. *Mystical Dimensions of Islam* (Chapel Hill: University of North Carolina Press, 1975).

_____. *Rumi's World: The Life and Work of the Great Sufi Poet* (Boston & London: Shambhala Press, 2001; originally published as *I Am Wind, You Are Fire*).

_____. *The Triumphal Sun* (Albany: State University of New York Press, 1993).

Tabatabai, Sassan. *Father of Persian Verse: Rudaki and His Poetry* (Leiden: Leiden University Press, Iranian Study Series, 2010).

Weatherford, Jack. *Genghis Khan and the Making of the Modern World* (New York: Crown Publishers, 2004).

Zarrinkub, A. H. *Step by Step Up to Union with God: Life, Thought and Spiritual Journey of Jalal-al-Din Rumi*, trans. by M. Kayvani (New York: Persian Heritage Foundation, 2009).

Notes

EPIGRAPH

xi "Love stole." Ghazal #940.

PROLOGUE

2 *Masnavi.* Its full title, *Masnavi-ye ma'navi,* is sometimes translated into English as "Spiritual Verses."

2 "Hearken to this reed." *Rumi: Poet and Mystic.* Translated by Reynold Nicholson (London: George Allen and Unwin Ltd., 1950), 31.

4 "I am the black cloud." #183. *Mystical Poems of Rumi.* Translated by A. J. Arberry. (Chicago and London: The University of Chicago Press edition, 2009), 197.

4 "Islam in New York City." A chapter of my book *Godtalk: Travels in Spiritual America* (New York: Alfred A. Knopf, 2002).

4 "best-selling poet." Ptolemy Tompkins, "Rumi Rules!" *Time Asia* 160, no. 13 (October 7, 2002), 62.

4 "Out beyond ideas of wrongdoing." *The Essential Rumi.* Translations by Coleman Barks with John Moyne, A. J. Arberry, Reynold Nicholson (Edison, New Jersey: Castle Books, 1997), 36.

4 "If you accustom yourself." *Signs of the Unseen: The Discourses of Jala-luddin Rumi.* Introduction and translation by W. M. Thackston Jr. (Boston: Shambhala Publications, 1994), Discourse 55, 210.

5 "paradise on earth." Ghazal #1493. All the lines from the *ghazals* and *robais* are taken from the *Divân-e Shams-e Tabrizi*.

6 "The mind is a caravanserai." *Masnavi*, V, 3644; 3646.

7 "calls me from the other side." Aflaki, *Manâqeb al-'ârefin*, III, sec. 579, 589.

8 "If you visit my grave." Ghazal #683.

8 "No one understood." Aflaki, III, sec. 333, 400.

CHAPTER 1: "IN A LIGHTNING FLASH
FROM HERE TO VAKHSH"

11 "In a lightning flash." *Masnavi*, IV, 3319.

11 "These are angels." Aflaki, III, sec. 1, 73.

11 "Let's jump." Ibid., III, sec. 2, 74.

12 "Love is your father." Ghazal #333.

12 "no name." Robai #1143.

12 "My Jalaloddin." Aflaki, III, sec. 2, 74.

13 "mean temper . . . ." Baha, *Ma'âref*, 2:62.

13 Vakhsh. An equation of Vakhsh with the medieval city of Lewkand, near the modern village of Sangtuda, is established in V. Minorsky, *Hudud al-'alâm: Translation and Commentary* (London: E. J. W. Gibb Memorial Series, New Series, XI, 1970), 359, 361. His findings are corroborated by Barthold, *Turkestan Down to the Mongol Invasion*, 69, and J. Marquart, *Eransahr nach der Geographie des Ps. Moses Xorenanc I*, Abh.kgl.Ges.Wiss.Göttingen, Phil.-hist. KLI.NJ Bd III, Nro. 2, 1901, 232–34, 236, 299, 303. Marquart writes that "as so often happens among the Arabs, the name of the country [Vakhsh] was carried over [to what] must have been considered its capital city [Lewkand]" (299). These studies are cited by Fritz Meier, *Baha-e Walad: Grundzüge seines Lebens and seiner Mystik* (Leiden: E. J. Brill, 1989), 15, footnote 7, the study that first established Vakhsh as the home of Baha Valad between 1204 and 1210. Meier deduces that if Minorsky is correct then Vakhsh was located on the thirty-eighth parallel of latitude. Franklin D. Lewis in *Rumi: Past and Present, East and West* (Oxford: A Oneworld Book, 2008, revised paperback edition), 47, further pinpoints the location of medieval Vakhsh/Lewkand near the modern-day village of Sangtuda, Tajikistan, on the east bank of the Vakhshab River, about sixty-five kilometers southeast of Dushanbe, thirty-five kilome-

ters northeast of Kurgan-Tyube, within five hundred kilometers of China.

13 "very fertile." Guy Le Strange, *The Lands of the Eastern Caliphate: Mesopotamia, Persia, and Central Asia from the Moslem Conquest to the Time of Timur* (New York: Cosimo Classics, 2010; first published in 1905), 438.

14 "your sweet scent." Ghazal #12.

14 "religion of lovers." *Masnavi*, II, 1770.

14 "If he is Turk or Tajik." Ghazal #58.

14 "Why is divine light." Ghazal #332.

15 "Joyful Prince." *Masnavi*, II, 929.

15 "Allah, Allah, Allah." Aflaki, III, secs. 159–61, 250–51.

16 "the light of God." *Fihe ma fih*, Discourse 2, 25.

17 "This arousal." Baha, 1:381.

17 "Maybe like the morning." Baha, 1:327.

18 "Embrace God." Baha, 2:28.

18 "I began to wonder." Baha, 2:138.

18 "Sometimes I feel." Baha, 1:374.

18 "Sultan al-Olama." Baha, 1:188–89.

18 "deviant." Baha, 1:82.

19 "useless." Ibid.

19 "But I have not found." *Encyclopedia of Islam*, New Edition, vol. 2, C-G, 1965, s.v. "Fakhr al-Din al-Razi."

19 "That philosopher." *Masnavi*, IV, 3354.

20 Journal. Known as *Ma'âref*, or "Intimations," this journal was held by Rumi, then recopied and circulated in private libraries of the Mevlevi order in Konya and Istanbul over seven centuries. When Rumi's Iranian editor Badi al-Zaman Foruzunfar obtained a handwritten copy in Tehran in the 1950s, he was impressed enough to publish a critical edition. He praised Baha Valad's "elegance of expression" as "one of the best examples of poetic prose" in Persian [Lewis, *Rumi*, 85]. A. J. Arberry, translating twenty sections into English, found his Persian "remarkably fine and eloquent" [Arberry, *Aspects of Islamic Civilizaion*, 228]. For the German Rumi scholar Annemarie Schimmel, the text was "rather weird" but the visions "astounding" [see Annemarie Schimmel, *The Triumphal Son: A Study of the Works of Jalaloddin Rumi* (Albany: State University of New York, 1993; first published in 1978 by FineBooks Ltd, Great Britain), 398].

20   "God inspired me." Baha, 2:138.

20   "I will be." Baha 1:354.

21   "You brother." Also translated as "Your sister's a whore." See Aflaki, III, sec. 417, 451.

22   "a grand Storybook." Rumi. *A Rumi Anthology,* trans. by Reynold A. Nicholson (Oxford: Oneworld Publications, 2000), Introduction, xxiii.

22   "Go ask Kalile." *Masnavi,* I, 899.

22   "You must have read." *Masnavi,* IV, 2203.

23   "No one has ever seen." Ferdowsi, *Shahname: The Epic of the Persian Kings,* trans. by Ahmad Sadri (New York: The Quantuck Lane Press, 2013), 347.

23   "sets the world on fire." Ghazal #975.

23   "Anywhere you find anger." Ghazal #2198.

24   "When the perfume of your grace." Ghazal #690.

24   "The hero gives a wooden sword." Ghazal #27.

25   "It occurred to me." Baha, 1:360.

CHAPTER 2: SAMARKAND

26   "1212." Yolande Crowe, "Samarkand," *The Encyclopedia of Islam,* Volume VIII (Leiden: E. J. Brill, 1993), 1033. Possible dates suggested elsewhere for the siege of Samarkand, which fixes the presence of Rumi and family in the city, are 1211 or 1213.

26   "Inside this month." Ghazal #2344.

27   "perpetually clear." Abul-Fida, cited in Afzal Iqbal, *Life & Work of Muhammad Jalal-ud-Din Rumi* (New Delhi: Kitab Bhavan, 2003), 29.

28   "Her pulse was beating." *Masnavi,* I, 167–70.

29   "Astonishing figures." Ibn Hawqal, cited in W. Barthold, *Turkestan Down to the Mongol Invasion* (Exeter, Great Britain: E. J. W. Gibb Memorial Trust. First published in English in 1928, 2012 reprint), 91.

29   "Spread out the paper." Ghazal #1.

30   *robai.* Ibn Sina (Avicenna), in the chapter on poetics in his *Mantiq al-shifâ',* mentions an alternative possibility that the *robai* might have been of Greek origin. See A. M. Damghani, "Persian Sufi Literature in Arabic," in *The Heritage of Sufism: Volume I: Classical Persian Sufism from Its Origins to Rumi* (Oxford: Oneworld, 1999), 53, fn. 35.

30   "Sugar." *Masnavi,* III, 3863.

30 "The death of a great man." Ghazal #1007.

30 "Now stirs the scent." Translation by the author from Persian
    text, in Sassan Tabatabai, *Father of Persian Verse: Rudaki and His Poetry*
    (Leiden: Leiden University Press, Iranian Study Series, 2010), 31.

30 "Now stirs the scent of the garden and the gardener." Ghazal
    #2897. (Cited in Usman Hadid, "Transformer," *The Friday Times*, Paki-
    stan weekly newspaper, vol. 25, no. 16, May 31–June 6, 2013, 24.)

31 "We were in Samarkand." *Fihe ma fih*, Discourse 44, 195.

31 "The word is an arrow." Ghazal #3073.

32 "Join together." *Masnavi*, IV, 3289.

32 "Someone said." *Fihe ma fih*, Discourse 41, 180.

33 "He went." Aflaki, III, sec. 246, 321.

33 "waving his hands." Aflaki, IV, sec. 84, 681.

33 high literacy rates. For a discussion of Muslim literacy, librar-
    ies, and schools and colleges in the Abbasid period in contrast with
    Europe, see Edmund Burke III, "Islam at the Center: Technological
    Complexes and the Roots of Modernity," *Journal of World History*, vol.
    20, no. 2 (June 2009) 177–82.

33 "That anxious mother." *Masnavi*, VI, 1433.

34 "Stay away." VI, 1436–37.

34 "At first." *Fihe ma fih*, Discourse 30, 151.

35 nurture over nature. The Mutazilites favored such teaching. Mu-
    tazila was an Islamic school of theology stressing rational thought over
    sacred precedent; they argued that the Quran was created, or written,
    rather than having been eternal or always coexisting with God.

35 "The opinions." *Masnavi*, III, 1542–43.

36 "The cleverest boy." III, 1526–28.

36 "Your love." III, 551.

36 "A window." VI, 3198.

37 "The flames." III, 3102–03.

37 "Some enjoy." *Fihe ma fih*, Discourse 43, 187.

38 "Amazing." *Masnavi*, III, 1858–59.

38 "That peerless." III, 1871.

39 "always lifting." Aflaki, II, sec. 1, 58.

39 "Go!" *Masnavi*, II, 1319.

39 "ability to argue." *Fihe ma fih*, Discourse 25, 129.

39 "just like a glass." Borhan, *Ma'aref*, 14.

40 "Closeness." *Masnavi*, III, 549–50.

40 "perfect saint." Aflaki, IV, sec. 84, 680.

40 "When God is taking." Baha, 1:354.

41 "from Rome to Khorasan." Rubai #1910.

41 rhythm. According to legend, Persian-Arabic poetic meters echo the different patterns of a camel's footfalls.

41 "Drunkenly pulling." Ghazal #302.

42 "Our voices." Ghazal #304.

CHAPTER 3: ON THE SILK ROAD

43 "Silk Road." I am indebted for this characterization of the Silk Road to Valerie Hansen, *The Silk Road: A New History* (New York: Oxford University Press, 2012), 5–7.

45 "Since I came." Ghazal #1373.

46 *The Conference of the Birds.* The original title is *Manteq al-tayr.*

46 "Your son." William C. Chittick, *The Sufi Path of Love* (Albany: State University of New York Press, 1983), 2.

46 *Book of Secrets.* The original title is *Asrarname.*

46 "to lose their heads." J. T. P. De Bruijn. *Persian Sufi Poetry: An Introduction to the Mystical Use of Classical Poems* (London: Routledge, 1997), 107.

47 "the unique Attar." Ghazal #824.

47 "the scent of Attar." Ghazal #24.

47 "Whatever you want." Ghazal #2634.

47 Sanai. For a critique of the story of Sanai's sudden conversion to Sufism and complete abandonment of court poetry as a simplification of the facts see Franklin D. Lewis, "Reading, Writing, and Recitation: Sanai and the Origins of the Persian Ghazal" (Ph.D. dissertation, University of Chicago, 1995).

47 *Garden of Truth.* The original title is *Hadiqat al-haqiqe.*

47 "The Royal Road." Quoted in J. T. P. de Bruijn, "Comparative Notes on Sana'i and Attar," in *The Heritage of Sufism. Volume I,* ed., Leonard Lewisohn (Oxford: Oneworld, 1999), 371.

48 parodied. See *Masnavi,* II, 2617 ff.

48 "Attar was the soul." Sultan Valad, *Divan,* 240.

48 "Whoever deeply." Aflaki, III, sec. 430, 458.

48 "Whether at Nishapur." Translation by Edward Fitzgerald, in *Persian Poets,* selected and edited by Peter Washington (New York: Everyman's Library, 2000), 16.

49 "bathing in his sweat." Quoted in de Bruijn, *Persian Sufi Poetry*, 12.

49 "Speak Persian." *Masnavi*, III, 3842.

50 "*qibla* of the friend's face." Quoted in Annemarie Schimmel, *The Triumphal Sun* (Albany: State University of New York Press, 1993), 292.

51 "On a rainy day." Quoted in Benson Bobrick, *The Caliph's Splendor: Islam and the West in the Golden Age of Baghdad* (New York: Simon & Schuster, 2012), 71–72.

51 "the young deacons." Quoted in Guy Le Strange, *Baghdad during the Abbasid Caliphate* (New York: Cosimo Classics, 2011; first published in 1901), 212.

52 "Bukhara is a mine." Ghazal #2168.

52 "Give up art and logic." *Masnavi*, III, 1146.

52 "Your Baghdad." Ghazal #344.

52 "The Bedouin's wife." *Masnavi*, I, 2716–17, 2719.

52 "hot sun." *Masnavi*, III, 1041.

52 "The Euphrates, Tigris, and Oxus would be bitter." Ghazal #214.

54 turban. See *Masnavi*, IV, 1578–79.

54 *The Revival of the Religious Sciences*. The original title is *Ehya olum al-din*.

54 "Had he possessed." Aflaki, III, sec. 128, 219.

55 "The term." Ahmet T. Karamustafa, *Sufism: The Formative Period* (Berkeley and Los Angeles: University of California Press, 2007), 7.

55 "We indeed created." *The Koran Interpreted*, translated by A. J. Arberry (New York: Touchstone, 1955), vol. 2, 234.

55 Rabia. Rumi is quoted, telling this story of Rabia, in Aflaki, III, sec. 331, 397.

56 "I am the Truth." The original, in Arabic, is *anâ al-Haqq*.

56 "In the world." Ghazal #731.

56 "A man traveling." *Fihe ma fih*, Discourse 10, 63.

57 "piling a few." *Fihe ma fih*, Discourse 61, 244.

57 "Say there is someone." *Fihe ma fih*, Discourse 43, 190.

58 "The glory." *Masnavi*, V, 3224.

58 "When you're inside." *Masnavi*, II, 1768.

59 Stoning of the Devil. This ritual involves throwing pebbles at three pillars thought to represent Satan, who was believed to have thrice tried to persuade Abraham to disobey God's command to sacrifice his son Ishmael.

59 "market full of fruits." *The Travels of Ibn Jubayr*, translated by Roland

Broadhurst (New Delhi: Goodword, reprinted 2011, first printed 1952), 103.

59 "became a great market." Ibid., 188.

59 "women's veils." Ibid., 132.

59 "cohesion." Quoted in W. M. Thackston Jr. *Signs of the Unseen* (Boston and London: Shambhala, 1999), 67, fn. 111.

59 Visting the Kaaba. *Fihe ma fih*, Discourse 14, 80.

59 "Oh you." Ghazal #648.

59 "I need." "Rabia," in *Early Islamic Mysticism: Sufi, Qur'an, Mi'raj, Poetic and Theological Writings*, translated, edited, and with an introduction by Michael A. Sells (New York and Mahwah, NJ: Paulist Press, 1996), 157.

60 "The pilgrim kisses." Ghazal #617.

CHAPTER 4: "FIRE FELL INTO THE WORLD"

61 "Fire." Ghazal #2670.

62 "sideshow." Amira K. Bennison, *The Great Caliphs: The Golden Age of the Abbasid Empire* (New Haven and London: Yale University Press, 2009), 203.

63 "Glory be to God!" Foruzanfar, *Zendegi-ye Mowlânâ Jalâl al-Din mashur be Mowlavi*, 43, fn. 2. While the Foruzanfar version places the story in Syria, Ibn Arabi's biographer argues that such a meeting would more likely have been in Malatya. See Stephen Hirtenstein, *The Unlimited Mercifier: The Spiritual Life and Thought of Ibn Arabi* (Ashland, OR: Anqa Publishing, 1999), 188.

63 *Meccan Revelations*. The original title is *Fotuhat-e makkiye*.

63 "Well." Aflaki, III, sec. 444, 470.

64 "Crazy." Majnun is a nickname, literally meaning "possessed by *jinn.*" His actual name is Qays.

64 "Majnun." Ghazal #947.

65 "Day and night." Ghazal #2670.

65 "Some of them." *Fihe ma fih*, Discourse 14, 80.

66 Genghis Khan. I am indebted for the full history of Genghis Khan's invasions to Jack Weatherford, *Genghis Khan and the Making of the Modern World* (New York: Crown Publishers, 2004).

66 "ready for war." Ala Ad Din Ata Malik Jovayni. *The History of the World Conqueror, Vol. I*, translated by John Andrew Boyle (Cambridge, MA: Harvard University Press, 1958), 81.

66 "laid waste a whole world." Ibid., 80.

66 "beheld." Ibid., 98.

66 "stands for." *Masnavi,* III, 3791.

66 "They came." Jovayni, 107.

67 "all the people." Ibid., 129.

67 "Wild beasts." Ibid., 131.

68 "the voice of pain." Quoted and translated from *The Conference of the Birds* by Annemarie Schimmel, *As Through a Veil,* 53. Schimmel was working from: Attar, *Mantiq ut-tair,* ed. M. Javad Mashkur (Tehran: Kitabfurush-i Tehran, 1962), 287.

68 "But for." Quoted in Le Strange, *The Lands of the Eastern Caliphate,* 401–2.

68 "effaced." Quoted in Edward G. Browne, *A Literary History of Persia, Vol.* 2 (Cambridge, UK: Cambridge University Press, 1969; first published in 1906), 432.

69 "the announcement." Ibid., 427.

69 "This period." Annemarie Schimmel, *The Triumphal Sun: A Study of the Works of Jalaloddin Rumi* (Albany: State University of New York Press, 1993; first published in 1978), 9.

70 "While everyone." Ghazal #1764.

70 "If you're afraid." Ghazal #1609.

71 "Today." Tarji-band #24, in *Divan.*

72 "The sky." Ghazal #1092.

72 "In childbirth." *Masnavi.* III, 3560–61.

73 "God is able." *Fihe ma fih, Discourse* 24, 125.

73 "Unless the baby." Ghazal #1156.

74 "Wars are like the fights." *Masnavi* I, 3435–36.

74 "They repented." Afklaki, I, sec. 47, 46.

74 "instructor." *Majâles-e sabe'e,* 62.

75 "The magician." Ibid., 108.

76 Najmoddin Razi. For a full comparison of the careers of Najmoddin Razi and Baha Valad, see Meier, *Bahâ'-i Walad,* 41–42.

76 "Like a baby." Ghazal #1372.

CHAPTER 5: KONYA

77 "Come." Ghazal #2905.

78 "Bahaoddin." Aflaki, III, sec. 148, 236.

79 "a dangerous dragon." Quoted in Tamara Talbot Rice, *The Seljuks* (London: Thames and Hudson, 1961), 172.

79 "embellishing." Ibid., 71.

80 "I prayed so much." Ghazal #903.

80 "If you turn into a lion." Ghazal #920.

81 "On all the roads." *Fihe ma fih*, Discourse 9, 54.

81 "At night." *Masnavi*, VI, 2381–83.

82 "The rose garden." Ghazal #1339. Of course spring was arguably the favorite season for all Persian poets and the depiction of the season a standard topos throughout all the lyrical poetry.

82 *The Acts of the Mystics.* The original title is *Manâqeb al-'ârefin.*

82 "Religious." Aflaki, I, sec. 21, 28–29.

83 "pleasant and polite." Ibid., 29.

83 "most learned." Borhân al-Din al-Zarnūjī, *Ta'līm al-Muta'allim: Tarīq at-Ta'allum; Instruction of the Student: The Method of Learning,* trans. G. E. Von Grunebaum and Theodora Abel (New York: King's Crown Press, 1947), 28.

83 "simple-hearted." Aflaki, I, sec. 36, 39.

85 "tongue," "walking stick." A. H. Zarrinkub, *Step by Step Up to Union with God: Life, Thought and Spiritual Journey of Jalal-al-Din Rumi,* trans. by M. Kayvani (New York: Persian Heritage Foundation, 2009), 61.

85 "Wait until." Aflaki, I, sec. 54, 52.

86 "After the mourning." Sultan Valad, *Valadname,* 195–96.

86 "He clearly heard." Aflaki, I, sec. 34, 38.

86 "The most effective." Baha, I: 152.

87 "Borhanoddin." Aflaki, II, sec. 22, 71.

87 "Your father." Ibid., sec. 1, 56.

88 "You are . . . If you don't know." Borhan, *Ma'aref,* 10, 18.

89 "God's seal." *Masnavi*, IV, 1923. By this time, Plato had become a standard symbol of wisdom generally in Persian poetry.

89 "Whatever." Ibid., VI, 4144.

90 "They said." *Fihe ma fih* Discourse 55, 229.

90 "Sayyed Borhanoddin." Ibid., Discourse 60, 242.

90 "The path." Borhan, *Ma'aref,* 14.

90 "root of spiritual joy." *Fihe ma fih*, Discourse 21, 113.

90 "Pharaoh." Borhan, *Ma'aref,* 26.

91 "I am the Truth." *Masnavi*, II, 305.

92 "God the Almighty." Borhan, *Ma'aref*, 26.

92 "And like." Sultan Valad, *Valadname*, 198.

CHAPTER 6: "I KEPT HEARING MY OWN NAME"

93 "I kept hearing." Robai #15.

93 "turbaned class." David Morray, *An Ayyubid Notable and His World: Ibn al-Adim and Aleppo as Portrayed in His Biographical Dictionary of People Associated with the City* (Leiden: E. J. Brill, 1994), 123.

94 "I'm the slave." Ghazal #3049.

95 "boundless compilation." Morray, *An Ayyubid Notable*, 10.

96 "innate poetic ability." Ibid., 181.

96 "the play." *Music of a Distant Drum: Classical Arabic, Persian, Turkish and Hebrew Poems*, translated and introduced by Bernard Lewis (Princeton and Oxford: Princeton University Press, 2001), 68.

96 "A heart." Ibid., 69.

96 "We can look." Ghazal #2266.

97 "sentinel." Morray, *An Ayyubid Notable*, 150.

97 "On the day." *Masnavi*, VI, 777, 782, 784.

97 "Have you been?" Ibid., 795.

98 "Mourn." Ibid., 802.

98 "In my youth." Aflaki, III, sec. 218, 301.

99 "Do not look." Cited in Michael Chamberlain, *Knowledge and Social Practice in Medieval Damascus, 1190–1390* (Cambridge, UK: Cambridge University Press, 1994), 129–30.

99 "I'm madly in love." Ghazal #1493.

101 "flashed." Cited in Michael Chamberlain, *Knowledge and Social Practice*, 155.

101 "his name." Ibid., fn. 25.

102 "When our Caesar." Ghazal #1921.

103 "The thinner." Borhan, *Maaref*, 14.

103 "fasting of the elite." Ibid., 20.

103 "Don't eat straw." *Masnavi*, V, 2473–74; 2477.

103 "Congratulations!" Ghazal #2344.

104 "tightening." Ghazal #2307.

104 "hidden sweetness." Ghazal #1739.

104 "During the *chelle*." *Masnavi*, V, 1445–46; 1448

105 "When he woke." Ibid., 1449–50.

105 "At that moment," Ibid., 1453–54.

106 "Some madness." Aflaki, II, sec. 4, 61.

106 "Undergo." Ibid., II, sec. 5, 61.

106 "Oh child." Ibid., II, sec. 12, 65.

106 "So I came." Ibid., II, sec. 23, 71.

106 "The stages." *Fihe ma fih*, Discourse 10, 62.

107 "If you prick." Cited in Zarrinkub, *Step by Step*, 91–92.

107 lists. See Chittick, *The Sufi Path of Love*, 2, as well as "Mawlana Jalaladdin Muhammad Rumi," by Adnan Karaismailoğlu, in *Rumi and His Sufi Path of Love*, eds., M. Fatih Çitlak and Huseyin Bingül (Somerset, NJ: The Light Publishing, 2007), 50.

108 "a second." Aflaki, III, sec. 14, 90. Partly due to Aflaki's description, she has sometimes been surmised to have been Christian, though no evidence exists.

108 "After today." Ibid., III, sec. 15, 93.

109 "God showed." *Fihe ma fih*, Discourse 19, 103.

109 "A woman." *Masnavi*, I, 2437.

110 "Dear son Bahaoddin." Rumi, *Maktubât*, Letter 64, 142.

110 "I was speaking." *Fihe ma fih*, Discourse 22, 115.

111 "Now that he stood." Sultan Valad, *Valadname*, 199.

111 "ten thousand." Ibid.

112 traps of fame. As Andrew Harvey wrote in *The Way of Passion: A Celebration of Rumi* (Berkeley, CA: Frog, Ltd. 1994), 20–21: "The ferocity and precision of Rumi's later attacks on mental pride and the hunger of fame show how intimately he knew and understood the dangers of both."

112 "For some time." Robai #15.

CHAPTER 7: "THE FACE OF THE SUN IS SHAMS OF TABRIZ"

115 "The face of the sun." Ghazal #310.

115 Shamsoddin. As *shams* is Arabic for "sun," his name could be translated "the Sun of Faith" or "the Sun of Tabriz."

115 "Parande." Aflaki, IV, sec. 3, 615.

115 "Aren't you coming?" Shams, *Maqâlât*, 141.

116 "My turban." Robai #1284.

116 "The first words." Shams, *Maqâlât*, 685; [Chittick, 210; Lewis, *Rumi*, 155]. Sepahsalar recounts their meeting as taking place in a little shop of the bazaar, where they stared at each other for hours before speaking. See Sepahsalar, *Resâle Sepahsalar*, 127.

117 "Was Bayazid." Aflaki, IV, sec. 8, 618–19.

117 "fell in a swoon." Ibid., 620.

117 "saw the veil." Sultan Valad, *Valadname*, 43.

118 "For lovers." *Masnavi*, III, 3847.

118 "After that." Aflaki, IV, sec. 9, 620.

119 "I already held." Ghazal #2669.

119 "I remember Mowlana." Shams, *Maqâlât*, 690.

119 "Salam." Ibid., 290.

119 "From the first day." Ibid., 752.

119 "I need it to be clear." Ibid., 686.

120 "Before me." Ibid., 730.

120 "Let's go." Ibid., 302.

120 "The tavern keeper." Ghazal #310.

120 "Where's your own?" Shams, *Maqâlât*, 744–45.

120 "Don't read!" Aflaki, IV, sec. 13, 623.

120 "He firmly commanded." Aflaki, IV, sec. 12, 623.

120 "That is not." Ibid., sec. 14, 623.

121 "This is the man." Ibid., sec. 15, 624.

121 "How sad." Lewis, *Music of a Distant Drum*, 71. Shams quotes a half-line of al-Maarri, "The high places will be earned in the measure of diligence," *Maqâlât*, 466.

121 "mixed-up." *Maqâlât*, 301.

122 "both father and son." *Maktubât*, Letter 130, 224.

122 "I rarely speak." *Maqâlât*, 290.

123 "He has a beautiful manner." Aflaki, IV, sec. 38, 636.

123 "He has two ways of speaking." *Maqâlât*, 104.

123 "Practice is practice." Ibid., 612–13.

123 "laid claim to love." Ibid., 231.

123 "When your love." Robai #616.

124 "When all the particles." Ghazal #1295.

124 "We will seek." Sultan Valad, *Valadname*, 195.

124 life story. Later Shams would refer in public with Rumi to past incidents, but presumably these comments were only quick references to background exchanged more fully between the two in private.

125 "the rose-garden district." *Masnavi*, VI, 3107–8.

125 "towering." *Maqâlât*, 369.

125 "greatest." Ibid., 822.

126 "The fault." Ibid., 625–26.

126 "You're not crazy." Ibid., 77.

126 "angels." Aflaki, IV, sec. 82, 680.

126 "spoiling." *Maqâlât*, 625–66.

126 "effeminate." Dowlatshâh-e Samarqandi, *Taz Kerrat al-sho'arâ*, ed. Mohammad Abbâsi (Tehran: Bârâni, 1337/1958), 216.

127 "The Sufi's book." *Masnavi*, II, 159.

127 "There were people." *Maqâlât*, 641.

127 "There were dervishes." Ibid., 687.

127 "With such a love." Ibid., 677.

128 "I used to have." Aflaki, IV, sec. 81, 679.

128 "They chose everybody." *Maqâlât*, 278–79.

128 "You used to come." Ibid., 729.

129 "If Abu Hanifa." Ibid., 304.

129 "I'm looking." Aflaki, IV, sec. 4, 616.

130 "When you see." *Masnavi*, III, 3753.

130 "Sheikh Mohammad." *Maqâlât*, 120. For a discussion of the likely identification of "Sheikh Mohammad" with Ibn Arabi, see Omid Safi, "Did the Two Oceans Meet?" *Journal of Muhyiddin Ibn Arabi Society*, vol. 26 (1999): 55–88.

130 "He was a mountain." *Maqâlât*, 239.

130 "You crack." Ibid., 239.

131 "He was compassionate." Ibid., 299.

131 "Our caravan leader." Ghazal #463.

131 "pearl." *Maqâlât*, 304.

131 "intellect." Ibid., 82.

131 "For me, death." Ibid., 286.

132 "I would say." Ibid., 635–36.

132 "This man." Ibid., 641.

132 "Though Shehab." Ibid., 225–26.

132 "You are asking." Ibid., 295.

133 "At first." Ibid., 249.

133 "Whenever you see someone." Ibid., 713–14.

133 "in Rum." Ibid., 760.

135 "Kerra Khatun." Ibid., 315.

135 "learning and knowledge." Cited in Lewis, *Rumi*, 135.

135 "alchemy, astronomy." Aflaki, IV, sec. 18, 625.

135 "beloved." Cited in Zarrinkub, *Step by Step*, 131.

137 "Be among." *Maqâlât*, 721.

137 "When I'm by myself." Ibid., 761.

137 "Sometimes Love." Ghazal #2231.

138 "The world." *Masnavi*, V, 1039.

138 "Whenever I write." Ghazal #1593.

138 "a sun has come up." *Maqâlât*, 223.

138 "be like the poor." Ibid., 778.

138 "I stop." *Maqâlât*, 761.

139 "The world." Ghazal #1095.

140 "We've met." *Maqâlât*, 93–94.

140 "I'm so happy." Ibid., 189.

140 "The first." Ibid., 779.

140 "God has not yet." Ibid., 777.

140 "I wanted." Ibid., 219.

140 "Now the water." Ibid., 142.

140 "Now rub." Ibid., 300.

141 "In the lane." Ibid., 646.

141 "The purpose." Ibid., 628.

141 "In the presence." *Fihe ma fih*, Discourse 20, 109.

141 "I do not revere." *Maqâlât*, 691.

142 "Which place." Aflaki, III, sec. 38, 121–22.

142 "Is wine." Ibid., IV, sec. 41, 639.

143 "What have you." Ibid., IV, sec. 89, 683.

143 "One of them claims." *Maqâlât*, 306.

144 "The lovely." Ibid., 736.

144 "jackasses" Ibid., 641.

144 "Who is this." Sultan Valad, *Valadname*, 44.

144 "Mowlana has." *Maqâlât*, 74.

144 "I'm all one color." Ibid., 106.

144 "I am only troubled." Ibid., 319.

144 "arrogant." Ibid., 774.

145 "You only." Aflaki, III, sec. 237, 314.

145 "During Majnun's time." *Fihe ma fih,* Discourse 15, 87.

145 "I'm not." *Maqâlât,* 774.

145 "On the Day of Resurrection." Aflaki, IV, sec. 80, 679.

146 "You were silent." Robai #1143.

CHAPTER 8: SEPARATION

147 "All wondered." *Valadname,* 43.

147 "His bird." Ibid., 47.

148 "Because." Aflaki, IV, sec. 26, 630.

148 "Please be aware." *Maqâlât,* 783.

148 "When you're not here." Ghazal #1760.

148 sonnet. The great historian of Iranian literature Jan Rypka writes of the "striking resemblance to the sonnet" of the *ghazal,* "the truest and most pleasing expression of lyricism, particularly of the erotic and mystical but also of the meditative and even the panegyric." Jan Rypka, *History of Iranian Literature* (Dordrecht-Holland: D. Reidel Publishing Company, 1968), 94–95.

149 "Oh you, light." Ghazal #1364.

150 "The sun of Truth." Aflaki, IV, sec. 24, 629.

150 "From the moment." Ghazal #1760.

151 "It's a wonderful." *Maqâlât,* 340.

152 "If they had said." Ibid., 756.

152 "I remember." Ibid., 340.

152 "Such praying." Ibid., 766.

152 "When I was in Aleppo." Ibid., 118.

153 "the work." Ibid., 766.

153 "When I found." *Valadname,* 49.

153 "Kissing Valad." Aflaki, IV, sec. 105, 695.

153 "All the companions." Ibid., 696.

153 "When you came." *Maqâlât,* 773.

154 "Comrades, go." Ghazal #163.

154 "It is not permitted." Aflaki, IV, sec., 105, 696.

155 "This time." *Fihe ma fih,* Discourse 19, 106.

155 "These people." Ibid., 105.

156 "and no one knew." Quoted in Annemarie Schimmel, *Rumi's World: The Life and Work of the Great Sufi Poet* (Boston and London: Shambhala Press, 2001; originally published as *I Am Wind, You Are Fire*), 18.

156 "With his beautiful." Robai #352.

156 "My sun and moon." Ghazal #633.

157 "The heart." *Maqâlât*, 610.

157 "Tolerate." Ibid., 260.

158 "In the book." Ghazal #327.

158 "They felt jealous." *Maqâlât*, 72.

158 "Mowlana became." *Resâle-ye Sepahsalar*, 132.

158 "I wish." *Maqâlât*, 353.

159 "If truly." Ibid., 757.

159 "pure and beautiful." Aflaki, IV, sec. 43, 641.

160 "Because it was winter." *Resâle-ye Sepahsalar*, 133.

160 "Shamsoddin said." Aflaki, IV, sec. 39, 637.

160 "I asked God." *Maqâlât*, 347.

162 "This is his study time." *Maqâlât*, 623.

162 "The second son." *Resâle-ye Sepahsalar*, 133.

163 "Did you see." *Maqâlât*, 198.

163 "He repeated." *Resâle-ye Sepahsalar*, 133.

163 "heart was after me." *Maqâlât*, 803.

163 "Whomever I love." Ibid., 219.

164 "Someone said." Ibid., 74.

164 "I become bored." Ibid., 740.

164 "I cannot blame." Ibid., 803.

165 "One day." Aflaki, IV, sec. 43, 641.

165 "When speaking." Ghazal #2179.

167 "I was restless." *Maqâlât*, 351.

168 "The dance." Ibid., 623.

168 "If you can." Ibid., 163–64.

169 "Was Mowlana." Ibid., 773.

169 "My entire life." Quoted in a slightly different translation in William
      C. Chittick, "Translator's Introduction," *Me & Rumi: The Autobiography
      of Shams-i Tabrizi* (Louisville, KY: Fons Vitae, 2004), xiv.

169 "My entire life." Ghazal #1768.

170 "He said." *Valadname*, 54.

170 "I cannot." *Maqâlât*, 334.

171 "As neither Mowlana." Ibid., 742–43.

171 "I became so upset." Ibid., 696.

171 "To be able." Ibid., 187.

172 "Bahaoddin." *Resâle-ye Sepahsalar*, 134.

172 "When Shamsoddin." *Valadname*, 54.

172 "Mowlana roared." *Resâle-ye Sepahsalar*, 134.

CHAPTER 9: "I BURNED, I BURNED, I BURNED"

173 "I burned." Ghazal #1768.

173 "the sheikh." *The Travels of Ibn Battutah*, ed., Tim Mackintosh-Smith (London: Picador, 2003), 106.

173 "Subsequently." Ibid.,107.

173 "his merciful presence." *Resâle Sepahsalar*, 134.

174 "a day or two." *Valadname*, 54.

175 "Perform." *Resâle-ye Sepahsalar*, 65.

175 "sang." Ghazal #1641.

175 tambourine. Ghazal #2083.

175 "Sometimes." Ghazal #302.

175 "Day and night." *Valadname*, 58.

176 "Mowlana." Aflaki, IV, sec. 92, 686.

176 "The night wears black." Ghazal #2130.

176 "bloody." Ghazal #2807.

176 "covered in blood." Ghazal #144.

176 "This earth is not." Ghazal #336.

177 "When the water." Ghazal #2514.

177 "They want to kill." Aflaki, IV, sec. 91, 684.

178 "The relationship." Schimmel, *Rumi's World*, 22.

178 "a more reciprocal." Janet Afary, *Sexual Politics in Modern Iran* (Cambridge, UK: Cambridge University Press, 2009), 98.

179 "One day." Aflaki, IV, sec. 51, 647.

179 "During." *Resâle-ye Sepahsalar*, 134.

179 "putting his head." *Valadname*, 60.

180 "For the third time." Ghazal #1493.

181 *The Trickery of Satan*. The original title is *Al-talbis Iblis*, written by Ibn al-Jawzi (d. C.E. 1201). For a fuller discussion, see Ali Asani, "Music and Dance in the Work of Mawlana Jalal al-Din Rumi," *Islamic Culture*, 60:2 (April 1986): 41.

181 stages. I am indebted to the analysis of Rumi's poetry about Shams in terms of such stages to Annemarie Schimmel, especially her chapter on "Rumi and the Metaphors of Love," in *As Through a Veil: Mystical*

Poetry in Islam (Oxford: Oneworld Publications, 2001, originally published 1982), 86–90.

182 "Since I am." Ghazal #1621.

182 "I gave him." Ghazal #600.

182 "Jalaloddin" Ghazal #1196.

183 "Be silent." Ghazal #1621.

183 "One night." Ghazal #757.

184 "Not alone." Ghazal #1081.

185 "Say the name." Ghazal #2807.

185 "I wonder." Ghazal #677.

186 "Speak." Ghazal #2056.

186 "there was probably." Lewis, *Rumi*, 167.

186 "the light." Ghazal #1526.

187 "It's not enough." Ghazal #2768.

187 "You speak for God." Ghazal #1310.

188 "When I went." Ghazal #2968.

188 "Joseph's shirt." Ghazal #997.

189 "If my eyes." Ghazal #2893.

190 "pious man." *Valadname*, 57.

190 "Each dawn." Ghazal #2152.

191 "loved dearly." Aflaki, V, sec. 13, 714.

191 "in himself." *Valadname*, 61.

191 "He said." Ibid., 63.

192 "son." Rumi, *Maktubat*, Letter 1, 59.

192 "angelic qualities." Ibid., Letter 23, 91.

193 "Just as water." Ghazal #232.

194 "This unfortunate." Aflaki, III, sec. 307, 376.

195 "My kindness." *Fihe ma fih*, Discourse 15, 89.

195 "He went." *Valadname*, 62.

196 "In every age." *Masnavi*, II, 815–16; 819–20.

196 "I grew old." Ghazal #207.

197 "one day." Aflaki, IV, sec. 110, 700.

197 "They feel" Ibid., III, sec. 297, 362.

197 "Morning rises." Ghazal #879.

198 "This was his clothing." Aflaki, IV, sec. 93, 687.

CHAPTER 10: "LAST YEAR IN A RED CLOAK . . . THIS YEAR IN BLUE"

201 "Last year." Ghazal #650.

201 "When Salahoddin." *Resâle-ye Sepahsalar,* 135.

202 "I passed on." Aflaki, V, sec. 3, 705.

202 "As Mowlana." Ibid.

203 "I see so many." Ibid., V, sec. 15, 715.

203 "No." Ibid., V, sec. 11, 712.

203 "That lion-hunting." Ghazal #594.

203 "Last year." Ghazal #650.

204 "The grace." Ghazal #1397.

202 "At the end." Ghazal #1210.

205 *"eshq bazi."* Aflaki, V, sec. 7, 711; John O'Kane translates the Persian as "amorous playfulness" in his translation of Aflaki, *The Feats of the Knowers of God* (Leiden: E. J. Brill, 2002), 495.

205 "It happened to me." *Fihe ma fih,* Discourse 20, 111.

206 *"nayeb."* For a discussion of Salahoddin and the position of *nayeb,* see Lewis, *Rumi,* 207.

206 delivering sermons. In a different account in Aflaki, the finality of Rumi's giving up sermons is presented as debatable: "He never again undertook to preach. According to others, he did continue to preach, but not consistently." Aflaki, III, sec. 86, 172.

206 "He said." *Valadname,* 66.

206 "Dedicate yourselves." Ibid.

207 "Words." Aflaki, V, sec. 18, 718.

207 "Again envy." *Valadname,* 73.

208 "nothing." *Fihe ma fih,* Discourse 21, 112.

209 "Without a mirror." Robai #1552.

209 "I'm a mirror." Ghazal #38.

209 "Take a polished." *Fihe ma fih,* Discourse 49, 209.

210 "Look at the face." *Valadname,* 67.

210 "If you become." Ibid., 106.

211 "Day and night." Ibid., 108.

211 "They are upset." Ibid., 78.

211 "When this news." Ibid., 77.

211 "with their faces." Aflaki, V, sec. 20, 719.

211 "Fateme is my right." Ibid.

212 "because of the extreme." Ibid., V, sec. 19, 719.

212 "May the blessings." Ghazal #236.

213 "Dance." Ghazal #31.

213 "His knowledge." Badi al-Zaman Foruzanfar, "Some Remarks on Rumi's Poetry," *Mawlana Rumi Review*, vol. 3 (2012): 183–84.

214 "One day." Aflaki, III, sec. 458, 483–84.

215 "If my dear son." *Maktubat*, Letter 56, 132–33.

215 "Because of the white." Ibid., Letter 6, 69–70.

216 "They collected." Aflaki, V, sec. 30, 727.

216 "my dear child." *Maktubat*, Letter 29, 98.

216 "my eloquent." Ibid., Letter 45, 117–18.

217 "May this wedding." Ghazal #2667.

CHAPTER 11: THE FALL OF BAGHDAD

218 Abbasid Caliph. He was a successor in a direct line from the Prophet Mohammad, though not by blood.

219 pope and emperor. See Weatherford, *Genghis Khan and the Making of the Modern World*, 180.

220 "When in the year." Aflaki, III, sec. 112, 202.

220 "in a sack." Ibid., III, sec. 113, 205.

220 "Oh seekers." Taqi al-Din ibn Abi al-Yusr, "[Burned to Ashes]," in *Baghdad: The City in Verse*, trans. and ed. Reuven Snir (Cambridge, MA: Harvard University Press, 2013), 155.

220 "loss for the kingdom." Al-Majd al-Nashabi, "[Turning a Child's Hair White]," ibid., 154.

221 "Now if not eating." Ibid., III, sec. 112, 203.

221 "The deputy." *Masnavi*, I, 2685.

222 "The Tatar armies." Ghazal #1839.

222 "taxes and camels." *Maktubat*, Letter 42, 114.

222 "During your absence." Ibid., Letter 61, 139.

224 "How would." Aflaki, III, sec. 37, 118.

225 "I hear." Ibid., III, sec. 82, 165.

225 "Day and night." *Fihe ma fih*, Discourse 2, 24.

226 "For my part." Aflaki, III, sec. 217, 299.

227 "premodern." Omid Safi, *The Politics of Knowledge in Premodern Islam: Negotiating Ideology and Religious Inquiry* (Chapel Hill: The University of North Carolina Press, 2006), 129.

228 "It's fine." Aflaki, III, sec. 374, 425.

228 "I want you." Ibid., III, sec. 384, 432.

228 "all alone." Ibid., III, sec. 468, 490.

229 "my brother." *Maktubat*, Letter 36, 104.

229 Ince Minareli. Annemarie Schimmel described the cursive Kufic architectural inscriptions as "the beginning of a new artistic consciousness." Schimmel, *Rumi's World*, 7.

230 "the people." *Fihe ma fih*, Discourse 22, 115.

230 "Your kingdom." *Maktubat*, Letter 102, 188.

231 "I wanted." Ibid., Letter 28, 97.

231 "Even though." Aflaki, IV, sec. 83, 680.

232 "Come let us go." Ibid., V, sec. 17, 718.

232 "For demolition." Ibid., V, sec. 23, 721.

232 "He accepted." *Valadname*, 113.

232 "The Sheikh said." Ibid., 115.

233 "Gabriel and the wings." Ghazal #2364.

234 "Ever since." Aflaki, III, sec. 147, 233.

CHAPTER 12: "SING, FLUTE!"

235 "Sing, flute!" Robai #1271.

235 "A human being." *Fihe ma fih*, Discourse 1, 23.

236 "as thin." Aflaki, III, sec. 204, 290.

236 "Look at Mowlana!" Ibid., III, sec. 99, 188.

236 "Is our religion." Ibid., III, sec. 459, 484.

237 "Mowlana." Ibid., III, sec. 296, 361.

238 "It is not proper." Ibid., III, sec. 542, 555.

238 "Boo!" Ibid., III, sec. 148, 234.

238 "Maleke." Ibid., III, sec. 249, 323.

238 "Why did you hit." Ibid., III, sec. 344, 406.

239 "Lord, wait for me." Ibid., III, sec. 68, 153–54.

239 "Why are you beating." Ibid., II, sec. 34, 116.

239 "happy union." Ibid., III, sec. 100, 190.

239 "The stench." Ibid., III, sec. 166, 258.

240 "The danger." *Fihe ma fih*, Discourse 1, 22.

240 "As my fame." Aflaki, III, sec. 138, 226.

241 "Make yourself thin." *Masnavi*, I, 1545–46.

241 "Words of praise." Ibid., I, 1855.

241 "I began to sweat." Aflaki, III, sec. 325, 394.

241 "affliction." Ibid., VII, sec. 14, 800.

241 "I am not keeping." Ibid., III, sec. 404, 441.

242 "I have never." Ibid., III, sec. 330, 395.

242 "One morning." Ghazal #649.

243 "Collections." Aflaki, VI, sec. 3, 740.

243 "Listen to the reed flute." *Masnavi*,   I, 1–4. An alternative translation of the last line of this section would be: "Longing to be joined together once again."

244 "Out of curiosity." Ibid., I, 6–9.

245 "When Hosamoddin." Aflaki, VI, sec. 2, 738.

245 "You are a ray." *Masnavi*, IV, 1.

246 "It's dawn." Ibid., I, 1807–9.

246 "One day Mowlana." Aflaki, III, sec. 544, 556.

247 "Mohammad." *Masnavi*, I, Prose Introduction.

247 "love's path." Ibid., I, 13.

247 "It's better the secret." *Masnavi*, I, 135–42.

249 "You blow into me." Robai #1273.

249 "You pick them out." *Maqâlât*, 180.

250 "I am a mountain." *Masnavi*, I, 3797–801.

251 "528 Quranic verses." Franklin Lewis cites this statistic from a talk given by Foruzanfar at the Rumi UNESCO Festival. See Lewis, *Rumi*, 291.

251 "When I first began." *Fihe ma fih*, Discourse 53, 221.

CHAPTER 13: "A NIGHTINGALE FLEW AWAY, THEN RETURNED"

252 "A nightingale." *Masnavi*, II, 8.

252 "In his emotions." Aflaki, VI, sec. 3, 743.

252 "spiritual ascension." *Masnavi*, II, 4.

253 "Having waged." Aflaki, VI, sec. 18, 766.

253 "my dear son." *Maktubat*, Letter 7, 71.

254 "Dear pride of professors." Ibid., Letter 67, 146.

254 "After he prayed." Aflaki, III, sec. 510, 523.

254 "At this time." Ibid., III, sec. 69, 154.

255 "If the sultan." Ibid., III, sec. 59, 147.

255 "Khodavandgar." Ibid., III, sec. 46, 129.

256 "These Sufis." Ibid., III, sec. 362, 416.

257 "What is poverty?" Ibid., III, sec. 190, 278.

257 "Such a blessing." Ibid., III, sec. 361, 415.

258 "He is a good man." Ibid., III, sec. 352, 412.

258 "No, I said." Ibid., III, sec. 185, 274–75.

259 "Why must this kind." Ibid., III, sec. 83, 165–66.

259 "requesting the remainder." Ibid., VI, sec. 3, 743.

259 "The light of God." *Masnavi*, II, 3–8.

260 "There was no further." Aflaki, VI, sec. 3, 744.

260 "When Salahoddin." *Valadname*, 116.

261 "Welcome my soul." Aflaki, VI, sec. 20, 770.

262 "Lovers are like waterwheels." *Masnavi*, VI, 911–12.

262 "If you had asked." Aflaki, III, sec. 381, 431.

263 "kept constant company." Ibid., III, sec. 591, 601.

263 "Come light of God." *Masnavi*, II, 2282.

264 "When friends." *Fihe ma fih*, Discourse 15, 89.

264 "What am I." Ibid.

265 a dozen core stories. I am indebted for insight into the structure of the *Masnavi* to Jawid Mojadeddi, "Introduction," *The Masnavi: Book Two* (Oxford: Oxford University Press, 2007).

265 "A fool believes." *Masnavi*, II, 2130.

266 "From love of Shams." *Masnavi*, II, 1122–23.

266 "Now father, I see." *Maqalat*, 77.

266 "You are the child." *Masnavi*, II, 3766–67; 3779.

266 "Shop of Unity." Ibid., VI, 1528.

267 "Beyond belief." Robai #395.

267 "opened the door." *Masnavi*, II, 3803.

267 "As he was praying." Ibid., II, 3805-7.

CHAPTER 14: THE RELIGION OF LOVE

268 "the religion of love." Rumi speaks of "the religion of love" in Ghazal #195 and Ghazal #232: "Reason is puzzled by the religion of love." He uses the Persian word for religion, "*din*" in Ghazal #195, and the Arabic word, "*mazhab*" in Ghazal #232.

268 "box of secrets." *Masnavi*, III, 2.

269 "Suddenly a fool." Ibid., III, 4232–35.

269 "When the Quran." Ibid., III, 4237–43.

270 "Why do they call." Aflaki, III, sec. 205, 291.

270 "People think." *Fihe ma fih*, Discourse 10, 58.

271 "Everyone who exhibits." Aflaki, III, sec. 196, 284.

271 "When Hallaj." *Masnavi*, VI, 2095.

271 *robai*. For a discussion of the robais as having been written later in Rumi's life, see Harvey, *The Way of Passion*, 54.

271 "He dove." Robai #422.

271 "I am the servant." Robai #717.

272 "Be empty!" Ghazal #1739.

272 "The mosque." *Masnavi*, II, 3111.

273 "the religion of love." Ibid., II, 1770.

273 "Since we worship." Ibid., III, 2124.

273 "My heart." Ibid., III, 2935.

274 "Youth is a garden." *Masnavi*, II, 1217–19.

274 "The eyebrows droop." Ibid., II, 1223–26.

276 "out of jealous anger." Aflaki, V, sec. 16, 717.

276 "How wonderful." Aflaki, III, sec. 598, 608.

276 "Take care of Mowlana." Ibid., III, sec. 43, 126.

277 "Why do these men." Ibid., VI, sec. 12, 755.

277 "I wish from this day." Ibid., VI, sec. 14, 759.

277 "Oh brother." *Masnavi*, II, 277–78.

278 "Although the sun." *Fihe ma fih*, Discourse 52, 218.

278 "People work." Ibid., Discourse 14, 79.

279 "All this I said." Ibid., "Introduction," 18.

279 "Shame on the companions." Aflaki, III, sec. 441, 468.

279 *Del ku*." Ibid., III, sec. 292, 356.

280 "He is the one." Ibid., III, sec. 291, 356.

280 "Extract." Ibid., III, sec. 256, 330.

280 "No clever doctor." Ibid., III, sec. 549, 563.

281 "At the Festival of Unity." Ghazal #202.

281 "You flee from death." *Masnavi*, III, 3441–43.

282 "God created." Ghazal #683.

282 "Squeezed in the womb." *Masnavi*, III, 3556–59.

283 "He said, 'My friends.'" Ibid., III, 3946–48.

283   "Death, its claws disease." Ibid., III, 3984.

283   "The bird." Ibid., III, 3977–3980.

284   "When you hear." Ibid., V, 1736–40.

CHAPTER 15: WEDDING NIGHT

285   "If a group." Aflaki, III, sec. 253, 328.

286   "Do not do." Ibid., VIII, sec. 3, 826.

286   "Faridun." Ibid., VIII, sec. 5, 828.

286   "The day." Ibid., VIII, sec. 5, 829; since the poem does not appear in most copies of Rumi's *Divan,* Sultan Valad has also been credited as its actual author.

287   "beautiful." Ghazal #16.

287   "Suddenly." Ibid., VIII, sec. 9, 832.

287   "The moment." Ibid., VIII, sec. 15, 838.

288   "Oh, Life of the Heart." *Masnavi,* VI, 1–3.

289   "glorious." Ibid., VI, 3109.

289   "He gave me a cap." Ibid., VI, 3126–28, 3130.

289   "the fairest." Sura XII, 1.3. *The Koran Interpreted,* trans. A. J. Arberry, vol. I, 254.

290   "And when she said." *Masnavi,* VI, 4023–27; 4030; 4032–33.

290   story of the three princes. See Shams's account, *Maqâlât,* 246–47.

291   "window between hearts." Ibid., VI, 4916.

291   "You should have." Aflaki, III, sec. 565, 579.

292   "I am thinking." Ibid., III, sec. 566, 580.

292   "Do you know." Ibid., III, sec. 567, 580.

292   "when the earth." Ibid., III, sec. 368, 420.

292   "Thank God." Ibid., III, sec. 568, 581.

293   "What excellent." Ibid., III, sec. 579, 587.

293   "It is hoped." Ibid., III, sec. 569, 581.

293   "I placed the cup." Aflaki, III, sec. 582, 594.

294   "When you see." Ghazal #911.

295   "Don't be sad." Ghazal #683.

295   "Sultan Valad." Aflaki, III, sec. 579, 589.

295   "last *ghazal.*" Ibid., III, sec. 579, 590.

295   "Go." Ghazal #2039.

295   "Who is suitable." Aflaki, III, sec. 578, 586.

296   "Will there appear." Ibid., III, sec. 571, 583.

297 "Don't be afraid." Ibid., III, sec. 570, 582.

297 "I recommend." Ibid., III, sec. 574, 584.

297 "Oh Lord God." Ibid., III, sec. 575, 585.

297 "My companions." Ibid., III, sec. 579, 589.

297 "pearl-shedding sea." *Masnavi,* VI, 1999.

298 "Place me." Aflaki, III, sec. 573, 584.

298 "The bats." *Masnavi,* II, 47.

299 "All the religious." Aflaki, III, sec. 580, 592.

299 "The people." Sultan Valad, *Valadname,* 124–25.

299 "The Muslims." Aflaki, III, sec. 580, 592.

300 "He was like." Ibid., III, sec. 580, 593.

300 "He came." Aflaki, III, sec. 333, 400.

301 "*Chuni?*" Ibid., III, sec. 588, 598.

301 "Serajoddin." Aflaki, III, sec. 587, 597.

AFTERWORD

302 "I feel sad." Omar, Facebook message to author, June 3, 2015.

303 "All those." Claude Cahen, *Pre-Ottoman Turkey: A general survey of the material and spiritual culture and history c. 1071–1330.*

303 "Most of these." Ahmet T. Karamustafa, in discussion with the author, May 15, 2015.

304 "Late in the evening." Schimmel, *Rumi's World,* 195–96.

305 "Animals grow fat." *Masnavi,* VI, 290.

305 collaborative. I collaborated with the Iranian-American writer Maryam Mortaz on translations of Rumi's poetry posted on Twitter under #RumiSecrets.

306 "This poem smells of roses." Şefik Can, "Rumi Studies in the West," in *Rumi and His Sufi Path of Love,* eds., M. Fatih Çitlak and Hüseyin Bingül (Somerset, NJ: The Light Publishing, 2007), 98.

306 "ear of the heart." Ghazal #837.

307 "Of Paradise." *The Topical Notebooks of Ralph Waldo Emerson,* vol. 2 (Columbia, MO: University of Missouri Press, 1992), 48; identified as a translation of lines of Rumi in Lewis, *Rumi,* 570.

307 "These poems need to be." Coleman Barks, "Releasing Birds to the Air," in *Robert Bly in This World,* eds., Thomas R. Smith with James P. Lenfestey (Minneapolis: University of Minnesota Press, 2011), 268.

307 "O Rumi." Cited in a translation by Mehmet Önder published in, "Rumi Studies in the West," in *Rumi and His Sufi Path of Love,* eds., Çitlak and Bingül, 100.

308 "the sunshine of the heart." Ghazal #968.

308 "Tell all the truth." Poem #1263. *The Poems of Emily Dickinson,* vol. 2, ed., R. W. Franklin (Cambridge, MA: Belknap Press of Harvard, 1998), vol. 2, 1089.

309 "Explanations." *Masnavi,* I, 113.

309 "Rumi resonates." Jawid Mojadeddi, in discussion with the author, June 11, 2015.

309 "When you discover." *Masnavi,* II, 45–46.

310 "I do believe." Coleman Barks, in discussion with the author, July 31, 2015.

310 "I felt befriended." Asma Sadiq, in discussion with the author, June 12, 2015.

311 "Don't speak." *Masnavi,* III, 1305.

Index

About the Author

BRAD GOOCH is a poet, novelist, and biographer whose previous ten books include *Flannery: A Life of Flannery O'Connor*, which was a National Book Critics Circle Award finalist, *New York Times* Notable Book of the Year, and *New York Times* bestseller; *City Poet: The Life and Times of Frank O'Hara*; *Godtalk: Travels in Spriritual America*; and the memoir *Smash Cut*. The recipient of National Endowment for the Humanities and Guggenheim Fellowships, he earned his PhD at Columbia University and is a professor of English at William Paterson University. He lives in New York City.